D0396925

TRASH TALKS

TRASH TALKS

Revelations in the Rubbish

Elizabeth V. Spelman

OXFORD
UNIVERSITY PRESS

OXFORD
UNIVERSITY PRESS

Oxford University Press is a department of the University of Oxford. It furthers
the University's objective of excellence in research, scholarship, and education
by publishing worldwide. Oxford is a registered trade mark of Oxford University
Press in the UK and certain other countries.

Published in the United States of America by Oxford University Press
198 Madison Avenue, New York, NY 10016, United States of America.

© Elizabeth V. Spelman 2016

Library of Congress Cataloging-in-Publication Data
Names: Spelman, Elizabeth V.
Title: Trash talks : revelations in the rubbish / Elizabeth V. Spelman.
Description: New York, NY : Oxford University Press, 2016. | Includes
bibliographical references.
Identifiers: LCCN 2015030985 | ISBN 978–0–19–023935–0 (hardcover : alk. paper)
Subjects: LCSH: Refuse and refuse disposal. | Values. | Material culture. |
Philosophical anthropology.
Classification: LCC TD793 .S64 2016 | DDC 306.4/6—dc23 LC record available at
http://lccn.loc.gov/2015030985

1 3 5 7 9 8 6 4 2
Printed by Sheridan, USA

to Mo,
fellow wastrel

CONTENTS

ACKNOWLEDGMENTS

Hearty thanks to the fine company of nourishing incubators for this project: Dear colleagues and students at Smith College, contagiously alive and abuzz. Delightfully inquisitive and unfailingly generous family and friends—Cornelia Spelman, Reg Gibbons, Jon Spelman, Liz Lerman, Anna Clare Spelman, Deborah Campert, Martha Minow, Joe Singer, Mira Singer, Lisa Heldke, Peg O'Connor, Frances Foster, Barrett Emerick, Adam Brady. Kaitlyn Willcoxon, puckish research assistant in the early days of exploration. Alert and demanding audiences at Georgetown University, Dartmouth College, Smith College, Southern Illinois University at Carbondale, St. Mary's College of Maryland, Allegheny College, and the University of Colorado at Boulder. At Oxford University Press, the wise and welcoming shepherd Peter Ohlin, the genial guide Emily Sacharin, vigilant manuscript referees, and the entire team crucial to producing what is now in your hands or on your screen. Along the path from start to finish, the hawk-eyed Monique Roelofs, who knows rubbish when she reads it.

TRASH TALKS

Introduction

It's not easy to think of trash other than as a ferociously growing menace. Across land and sea, communities face crises over what to do with the mountains of garbage and rubbish we routinely and relentlessly produce, the enormous amount of biological waste generated by humans and animals, the truckloads and shiploads of electronic equipment we have judged to be obsolete. All this refuse poses widespread problems for human health, the well-being of the planet, and the quality of lives people lead—especially those in whose neighborhoods or on whose shores it is unceremoniously dumped.

Even apart from such concerns and threats, it's clear that there are many kinds of things in the world we don't want anywhere near us, and we have ready at hand a family of trash-related words to mark our disgust, disdain, or distance: "Those oranges belong in the garbage." "This computer is a piece of junk." "What a colossal waste of time." Or the fierce battle cry of the warrior philosopher, "That argument is pure rubbish."

However, our relation to our rejects is considerably more complex, more curious, than these worries and linguistic habits may suggest. We have remarkably intimate ties to waste and trash: they not only bear the stamp of our creation but figure prominently in accounts of the kinds of beings we are and in the crafting of our relations to each other. The chapters that follow offer a portrait of the rich and enduring fellowship we maintain with the scrapped and discarded.

Humanity leaves its footprint in the very designation of something as trash: matter becomes trash in virtue of our having thrown it away, tossed it out, abandoned it, treated it as something for which we no longer have any use, debris we don't want among our belongings. But what we anoint as trash and thereby hope to propel out of our personal orbit may come back to haunt us. Trash talks, and there is much of which it speaks. In Chapter 1, "Combing through the Trash," we are reminded that snoops of various stripes—celebrity watchers, forensic investigators, archaeologists specializing in what has come to be known as garbology—are happy to paw through our rubbish in search of what they hope to be juicy information about us. Just what is it about the very stuff we have thrown out that makes it appear to be such a treasure trove?

Probably most of us don't much like our trash being combed through by those determined to get the dirt on us. At the same time, some of us are eager for the public to see and admire our capacity to be wasteful. If actual trash and waste make us vulnerable to unwanted probing by those hoping to tarnish our reputations, unabashed wastefulness sometimes has been just the ticket to creating and keeping well burnished a shining social status.

How and why such wastefulness comes to be proudly broadcast is at the heart of Chapter 2, "A Taste for Waste." Our guide is Thorstein Veblen, whose still classic though hardly uncontested exploration of conspicuous consumption in *The Theory of the Leisure Class* and related works constitutes a sustained examination of what he described as conspicuous wastefulness—a predilection for, indeed a commitment to, wasteful excess pervading late 19th- and early 20th-century life, especially in the United States. Veblen found such devotion in the vast array of products and personnel on display in leisure class households. But he also saw a principle of waste as tightly woven into aesthetic standards, religious practices, the aims of higher education, and the business practices of mighty "captains of industry."

Trash and garbage are stuff—often quite unappealing or unhygienic stuff—to be removed and disposed of. It is not uncommon for those who actually deal with the castoffs of daily life to be considered contaminated in some way by their association with what they handle. But the nature and extent of such alleged defilement varies, as does the ability and authority of trash handlers to escape from being thought sullied by their task. In Chapter 3, "On Taking Out the Trash," we explore three of those variations. In one of her early novels, Iris Murdoch implicitly invites us to meditate on a commonly made assumption that a lack of capacity or absence of desire to keep one's household minimally clean points to a troubling flaw in character. An illuminating complement to this mode of assessment appears in "La Poubelle Agréée," the fabulist Italo Calvino's nonfictional account of the pleasurable challenges and contemplative rewards of meditating on his family job as garbage handler-in-chief. Though it is not by any means his primary intention, Calvino in effect preempts any attribution of contamination based on the nature of his daily chores. As is well known, such distance from personal pollution is not possible for the so-called untouchables or Dalits in India. In their case there is alleged to be an unbreakable link between the kind of labor to which they are assigned and the impure nature imputed to them. What is it about the cultural context and the particular standing of individuals that allows, requires, or prevents inferences to be made about their character or nature on the basis of their taking out (or failing to take out) the trash?

Around the world and across time, people who handle and haul rubbish have been among those treated like trash: though the work they do may be indispensable for the community of which they are a part, they are regarded as disposable. Such expendability takes on a much broader cast in the prospect of *Homo sapiens* having to face up to the possibility that as a species it is in fact not just *like* trash; it is trash-in-waiting. The unwanted realization is not merely that individuals die, that we become, as we are wont to put it, "human remains"; we also have to acknowledge that our species hasn't been around very long and like other species will eventually end up in the evolutionary landfill. Moreover, as we shall see in Chapter 4, "Evolutionary Trash," prominent evolutionary theorists tell us that the very process by which our species emerged is enormously wasteful. This has been especially shocking for those who believe that we humans came into being as a result of a divinely designed plan of which our species is the signal and crowning achievement. Indeed Charles Darwin found it difficult to reconcile his observations of the abundant waste in nature with his inclination to see the natural world as the product of intelligent design. Whether such reconciliation is achievable continues to be a matter of intense concern among current proponents of "Intelligent Design" and evolutionary theorists. Waste long ago wormed its way into accounts of humanity's origins and our place in the natural world, and that fact continues to be a source of considerable anxiety in some pockets of our trepidatious species.

Our penchant for giving things the heave-ho points to a condition of human existence about which there has been no small amount of reflection in the history of both Western and Eastern philosophy: the state of dissatisfaction. As we note in Chapter 5, "Desire, Dissatisfaction, and Disposability," neither Plato nor the Buddha was explicitly concerned about trash. But both were highly attentive to causes and consequences of the dissatisfaction they believed accompanied the insatiability of appetitive desire and the specious promises of what we crave. While neither Plato nor the Buddha would be surprised to learn how close we seem to have come to littering ourselves to death, they might not have anticipated the extent to which dissatisfaction's star has risen: clever entrepreneurs in hyper-consumerist economies have not let dissatisfaction itself go to waste. Our wizards of wile appear to have transformed this commonly occurring condition of human life into a consumer's high calling, a crucial piece of the machinery powering a nation's economy. Good shoppers aren't supposed to be disappointed by dissatisfaction but to welcome it as a sign that 'tis time to go back merrily for more.

Not all trash and waste are the result of dissatisfaction. Much food waste, for example, arises from carelessness or inattention or greed. This would seem to reflect badly on humanity, given the inarguable need for food in order to survive. But as we are reminded in Chapter 6, "On Knowing Waste When You See It," the tales told by the waste of food are not as simple as a set of variations on human irrationality and irresponsibility. For it turns out that much has been thought to be at stake in deliberations over what actually constitutes the waste of food and over who is or is not a reliable judge of such matters. In John Milton's *Paradise Lost*, for example, central to Eve's fateful act of disobedience is her confident judgment that not eating from the tree of knowledge would be a waste of resources.

It was thus she plucked, thus she ate. John Locke, a near contemporary of Milton, argued in *The Second Treatise of Government* that the "wretched inhabitants" of the Americas did not have the good sense to cultivate land rather than let it go to waste. Milton's God did not give humans the capacity to be good judges of what constitutes waste, and Eve's arrogant assumption to the contrary precipitated our expulsion from Paradise. Yet Locke's God not only blessed humanity with such a capacity but thereby offered a justification, to humans who presume they do know waste when they see it, for undertaking to build a paradise they deemed unimaginable to those lacking such knowledge.

Locke, and Locke's God, no doubt would be alarmed by the waste that is at the heart of the common human activity of feasting. But to many students of human behavior, the waste of food and other human resources characteristic of feasts is central to vital psychological, social, political, and economic functions that feasts perform. Food waste thus puts us at the very nub of intriguing battles over who is and is not a good judge of the proper use of the resources upon which our lives depend.

What follows, then, is an account of a variety of tales told about humans through our close and complex relations to trash and waste. The intimacy of those relations shows up in our rejectamenta being used to generate hypotheses about who we are and what we value; in the fact of our embracing wastefulness as a means of signaling social status; in our taking the occupation of handling trash and garbage as revelatory of possible moral or spiritual shortcomings; in the proposal that waste is a prominent feature of the process by which humans evolved and in the reminder that it is to the dustbin that each of us, and our species, shall ultimately repair; in our trash and related discards as the inevitable corollary of our oh-so-human state of dissatisfaction; and in the wasting of food as an entrée into explorations of cardinal differences alleged to exist between God and humanity and among humans.

To be sure, the portrait of our intimate connections to trash and waste drawn here is incomplete. It not only has drawn inspiration from the labors of other trash mavens but cries out to be enlarged upon, perhaps especially by those who enjoy the irony in our having such close connection to the very stuff we hope to put out of mind, out of sight, out of smell. Each of the following chapters could well be the beginning of a much longer treatment of the particular subject under consideration. I'm hoping that readers will feel not shortchanged but enticed by the relatively brisk discussions of a rather large number of figures and topics. This depiction of the chummy and intricate relation between humans and our trash includes a promiscuous but not unwarranted commingling of US Supreme Court justices, archaeologists, narcotics agents, psychoanalysts, philosophers, fiction writers, sanitation workers, economists, and evolutionary theorists: veritable co-investigators of trash, waste, rubbish, garbage, and other members of the large flotsam/jetsam family.

The terms "trash," "waste," "junk," and their many semantic siblings sometimes are used as if they are synonymous. But in the various contexts in which they arise here, they typically are not so readily interchangeable. Reasons for preferring the use of one to another will emerge as portions of the portrait are filled out. In the meantime readers can rest assured that the abundance of terms included in what we might call the trash lexicon is not a matter of wasteful excess. They earn their keep.

Chapter 1

Combing through the Trash

It's an aphorism almost in tatters from overuse: one person's trash is another person's treasure. A friend of mine has never purchased a pencil—not because she doesn't use pencils or can't afford a new one, but because early in her life she realized that she prefers stubs found on schoolroom floors to any other version of that handy implement. It has long ceased to be a novelty for artists to grasp the aesthetic potential in abandoned city lots, defiled beaches, and other rich sources of refuse. Cities such as Oslo actually import waste and trash from other countries, seeing in landfills the promise of an endless supply of energy-generating fuel.[1]

The trash-to-treasure journey of special interest here begins with the rifling through of rubbish bags and bins in the expectation that they will yield quite personal information—perhaps good old dirt—about individuals, communities, civilizations. But just what and just how much can be gleaned from combing through the trash?

---

1. Serious questions remain concerning the safety of processes used to convert waste into energy.

TRASH AS FORENSIC EVIDENCE

The assumption that our trash speaks volumes about us—or at least significant paragraphs—is firmly held by both those who make it their business to rummage through other people's garbage and those who insist that such searches constitute an unjustifiable invasion of privacy or unreasonable appropriation of property. (It also is an assumption crucial to the work of some archaeologists, as we shall learn a bit later.)

There are probably few statistics about how frequently or with how much fervor the activity sometimes referred to as "trash reconnaissance" goes on. I'm speaking here not of those scavengers and dumpster divers looking for food to eat and castoffs to use but of those seeking insight about their targeted subjects based on what's in the trash. The fact that some cases of garbage-rummaging have captured the attention not only of celebrity watchers but the justices of the Supreme Court of the United States suggests that we're anxious and uncertain about just what our garbage does or doesn't tell about us, should or should not be used to reveal about us.

In the early 1970s an obsessed fan of Bob Dylan, A. J. Weberman, began sifting through the garbage can outside the home of Dylan and his family in New York City's Greenwich Village. Weberman reportedly had become disenchanted with his former hero for allegedly abandoning his radical roots and betraying the legions of fans who supported his rise to stardom. Not content simply to write abusively about Dylan and find out ways to get him on the phone, Weberman started practicing what he called "garbology" to get the dirt on Dylan. ("Garbology" was defined by one follower of the affair as the "study of human refuse in an attempt to divine ill-begotten truths";[2] the term quite recently was beatified for inclusion in the *Oxford English Dictionary, OED*.)

Whatever is yielded by searches such as Weberman's—the likes of which continue to be one of the perils of the trade for celebrities—something remarkable emerges from public reaction to such investigations. Those disturbed by someone pawing through another person's garbage often describe the trash as "sacred." For example, a neighbor of celebrity garbology victims is reported to have found the activity "incredibly creepy. It's like nothing is sacred."[3] Weberman himself took pains to say that he did not find Dylan's garbage "sacred, the way some people do."[4]

Moreover, Weberman and other trash prowlers typically have been depicted as being not just "creepy" but also "pathetic" or "unnaturally curious."[5] For example, the main character in Ryuichi Hiroki's 2000 film *Tokyo Trash Baby*[6] is a young woman with an obsessive crush on a young man living in her apartment building. She routinely retrieves his trash bag from the basement and spends most of her free time adoringly going through it, convinced that despite not having met him she can come to know him intimately, to be in touch with him through examining his trash; at the same time she can protect herself from being rejected by him, from being herself treated as disposable.

There appear, then, to be some robustly held views about the special nature of the relation between us and our garbage, and

2. Seth Rogovoy, "The Bob Dylan's Who's Who," http://expectingrain.com/dok/who/w/webermanaj.html.
3. PageSix.com Staff, "Prowlers Target Celebs' Trash," *New York Post*, October 27, 2008, http://pagesix.com/2008/10/27/prowlers-target-celebs-trash/.
4. Robert Mayer, "Dylan's Having a Heap of Trouble with His Garbage Can These Days," *Toledo Blade*, May 30, 1971, C 6.
5. JayBird, "Someone Went through Mary Louise Parker's Trash and Told Page Six about It," *Celebitchy*, October 27, 2008, http://www.celebitchy.com/18327/someone_went_through_mary-louise_parkers_trash_and_told_page_six_about_it/.
6. *Tokyo Trash Baby*, directed by Ryuichi Hiroki (Arcimboldo, 2000), DVD.

accordingly about the character of people who don't understand or honor that relation. What is it about us, and about our trash and garbage, that might account for this rather fierce sense of offense or intrusion or over-stepping of boundaries?

Most of us probably don't want other people combing through our trash. If pressed, we may not be able to be very articulate about just why. But it seems less hard to figure out why someone engaging in illegal behavior would be bothered by such searches, especially when carried out by or for law enforcement officials. Your trash could provide damning evidence of your law-breaking activities. Should it be allowed to do so?

The conditions under which one's trash could be incriminating is at the heart of a case decided by the Supreme Court of the United States in 1988. William Greenwood was living in Laguna Beach, California, when he came under suspicion from a local police investigator for drug trafficking. The police officer, Jenny Stracner, had no hard evidence against Greenwood but had received information that a truckload of drugs was en route to his house, and she knew that a neighbor had been calling to complain about frequent late-night traffic there. Stracner did some of her own firsthand surveillance, observing considerable coming and going of visitors in the wee hours and following a truck from the Greenwood residence to a house already under investigation for similar reasons.

At this point Stracner decided that to gather enough evidence to obtain a search warrant for Greenwood's house she would find a way into the next best thing: his garbage. But, perhaps concerned about evidence tampering or the appearance thereof, she didn't pick up the trash herself. She simply asked the regular trash collector to do so and to make sure that it did not get mixed into the more general collection. The trash collector complied, and Stracner at last had enough dirt on Greenwood to be granted a search warrant for his house. Greenwood and someone else residing there at the time were arrested, but returned to the house after posting bail.

Greenwood sued the state, insisting that searches of one's trash need a warrant no less than searches of one's home. The Superior Court of California decided in his favor, holding that both the state's own constitution and the Fourth Amendment to the US Constitution prohibit warrantless searches of trash. The police indeed had had warrants for searches of Greenwood's house, leading to his arrest, but those warrants were based on unwarranted searches of his garbage. The prosecutor took the case to the next level, but the Court of Appeal affirmed the lower court's ruling. The California Supreme Court found no reason to review the decision reached by the Court of Appeal. Greenwood appeared to be free and his garbage to be safe from further unwarranted snooping.

The Supreme Court of the United States, however, taking note of a number of cases like Greenwood's popping up across the country, thought that the time had come to clarify the law of the land concerning the nature of a person's relation to her trash. And so arose the 1988 US Supreme Court case *California v. Greenwood*.[7]

The primary legal instrument employed by Greenwood's lawyers was the Fourth Amendment to the Constitution of the United States (and its all but identical cousin in Article I, Section 13, of the California State Constitution):

The right of the people to be secure in their persons, houses, papers, and effects, against unreasonable searches and seizures, shall not be violated, and no Warrants shall issue, but upon probable cause, supported by Oath or affirmation, and

---

7. *California v. Greenwood*, 486 U.S. 35 (1988). Hereafter cited as *Greenwood*.

particularly describing the place to be searched, and the persons or things to be seized.

Presumably Greenwood's case would have been a non-starter if trash were not considered a plausible candidate for the kind of protection the Fourth Amendment is meant to provide. The question the Supreme Court took itself to be answering was whether in this particular case the warrantless seizure and search of Greenwood's garbage by the police was permissible under the Fourth Amendment. Justice Byron White, writing for the majority, ruled that it was allowed; Justice William Brennan, writing for himself and Justice Thurgood Marshall, argued in dissent that it was not. How did the majority reach its decision? On what grounds did the dissenting justices disagree? What do their deliberations have to tell us about just how sacred, or in any event inviolate, is our relation to our garbage?

The Fourth Amendment does not prohibit all searches and seizures of personal belongings and effects. Those undertaking such searches must be prepared to demonstrate that their proposed actions are not "unreasonable," neither baseless nor vaguely defined. Those requesting Fourth Amendment protection also have to meet certain requirements: their expectation of privacy must be accepted by society as "objectively reasonable" (*Greenwood*, 40).

Think for a moment about the following routine, familiar to millions of household trash-makers around the country: you put your garbage and other unrecyclable stuff in opaque plastic bags (except in those communities in which you are required to use transparent ones), seal them, and try to remember to get them to the curb in time for the regular pickup. All going well, the waste collectors swing by and toss your rejects, along with those of others, into the cauldron at the back of their truck. Further commingling of individual household trash occurs at the dump or landfill, where similar trucks disgorge their contents.

On the basis of such familiar routines, Greenwood's lawyers maintained that his having put his trash and garbage in sealed opaque plastic bags entitled him to expect that the contents of the bags, identifiable as his, would remain private even though placed, as in fact required by municipal rules, on public ground; they insisted that he had every right to expect that the bags would be tossed in with those of others, and then be left at the dump.

The majority concluded that Greenwood's expectation of privacy was not "objectively reasonable," that Greenwood "exposed [his] garbage to the public sufficiently to defeat [his] claim to Fourth Amendment protection." Here's why:

> It is common knowledge that plastic garbage bags left on or at the side of a public street are readily accessible to animals, children, scavengers, snoops, and other members of the public.... Moreover, respondent placed [his] refuse at the curb for the express purpose of conveying it to a third party, the trash collector, who might himself have sorted through respondent's trash or permitted others, such as the police, to do so. Accordingly, having deposited [his] garbage "in an area particularly suited for public inspection and, in a manner of speaking, public consumption, for the express purpose of having strangers take it,"... respondent could have had no reasonable expectation of privacy in the inculpatory items that [he] discarded. (*Greenwood*, 40)

In short, everybody knows or certainly could easily and should know that the imagined smooth and uninterrupted journey of one's trash from inside the house, to the curb, to the truck, and finally to the dump, is an illusion. Even if you've spent extra money for stronger bags, you shouldn't forget about the habits of raccoons, rats, dogs, and cats; you shouldn't rule out possible meddling by intrusive types such as children, scavengers, and snoops. And for all you know—and apparently should know—the trash collector may start pawing through your stuff or willingly offer up the goods to the police. It's just not reasonable of you to think otherwise, given such common knowledge.

The majority insisted that its decision was fully consistent with earlier Supreme Court cases involving the Fourth Amendment. Many lower level courts, the majority claimed, did not hesitate to deny the applicability of privacy rights in the case of trash. During that period of time in which your trash is still identifiable as yours but placed by you "outside the curtilage," beyond the boundaries, of your property, you have no claim to Fourth Amendment rights against search and seizure. The trash is yours in the sense that it can be traced to you, but it is no longer yours in the sense that once you put it on public grounds not only is it likely to be open to inspection and even appropriation by others, but police need not seek a warrant to take it and open it and use it against you. Having disposed of it, you've lost control over its disposition. So sayeth the majority of justices.

Writing for the dissent, Justice Brennan expressed considerable chagrin over the decision of his colleagues in the majority:

> Scrutiny of another's trash is contrary to commonly accepted notions of civilized behavior. I suspect, therefore, that members of our society will be shocked to learn that the Court, the ultimate guarantor of liberty, deems unreasonable our expectation that the aspects of our private lives that are concealed safely in a trash bag will not become public. (*Greenwood*, 45–46)

Trash can talk, but, Justice Brennan insists, that doesn't mean that just anyone has the right to make it squeal. He is confident that most of his fellow citizens would agree. He also argues that careful consideration of earlier cases shows that the Supreme Court in fact has understood the Fourth Amendment to protect one's privacy in matters as intimate as the contents of one's garbage.

After all, Justice Brennan points out, people put sealed letters and packages in the mail, sending them off to be carried by public means to their intended recipients, and Fourth Amendment jurisprudence has consistently required warrants for searches of them. The Court has refused to distinguish between "worthy" and "unworthy" containers of personal effects—a closed paper bag is no different in this regard from a locked suitcase; what matters is whether the container has been closed to "conceal the contents from plain view" (*Greenwood*, 47). If I were carrying a closed garbage bag, any representative of the law wanting to peep into it without my consent would have to get a warrant; surely the same is true if someone happens to be using such bags "to discard, rather than transport, his personal effects. Their contents are not inherently any less private, and Greenwood's decision to discard them, at least in the manner in which he did, does not diminish his expectation of privacy" (*Greenwood*, 49).

Nor, Justice Brennan continues, should the Court judge such expectation to be diminished in light of the possibility that some two- or four-legged creature *might* meddle with one's trash. The law doesn't consider the mere possibility that a burglar might break into one's home to be adequate grounds for dismissal of Fourth Amendment protection against such intrusion (*Greenwood*, 54).

Justice Brennan thinks the majority at least avoided one wrong turn in its judgment: it did not rely on a theory of "abandonment" that the Court discredited in earlier cases (*Greenwood*, 51). While discarding one's trash might seem to amount to abandonment of it and thus abandonment of the very grounds on which to claim

Fourth Amendment protection, there is a strong strand in the history of "trash search doctrine"[8] according to which it is *privacy* and not only *property* for which protection is provided (for example, the Court had ruled in *California v. Rooney*[9] that the fact that a telephone call is made in a public phone booth does not mean that its contents are open to surveillance absent a warrant). Placing one's trash in a sealed opaque container on the curb so that it will be picked up by a designated collector at a specific time in order to reach a specific destination constitutes abandoning it in the sense of putting it out of one's immediate control but hardly constitutes behavior exhibiting no intent to preserve the privacy of its contents.

Moving beyond Court precedent, Brennan cites non-judicial support (including an article in *Esquire* written by Mr. A. J. Weberman himself) for the view that

> a single bag of trash testifies eloquently to the eating, reading, and recreational habits of the person who produced it. A search of trash, like a search of the bedroom, can relate intimate details about sexual practices, health, and personal hygiene. Like rifling through desk drawers or intercepting phone calls, rummaging through trash can divulge the target's financial and professional status, political affiliations and inclinations, private thoughts, personal relationships, and romantic interests. It cannot be doubted that a sealed trash bag harbors telling evidence of the "intimate activity associated with the 'sanctity of a man's home and the privacies of life,'" which the Fourth Amendment is designed to protect. (*Greenwood*, 50)

---

8. Gordon MacDonald, "Stray Katz: Is Shredded Trash Private?" 79 *Cornell Law Review* 452 (1994): 455, 477.
9. *California v. Rooney*, 483 U.S. 307 (1987).

In closing, Justice Brennan expresses alarm at the picture of society he thinks the majority has sketched: one in which

> local authorities may command their citizens to dispose of their personal effects in the manner least protective of the "sanctity of [the] home and the privacies of life" . . . and then monitor them arbitrarily and without judicial oversight—a society that is not prepared to recognize as reasonable an individual's expectation of privacy in the most private of personal effects sealed in an opaque container and disposed of in a manner designed to commingle it imminently and inextricably with the trash of others. (*Greenwood*, 55–56)

The Greenwood case was neither the beginning nor the end of judicial deliberation about whether people are entitled—in the United States, anyway—to think that their sealed trash is not to be searched and seized by police or other authorities without a warrant. The stories behind such cases can be both entertaining anecdotes and cause for alarm. For example, not long after Greenwood was decided, a Federal Appeals Court, in *United States v. Scott*,[10] refused to consider it a violation of the Fourth Amendment when police painstakingly put back together the carefully shredded records of a bookkeeper accused of fraud against the IRS.

Greenwood and *Scott* certainly shore up the case to be made for the revelatory power of trash and garbage. But at the same time they bring to our attention ways in which our relation to trash can be quite perplexing. On the one hand, as Justice Brennan pointed out, trash is thought to "testify eloquently" to the personal habits of those who generate it, to their political preferences, romantic

---

10. *United States v. Scott*, 975 F.2d 927 (1st Cir. 1992).

inclinations, and all manner of thoughts and attitudes and activities not necessarily meant for public consumption. On the other hand, trash is by definition what we have thrown out. We have deliberately distanced ourselves from it, cast it out of the orbit of our care, implicitly declared that we are or must be done with it. We might be sorry to have done so, or might be glad, but such a distinction won't be apparent in the higgledy-piggledy pile in the trash can. Indeed, long before our trash comes to be commingled with that of others, the once disparate elements of our own rejectamenta[11] are unceremoniously commingled at home. The severance of our former relation to them is reflected in the absence of any preferential differentiation obvious among them: there's little indication of how well or how poorly we thought of each piece, of how welcome or unwelcome they were, of their relative desirability, their standing as items of endearment or disgust. The carton that once contained the delicious peach cobbler ice cream might well be cradling within it scraps of the dutifully eaten but unseductive broccoli. (Celebrity garbologists may lament this loss of preferential detail; legal authorities probably don't care.)

Trash speaks of us, even as its status as trash signals a significant distance between it and us. We can get rid of our trash, but it doesn't quite get rid of us. That is why it lends itself so readily yet confoundedly to arguments over what is to be considered private. We may well not be concerned if others know, search through, or make use of what we toss out—we may just not care whether it remains private, whether its knowability remains subject to our control. But when we do care—even though we consider the trash

---

11. I first came across the wonderfully vivid word *rejectamenta* when reading Heather Rogers's *Gone Tomorrow: The Hidden Life of Garbage* (New York: New Press, 2006).

no longer to be part of us (we're tossing it out, after all)—we may not want others to know what it still has the power to reveal.

Still, beyond yielding potentially embarrassing or incriminating information, exactly *what or how much* do searches through our trash have the power to uncover? Quite a lot, according to the researcher whose work in garbology is cited in the *OED*'s entry for the term—and, he insists, it's primo stuff, of incomparable value.

TRASH AS "SETTING THE STORY STRAIGHT"

It is clear that A. J. Weberman and Justice William Brennan were guided by firm beliefs about the nature and significance of what a person's trash can tell us about him or her. Weberman was assuming that as a result of rummaging through Dylan's trash he could paint an unfavorable portrait of Dylan's character—one at odds with Dylan's public persona. Justice Brennan's dissent articulates a belief not incompatible with but much broader than Weberman's: our trash offers eloquent evidence of all aspects of our lives, whether what is revealed puts us in a negative or a positive light. No matter what it might say about us, it qualifies for Fourth Amendment protection of "the right of the people to be secure in their persons, houses, papers, and effects, against unreasonable searches and seizures."

Justice Brennan's impassioned plea implies that what is in a person's trash is at least as revelatory of that person as what she might choose to put on display for all to see. Weberman's approach has a further implication: that the contents of trash can tell not just a different but a closer, more accurate, more complete story about a person than what she is inclined to present for public consumption. Weberman's belief finds firmer and more explicit expression in the work of garbage archaeologist William Rathje, according to whom trash provides an epistemologically *privileged* resource for understanding the nature of human life.

Rathje for many years led teams of graduate students at the University of Arizona in the Garbage Project, a long-term examination of local landfills. He and Cullen Murphy published the results of the Garbage Project's research in *Rubbish! The Archaeology of Garbage*.[12] In addition to the *OED* reference to Rathje and the Garbage Project in connection with its definition of "garbology," references to Rathje's work abound in the growing body of literature on garbage and waste.[13] How well do this über-garbologist's enticing claims about the special epistemological riches of the landfill stand up?

Unlike A. J. Weberman or narcotics agents in southern California, Rathje and his team engaged in social science–sanctified snooping: though they did not identify garbage as belonging to any given individual or family, they explored such matters as demographic differences in what people throw out and possible discrepancies between what people say they eat and what their garbage reveals about their actual consumption (not surprisingly, we under-report how much candy, ice cream, and bacon we eat and over-report our intake of cottage cheese, skim milk, and high-fiber cereal [Rathje, 71]).

Rathje makes some striking claims about the particular kind of epistemological access garbage provides. He does not stick to

---

12. William Rathje and Cullen Murphy, *Rubbish! The Archaeology of Garbage* (Tucson: University of Arizona Press, 1992).

13. Rathje's admirers include not only food waste investigators such as Jonathan Bloom, *American Wasteland: How America Throws Away Nearly Half Its Food (And What We Can Do about It)* (Cambridge, MA: Da Capo, 2010), 186, but those with broader philosophical concerns such as John Scanlan, *On Garbage* (London: Reaktion, 2005), 138.

modest remarks such as saying that landfills provide "valuable insights" (Rathje, 4) or that archaeology might be understood as "the discipline that tries to understand old garbage" (Rathje, 10). No, Rathje argues more strongly that the garbage in which archaeologists traffic actually produces more reliable evidence than the stuff gleaned, for example, by historians: historians are "understandably drawn" to evidence such as the "remains of the tombs, temples, and palaces of the elite . . . filled with personal histories as recorded by admiring relatives and fawning retainers." But "garbage has often served as a kind of tattle-tale, *setting the record straight*" (Rathje, 12 [my emphasis]). Indeed, against what he sees as the pretensions of the historians, Rathje insists that "what people have owned—and thrown away—can speak *more eloquently, informatively, and truthfully about the lives they lead than they themselves ever may*" (Rathje, 54 [my emphasis]).

At various points in *Rubbish!* Rathje offers arguments to back up his view about the superior epistemological advantages of garbage archaeology. He notes the well-known tension often found between our "beliefs, attitudes, and ideas" on the one hand and "the picture embodied in the physical record" (Rathje, 12–13) on the other: the archaeological record of 18th-century life in "Colonial Williamsburg," for example, belies the tourist image of it as a pristine, garbage- and manure-free village (Rathje, 52–53). At the same time, he acknowledges that physical evidence should not be thought to point unambiguously to people's behavior or the conditions under which they live. Savvy garbologists know that the absence of a magazine such as *Playboy* in household trash doesn't necessarily mean that no one in that household reads it, but that perhaps it is to be found in a nonidentifying trash bin down the road (Rathje, 57–58).

Rathje also points out that most of the research conducted by his team was unobtrusive in the sense that the people whose behavior was being assessed were not aware of that fact, certainly not when they were actually throwing out the trash and garbage (Rathje, 20). In thereby reducing "one of the great biases inherent in much social science" (Rathje, 20)—the tendency of interviewees to skew their responses to protect themselves or please investigators, for example, or simply the fact that people are bad judges of how much they waste even when they are explicitly asked to keep track of it (Rathje, 69–70)— Rathje claims to have produced more accurate and reliable information about people's actual practices than would have been possible if the investigations had not been carried out "from the back end" (Rathje, 14).

Moreover, Rathje suggests that on the whole, people are so uninterested in or concerned about what they throw away that they are likely to be puzzled by what garbage archaeologists discover:

> The profligate habits of our own country and our own time— the sheer volume of the garbage that we create and must dispose of—will make our society an open book. The question is: Would we ourselves recognize our story when it is told, or will our garbage tell tales about us that we as yet do not suspect? (Rathje, 11)

There is no doubt that "we do not necessarily know many things that we think we know" (Rathje, 245)—including how much garbage we actually generate ("the sheer volume of the garbage that we create and must dispose of" [Rathje, 11]). And perhaps it is true that "what people have owned—and thrown away—can speak more eloquently, informatively, and truthfully about the lives they lead than they themselves ever may" (Rathje, 54), though this presumably depends upon garbologists being around to channel what the stuff says. As Rathje tells it, garbologists emerge as more reliable sources concerning significant features of people's habits and activities than people themselves or the dissimulating historians who write about them. Rathje doesn't seem to consider the possibility that there might be other claimants to bragging rights as deliverers of profound revelations about our lives. Are trashmakers, garbologists, and historians the only possible contestants or the only plausible winners? What is the nature and scope of the knowledge that garbage-sifting yields?

Rathje does lay out some fairly specific ideas about the particular kind of information garbage archaeology offers that goes beyond pointing out that people have a foggy, sometimes self-serving notion of their own waste practices. Demographic studies of garbage serve some very practical ends. For example, makers of a specific brand of cat food can find out just how loyal their customers are from a systematic haul of their trash (Rathje, 16); garbage studies can assist in the "rational governance of communities": municipalities need to know how much waste they actually generate, what they actually do with it, and how it might be reduced; garbage statistics can be of use in "any endeavor that demands detailed knowledge of the behavior (including the relatively private behavior) of large groups of real people" (Rathje, 135): are upper-class families more likely than middle-class families to purchase and use canned soup? (Rathje, 135–136).

Rathje provides much sturdier support for these modest findings than he does for his bold claims about the superior eloquence and broad truth-revealing properties of trash. What might account for his splashier proposals? Disciplinary pride may be a factor, but such pride is hardly peculiar to garbage archaeology. Nor are claims along the lines of "if you want to know what people are *really* like, look at _____." Candidates for filling in the blank have included "their cities," "their architecture," "their food," "their garbage," "their art," "their laws," and "the condition of their women and children." If the presence of "their garbage" on the list is at least prima facie plausible, it is in part thanks to the kind of work done by Rathje and his teams of hermeneutically inclined garbologists.

> Disdained commodity though it be, garbage offers a useful, if ironic, reminder of one of the fundamentals of critical self-knowledge—that we do not necessarily know many things that we think we know. (Rathje, 245)

Rathje has presented some good reasons for thinking that important information lurks in our landfills. But he hasn't yet provided convincing evidence for the more extravagant claims he makes about the epistemological access garbage offers—its alleged unique capacity to render humanity an "open book."

GARBAGE IN, GARBAGE NOT OUT

The job of trash haulers puts them in a professional relationship to garbage different from that of researchers such as William Rathje and his crew. That doesn't mean they never engage in the kind of hermeneutical and epistemological speculation characteristic of their garbology counterparts. A sanitation worker interviewed by television reporter Charles Kuralt some years ago described what his work enabled him to glean about his customers: it's "better'n being a psychiatrist. I can tell you anything you want to know" (Rathje, 55).

This vivid comparison echoes a not uncommon image of psychiatrists or psychotherapists as trained to "get the dirt" on people (whether or not such people are the analysts' willing patients). The familiarity of the comparison might well pique the interest of trash mavens: in boasting that the physical stuff people toss out provides even better insight into their lives than the psychological material a therapist or analyst might unearth, the sanitation worker's analogy invites us to think of our complex psychological furniture as including a mental trash bin—as if there's a lot on our minds or in our hearts we wish to get rid of but unlike our trash and garbage it cannot be seen or smelled or put into plastic bags.

The wry trash hauler is not alone in thinking that such psychological stuff might, along with the physical matter we discard, be thought of as matter fit for the trash. As we shall see, Sigmund Freud's descriptions of his patients' efforts to banish unwelcome thoughts and wishes from consciousness are filled with images of expelling, rejecting, or otherwise trying to discard and disown those thoughts and wishes. Indeed, Freud implies that there is a strong resemblance between the processes by which we try to keep physical waste and garbage out of sight, or at least out of mind, and those by which we try to keep what we fear is unsavory or undesirable about ourselves out of consciousness. This is not to suggest that Freud saw himself as a kind of sanitation worker, combing the trash bins or scouring the sewers of the psyche. On the contrary, he was acutely aware that the kinds of explorations he was opening up as a psychoanalyst were widely considered disreputable because of the nature of the material he claimed to be uncovering.

What follows hardly constitutes a detailed examination or critique of Freud's voluminous writings on the nature and goals of psychoanalysis (let alone the massive secondary literature on Freud and Freudianism). But given the importance of the notion of "repressed" psychic material in Freud's work, the sanitation worker's analogy invites us to wonder: did Freud in any way treat such repressed material as resembling more familiar and more visible examples of trash or garbage? Did he think such material provided especially revelatory information about a person?

Repression: Where Does That Repressed Material Go?

A relatively early version of Freud's account of repression can be found in "Five Lectures on Psychoanalysis,"[14] a series of talks Freud delivered at Clark University in 1910. In cases of hysteria and other neuroses, he argued, there emerged.

a wishful impulse which was in sharp contrast to the subject's other wishes and which proved incompatible with the ethical and aesthetic standards of his personality. There had been a short conflict, and the end of this internal struggle was that the idea which had appeared before consciousness as the vehicle of this irreconcilable wish fell a victim to repression [*Verdrängung*], was pushed out of consciousness with all its attached memories, and was forgotten. (*Lectures*, 23)

14. Sigmund Freud [1910], "Five Lectures on Psychoanalysis, Leonardo da Vinci and Other Works," in *The Standard Edition of the Complete Psychological Works of Sigmund Freud*, translated from the German under the general editorship of James Strachey, in collaboration with Anna Freud, assisted by Alix Strachey and Alan Tyson, 11: 1–56, http://www.pep-web.org.libproxy.smith.edu:2048/document.php?id=se.011.0001a#p0003. Hereafter cited as *Lectures*. Freud's many queries about the nature of repression began at least as early as "The Interpretation of Dreams" [1900], *Standard Edition* 5: 588–609, and include an essay entitled simply "Repression" [1915], *Standard Edition* 14: 141–158. But it is in the *Lectures* and, as we are about to see, in "Civilization and Its Discontents," that he offers vivid analogies in hopes of depicting the mechanics of repression.

The repression allows the patient to avoid the pain of mental conflict. For example, a young woman whose older sister has just died becomes aware of entertaining the idea that the sister's husband would now be free to marry her. But this realization revolts her, and she banishes the thought. However, she pays a heavy price for doing so: she falls ill "with severe hysterical symptoms" (*Lectures*, 24).

Freud then offers this analogy to help provide "a more vivid picture of repression and of its necessary relation to resistance" (*Lectures*, 25):

> Let us suppose that in this lecture-room and among this audience . . . there is nevertheless someone who is causing a disturbance and whose ill-mannered laughter, chattering and shuffling with his feet are distracting my attention from my task. I have to announce that I cannot proceed with my lecture; and thereupon three or four of you who are strong men stand up and, after a short struggle, put the interrupter outside the door. So now he is "repressed" [*verdrängt*], and I can continue my lecture. But in order that the interruption shall not be repeated, in case the individual who has been expelled [*Herausgeworfene*] should try to enter the room once more, the gentlemen who have put my will into effect place their chairs up against the door and thus establish a "resistance" [*Widerstandt*] after the repression has been accomplished. If you will now translate the two localities concerned into psychical terms as the "conscious" and the "unconscious," you will have before you a fairly good picture of the process of repression. (*Lectures*, 24)

Much closer to the end of his career, in *Civilization and Its Discontents*,[15] Freud uses somewhat similar terms to describe attempts to get rid of unwanted thoughts or wishes:

A tendency arises to separate from the ego [*vom Ich abzu-sondern*] everything that can become a source of such unpleasure, to throw it outside [*nach aussen zu werfen*] and to create a pure pleasure-ego which is confronted by a strange and threatening "outside." . . . [S]ome sufferings that one seeks to expel [*hinausweisen will*] turn out to be inseparable from the ego in virtue of their internal origin. . . . In order to fend off [*zu erwehren*] certain unpleasurable excitations arising from within, the ego can use no other methods than those which it uses against unpleasure coming from without, and this is the starting-point of important pathological disturbances. (*Civilization*, 66–67)

Throw the boisterous disruptive impertinent man out of the lecture hall; throw the noisy disruptive shameful thought into the unconscious.[16]

Notice that though the noisy interrupter is tossed out of the hall, he does not disappear. Indeed if he had, there would have been no need for anyone to stand at the door to make sure he couldn't get back

15. Freud [1930], "Civilization and Its Discontents," *Standard Edition* 21: 57–146. Hereafter cited as *Civilization*, http://www.pep-web.org.libproxy.smith.edu:2048/document.php?id=se.021.0057a#p0064.

16. Anthony Storr has pointed out that Freud was not committed to the view that there was a piece of mental equipment called the "unconscious," and that he was content to treat "unconscious" as an adjective rather than a noun. *Freud: A Very Short Introduction* (New York: Oxford University Press, 1989), 60.

in. This is not an insignificant detail, since according to Freud, what gets repressed is in a sense out of sight but not out of mind: it is out of consciousness, yes, but there is more to the mind than consciousness. As we've just been reminded, Freud suggests that we use the same or something like the same methods to try to "fend off" or "expel" unwanted mental contents as we do to avoid or get rid of unwanted stimuli from without. But that doesn't mean that employing those methods necessarily leads to successful results, if the measure of success is the degree to which the unwanted matter actually is expelled. The man in Freud's analogy has been successfully rejected from the hall, but he remains outside. He hasn't disappeared.

That a painful event can be lost to memory doesn't mean it has ceased to exist. It remains "in the patient's possession" (*Lectures*, 22): "*But the repressed wishful impulse continues to exist in the unconscious. It is on the look-out for an opportunity of being activated, and when that happens it succeeds in sending into consciousness a disguised and unrecognizable substitute for what had been repressed, and to this there soon become attached the same feelings of unpleasure which it was hoped had been saved by the repression*" (*Lectures*, 26, emphasis in the original). Wishes may "have undergone repression, but have been able, in defiance of it, to persist in the unconscious" (*Lectures*, 46); "in mental life nothing which has once been formed can perish" (*Civilization*, 68). And far from weakening its force and influence, repression strengthens a wish, since once repressed it "cannot be influenced and it is independent of any contrary tendencies" (*Lectures*, 53). However, it need not stay repressed and can be retrieved, for "in suitable circumstances . . . it can once more be brought to light" (*Civilization*, 68). Those "suitable circumstances" can be provided by the well-trained psychoanalyst.

In an attempt to further illuminate how repression works, Freud draws upon archaeological images to describe the way in which unwanted mental phenomena get buried in the unconscious. Recounting the preservation of Rome's history in the ruins and remnants of walls and buildings, he remarks: "Remnants of ancient Rome are found dovetailed into the jumble of the great metropolis which has grown up in the last few centuries since the Renaissance. There is certainly not a little that is ancient still buried in the soil of the city or beneath the modern buildings" (*Civilization*, 69). But Freud is not fully satisfied with the analogy. He notes that if contemporary Rome contained as much of the past as in fact is retained in the human psyche, "in which nothing that has once come into existence will have passed away and all the earlier phases of development continue to exist alongside the latest one," we'd find not only the "Pantheon of to-day, as it was bequeathed to us by Hadrian, but, on the same site, the original edifice erected by Agrippa" (*Civilization*, 69), which is not and could not be the case. Moreover, routine demolition and replacement are characteristic even of cities with relatively peaceful pasts. So while the preservation of Rome's history in its buried remains provides an image of the psyche with its forgotten but still existing memories, at the same time what is known about the psyche and its workings reveals some of the limitations of the analogy, showing us "how far we are from mastering the characteristics of mental life by representing them in pictorial terms" (*Civilization*, 70).

Freud considers one or two other possible images or models only to caution, in the end, "we are not in a position to represent this phenomenon [the "forgotten" wishes and dreams deep-sixed in the psyche] in pictorial terms" (*Civilization*, 70). But at the same time attempts to do so have not proved fruitless, for they serve to temper the certainty of the belief that all forgotten memories still exist and encourage us to embrace the more qualified claim that "it is rather the rule than the exception for the past to be preserved in mental life" (*Civilization*, 71). But "preservation" [*Erhaltung*] can be misleading: the symptomatic expression of what is buried in the psyche is deferred, and the very process of unearthing it transforms or disguises many of its features. Neither the patient nor the analyst is in the fortunate and highly unusual situation of those who dug into the volcanic ash covering Pompeii and found the inhabitants and their city in much the same condition they were when Mount Vesuvius erupted.

According to Freud, then, when thoughts or wishes conflict with our strongly held ideals, we may succeed in forgetting the thoughts and wishes to avoid the pain of such conflict. But that does not mean they disappear. Though certain pictorial analogies may help us begin to understand the repression of those wishes and the relocation of them in the psyche despite our earnest efforts to expel them, such analogies—the man thrown out of the lecture hall, the enduring remnants of a city such as Rome—aren't adequate to the task.

In addition to analogies explicitly drawn by Freud, images of expelling and tossing out appear regularly in his descriptions of the manner in which the person feeling under threat by her wishes or ideas tries to rid herself of them. This should not be surprising. According to psychoanalytic theory, the patients were repressing material they thought so disgraceful or shameful or frightening that to keep it out of the sight of others was not sufficient; they had to hide it from themselves.

Recall Freud's example in the *Lectures* of the disruptive man being tossed out of the room: "Strong men stand up and, after a short struggle, put the interrupter outside the door. So now he is 'repressed'" Or his account in *Civilization* of how a patient "seeks to dispel" "displeasure" coming from inside, to "throw it outside." Freud's descriptions of attempts to banish unwanted wishes often carry a strong sense of urgency and intensity. For example, in the essay "A Childhood Recollection from 'Dichtung und Wahrheit,'" Freud recounts at some length what seems to be a common reaction of young children to the unwanted arrival of younger siblings: with a vehemence bordering on violence, they throw crockery or other breakables out the window. Freud argues that it is not just the pleasure of doing something naughty or of making something break that accounts for such behavior. No, "this 'Out!' seems to be an essential part of the magic action and to arise directly from its hidden meaning. The new baby must be got rid of [*fortgeschafft*]."[17] And if for any reason the child fears entertaining such a notion, the very thought of throwing out the new sibling must itself be thrown out. Unlike the defenestrated dishes, however, the unwanted wish can't be flung out the window. Recall:

> In order to fend off certain unpleasurable excitations arising from within, the ego can use no other methods than those which it uses against unpleasure coming from without, and this is the starting-point of important pathological disturbances. (*Civilization*, 66–67)

So, then, Freud's descriptions of patients as expelling unwanted material from consciousness, trying to dispose of it, get rid of it, are not at all unlike, indeed sometimes are compared by him to, familiar gestures of throwing stuff out, of marking material as rejectamenta ready for removal, for being hauled away, transported out of sight, rendered virtually nonexistent.

17. Freud [1917], "A Childhood Recollection from *Dichtung und Wahrheit*," in *Standard Edition* 17: 151.

There are differences, of course, between everyday gestures of tossing stuff out and the rejection of unwanted wishes and thoughts: not all our ordinary trash is stuff we are desperate to remove out of fear that it will provide evidence of our shameful ways. And throwing out the trash typically is something we knowingly and intentionally do. Moreover, if it isn't pawed through and confiscated by scavengers, snoops, or social scientists and other garbologists, the trash does get hauled away, probably to be commingled with that of others at the landfill or incinerator. In these ways, discarding stuff no longer wanted around the house is different from expelling thoughts and wishes so threatening that their being tossed out of consciousness does not depend, cannot depend, on our being aware of trying to do so, and the removal of which from the psyche is in fact not achieved.

Still, gestures of tossing, expelling, expurgating, and rejecting occur in descriptions of how both physical stuff and psychological matter are treated. And as an image of repressing psychological material, throwing out trash has some advantages over pitching out the boisterous audience member Freud described in the Clark Lectures: the disruptive person is depicted as distracting and unpleasant, but the image doesn't capture the fear or shame Freud suggests is so often associated with unwanted thoughts and wishes. There are lots of reasons for wanting to get something out of sight, hearing, or awareness; the reasons for the patients Freud describes include a strong sense of revulsion or shame or threat. The kinds of conflicts he notes seem to involve something like a desire to get rid of moral or aesthetic trash or rubbish, threatening proof of one's own trashy self. Though the interrupter is tossed out, he is not treated in a way that suggests his behavior was considered shameful or fear-inducing.

Another comparison comes to mind, especially in connection with Freud's interest in archaeology and the layered history of cities. Given his views that what gets dispatched to the unconscious moils and rumbles about, making its continued presence known through the patient's symptoms, one might compare the unconscious to a poorly functioning sewage system. We fill the latter with biological and other wastes that we flush away in hopes of never seeing or smelling them again. But when malfunctioning, such a system gets all clogged up, and our earnest efforts at expulsion are rewarded with foul odors and stinky seepage. The return of the repressed.

The suggestion being made here is not that Freud included explicit allusions to trash or waste or garbage or sewage in his efforts to illuminate the process of repression. But such analogies seem apt in capturing the nature of what he describes when thoughts and desires are repressed. That a similarity might in fact have occurred to Freud seems quite possible, given his great interest in the history of Rome, whose ancient water and sewage systems long have been among the wonders for which the city is renowned, and his rich acquaintance with London and Paris, whose notorious garbage and sewage crises involving the fouling of the Thames and the Seine must have been known to him.[18] Moreover, punning on the German word for filth, in letters to his friend Fliess he described aspects of his work (including that in connection with his self-analysis) as "tramping along in the *Dreckology*," and creating "'dreckological [*Dreckologisch*] reports."[19]

---

18. This possibility is not included, however, in Carl Schorske's delightful description of Freud's complex feelings about differences among Vienna, London, Paris, and Rome. Carl E. Schorske, "Freud: The Psycho-Archaeology of Civilizations," *Proceedings of the Massachusetts Historical Society*, Third Series 92 (1980): 52–67.

19. *The Complete Letters of Sigmund Freud to Wilhelm Fliess 1887–1904*, translated and edited by Jeffrey Moussaieff Masson (Cambridge, MA: Belknap, 1985), 290, 291, 294, 295, 300.

At the same time, though concepts of expelling, rejecting, and tossing out appear frequently in Freud's accounts, he would have been eager to downplay any suggestion that what his patients created and he treated was material fit for the trash. For several reasons he would have been very reluctant to publicly and explicitly draw attention to similarities between the contents of what his patients tried to expel and the trash and garbage and waste in backyards or front yards, on the streets or in sewers and rivers. Though it may be hard to imagine now—decades after accounts of "the triumph of the therapeutic" and debates over the powerful effects on public life of "therapeutic culture"[20]—Freud and his professional colleagues were vulnerable to charges that the work they were engaged in was disreputable. One reason that the reputation of psychoanalysis as a serious profession was far from well established was the assumption that Freud and others were trafficking in what was filthy, dirty, and scandalous; they delved into matters such as sexuality and excrement that were considered not proper or worthy objects of inquiry.[21] Freud himself had said, "Dirtiness of any kind seems to us incompatible with civilization," and "We do not think highly of the cultural level of an English country town in Shakespeare's time when we read that there was a big dung-heap in front of his father's house in Stratford" (*Civilization*, 92).

---

20. See, for example, Philip Rieff, *The Triumph of the Therapeutic: Uses of Faith after Freud* (New York: Harper, 1966); Christopher Lasch, *The Culture of Narcissism: American Life in the Age of Diminishing Expectations* (New York: Norton, 1978).

21. In an entry on Psychoanalysis that Freud contributed to the 13th edition of the *Encyclopedia Britannica*, he posits that the "strongest reason" for the "forcible rejection of the new teachings" of psychoanalysis "was undoubtedly the general disinclination of mankind to concede to the factor of sexuality the importance that is assigned to it by psycho-analysis." "Psycho-Analysis," *Standard Edition* 20: 269. Freud thought that the achievement of "adult sexuality" required the repression of "coprophilic elements" in

In response, Freud tried carefully to dignify the psychoanalytic project through his characterizations of the work involved. In comparing the ruins of Rome's past excavated by archaeologists to repressed material in the unconscious unearthed by psychoanalysts, he arguably was hoping to burnish psychoanalysis with a reputation for scientific aspiration (Freud did a considerable amount of undeniably scientific work early in his career).[22] As Sabina Hake points out, a connection with the "historical significance" of a profession such as archaeology "validate[d] . . . [psychoanalysts'] cultural preferences as members of the educated middle class." Given the "scandal of psychoanalysis," Freud usefully based "his daring advances into the realm of the unconscious on the solid foundation of tradition, at least with regard to his choice of tropes. In so doing, he gave psychoanalysis an aura of respectability."[23] And indeed, how could anything unseemly or suspect be going on if the investigations of the psychoanalyst resembled those of the archaeologist, and if Freud could explain repression using perfectly innocent scenes such as disruptive people being sent from the lecture hall?

Moreover, if Freud believed that his patients already felt shame about what they were trying so hard to keep from their own awareness, he would not want to further burden them with the possibility that the material they hoped to expel was too far outside the range of acceptable topics of conversation to be alluded to, let alone examined. Indeed, Philip Rieff has pointed

the sexual instinct. "On the Universal Tendency to Debasement in the Sphere of Love," *Standard Edition* 11: 188. Ridding ourselves of intense interest in our own biological waste is among the requirements of "civilized" sexuality.

22. See "Abstracts of the Scientific Writings of Dr. Sigm. Freud (1877–1897)," *Standard Edition* 3: 223–257.

23. Sabine Hake, "*Saxa Loquuntur*: Freud's Archaeology of the Text," *boundary 2*, 20, no. 1 (Spring, 1993): 155–156.

out that Freud's comparison of the work of the psychoanalyst to that of the archaeologist exhibited a kind of respect for the patient.[24]

In addition, Freud thought it crucial to retrieve what had been expelled, to uncover what had been buried: in that sense he was refusing to regard it as the kind of thing that ought to be got rid of, that was fit for the trash or the sewer. He thought that bringing it back to consciousness was crucial to the patient's recovery. There is valuable treasure there. The patient may have thought it must be trashed, that it was fit only for the rubbish bin, but the analyst knew otherwise. It was treating the material as trash that was the problem.

The Repressed as Psychic Pay Dirt?

This takes us to our second main question about Freud: did he think of the contents of the unconscious as providing epistemologically privileged information about the patient? Was combing through the detritus hauled up from the unconscious going to yield primo pay dirt about the patient?

In considering this, let's look again briefly at the various elements of the psychoanalytic picture of the patient and the analyst:

1. The patient regards something that she has thought or wished to be so repugnant, so at odds with her consciously expressed values, that it must be expelled.

---

24. Philip Rieff, *Freud: The Mind of the Moralist* (New York: Anchor, 1961), 45. But Rieff also points to an aggressive side of the comparison: the analyst but not the archaeologist sees the past as "an incubus on the present," an enemy of both patient and analyst and needing to be taken control of.

2. The undesirable material is dispatched to the unconscious, but it has not thereby been got rid of: it remains in the deep recesses of the psyche.

3. The repressed material pushes to emerge from those recesses, and is resisted.

4. Nevertheless it re-emerges, albeit in a disguise: neurotic symptoms.

5. However ingenious the disguise, it can be seen through by appropriately trained and skilled analysts, who can also provide ways of dealing consciously and fruitfully with the conflict that is its cause.

The job of the analyst, as Freud saw it, is to retrieve, with the help of the patient, what has been banished to unconsciousness and make it available for inspection and possible use. Did he think that the analyst is thereby in a position to reveal information about the patient that is in some sense "truer," "deeper," more epistemologically privileged than anything else about her?

There is no doubt that Freud thought of repressed material as importantly revelatory of a person's thoughts and wishes, significant precisely because it had been rendered inaccessible to the person herself and those close to her. But it's not clear that he regarded what was repressed as somehow *more* revelatory of the person than what she and others were more readily and consciously aware of. What gets tossed into the unconscious is in the patient's eyes a source of shame or fear. The shame or fear arises from a perception of conflict between what one has thought or wished and strong norms making such wishes taboo. The conflict has to be recognized and dealt with to get rid of the debilitating symptoms that are caused by it and betray its continuing existence. All going well, the psycho-analytic method of treatment is then able to subject this process of repression to revision and to bring about a better solution of the conflict, one compatible with health.[25]

The aim of the analysis is to help "effect a recovery" (*Lectures* 22). The recovery requires the unearthing of the truth that one has had certain thoughts or wishes. Also, as a result of the analysis a more complete picture of the person becomes available and in that sense a better, fuller picture of her emerges. But Freud doesn't seem to have regarded the forgotten truths retrieved in psychoanalysis as more significant than those more readily acknowledged by the patient. They are necessary to the whole picture of the patient but do not occupy its center, however much damage their interment has done. In fact, reducing the sense of the patient's shame or fear in having certain thoughts and wishes seems an unlikely outcome if as the result of the analysis the patient concludes that what has been revealed about her tells the "real" story about her, the big story, the heart of the story, "the dirty truth." Freud may believe that psycho-analysis provides the best access to what has been festering in the unconscious, but that doesn't mean he treats what is thereby unearthed as "truer" of the patient than what is more readily accessible. The patient on her way to health has integrated the formerly banished information into her understanding of herself, not decided that she is after all simply and only the nasty girl she feared she was.

Was Freud as sanguine as William Rathje about trash providing epistemologically superior access to people's lives? Much of

---

25. Freud, "A Difficulty in the Path of Psycho-analysis," *Standard Edition* 17: 137.

what Freud says suggests that the aim of psychoanalysis as he understood it was not the "gotcha" of celebrity trash reconnaissance, or the "*j'accuse*" of narcotics agents, or the "we've got a leg up on all the other professions" of some garbage archaeologists, but rather the promise of removing a patient's neurotic symptoms, of dissolving a sense of shame rather than trying to induce it.[26]

Attempts to "get the dirt" on someone by combing through their trash may end up throwing some "dirt" back onto the investigator. Though the cases of A. J. Weberman, the Tokyo Trash Baby, Kuralt's sanitation worker, and Freud are not the same, in each case, being understood to be a collector or scavenger of the trash of others threatens to sully one's reputation or standing. Weberman and the Trash Baby have to fight off the impression that they are just plain creepy; Kuralt's garbage hauler is eagerly presenting an interpretation of his work at odds with a much less favorable understanding of the nature of his labor; Freud hoped to benefit from having his work compared to that of an archaeologist but not to that of a sanitation worker. On the other hand, neither the narcotics agents who went after Billy Greenwood's trash, nor Rathje and his crew appear to have had to fight off being contaminated by their working closely with

---

26. In *Darwin's Worms* (New York: Basic Books, 2000), Adam Phillips has argued that Freud was deeply skeptical about "the whole notion of getting at the truth about a person's life" (85). Indeed, Phillips goes on, "the more Freud elaborated psychoanalytic theory the less impressed he was by the knowability of the human subject" (94). Phillips develops this view at greater length in *Becoming Freud: The Making of a Psychoanalyst* (New Haven, CT: Yale University Press, 2014).

others' discards. We shall consider the imputation of such contamination at much greater length in Chapter 3. But first we pause to explore a tendency in humans quite at odds with worries about people going through one's trash: unmitigated boasting over how wasteful one can afford to be.[27]

27. The New York Metro American Studies Association conference on DIRT in December 2010 provided me a welcome opportunity to give a brief presentation of some of the ideas discussed here and to meet a particularly congenial group of DIRT mavens. A considerably shorter version of this essay was delivered as the 53rd Katharine Asher Engel Lecture at Smith College and published in *The Massachusetts Review* 52, no. 2 (Summer 2011): 313–325. I'm very grateful to members of the DIRT conference, especially organizers Hildegard Hoeller and the late Patricia Yaeger, the Engel Lecture audience at Smith, and to Jim Hicks and Michael Thurston at *The Massachusetts Review*.

Chapter 2

A Taste for Waste

On the whole, we probably don't want other people to have license to go through the stuff we discard. Whether or not we think of our trash as "sacred," we may well find such snoops "creepy" (to retreat to the language of everyday reaction to such searches noted in Chapter 1). Even if our trash contains nothing embarrassing or incriminating, it is fair to say, surely, that it doesn't reveal us at our best. It's not usually what we want the neighbors to see—or smell. Pictures of our garbage and trash probably are not among those we proudly send to friends and relatives.[1]

At the same time, it's not unusual in the history of *Homo trasho* for people to use their capacity to produce waste as evidence of their economic prowess or social status. Snoopy rummaging notwithstanding, not all combing through other people's rubbish bins reflects a desire to glean information about an individual's

---

1. Plausible exceptions include instructive blogs about how much trash a single household generates in, say, a month or a year. See, for example, David Chameides, "365 Days of Trash: One Man's Attempt to Throw Nothing 'Away' for a Year . . . and Beyond," http://365daysoftrash.blogspot.com/2007/12/365-days-of-trash.html.

personal habits or intimate activities. Scavenging may simply be a function of a searcher's desperate need to obtain adequate food, clothing, and shelter. One measure of the extent to which a person lives in penurious conditions is having to survive on the rejects of others and needing to use whatever goods one does have as long as possible.

A vivid measure, on the other hand, of not being in such reduced circumstances is conspicuous consumption, a sustained demonstration readily intelligible to others that far from living in such straits one is in a position to enjoy an abundance of goods as well as the services of people who take care of them and of you. The notions of "conspicuous consumption" and the closely related "conspicuous leisure" were introduced by Thorstein Veblen in *The Theory of the Leisure Class*, published in 1899.[2] At the heart of such sustained exhibitions of lavish consumption and unencumbered leisure, according to Veblen, is a principle of conspicuous waste.

Veblen's point was not that people eager and anxious to make a conspicuous exhibit of their wealth go about displaying their garbage, trash, and other discards; he surely doesn't suggest that they would welcome "curbside trash reconnaissance" of the sort described in Chapter 1. But their mode of living functions to get others to notice and appreciate a more general kind of capacity to waste—a wastefulness available to, indeed incumbent upon, those who have not only more than they need (by any reasonable standard) but more than they can productively use unless they go to Herculean lengths. Their capacity to waste is not meant to be out of sight or out of mind.

---

2. Thorstein Veblen, *The Theory of the Leisure Class: An Economic Study of Institutions* (New York: Modern Library, 1931 [1899]). Hereafter referred to as *Leisure*.

In working out the meaning and the function of "conspicuous waste," Veblen offers trash mavens a reminder that not only can trash talk: waste can proclaim. But "waste" in what sense? Waste of what? To whom is the proclamation made, in what manner, to what end? And why use *waste* for such purposes?

Before turning to those questions we must spend a few moments asking another question: why Veblen? After all, *The Theory of the Leisure Class* is well more than a hundred years old, and the last of the works published in Veblen's lifetime appeared in 1925; his views about the nature of consumption and the social norms and economic conditions in which it is embedded have been judged by some of his more sympathetic critics to be outdated and by his least enthusiastic ones to be excellent candidates for the trash heap of satirical but unserious broadsides.[3] Moreover, as already indicated, Veblen's focus did not include the actual production and disposition of garbage and trash; it's not as if he foresaw our drowning in the sea of our own disposables and discards. On top of that, his sometimes antique and idiosyncratic use of the English language, and the evident acerbity of his commentary on the predilections and habits endorsed in the "leisure class regime" (he didn't think you actually had to be a member of the "leisure class" to be in the thrall of its canons of taste and behavior) may appear too fusty and fogeyish to some contemporary readers for his analysis to have any serious hold on us.

But for anyone interested in exploring humanity's complex relation to waste and trash, a close and careful look at Veblen is hardly a waste of time. As will become clear, Veblen offers a portrait

3. For a useful survey of some of the central complaints about Veblen's analysis, and to what extent they might be countered, see Andrew B. Trigg, "Veblen, Bourdieu, and Conspicuous Consumption," *Journal of Economic Issues* 35, no. 1 (March 2001): 99–115.

of societies built on industrial technology and private property as shot through with what amounts to a commitment to and elevation of wastefulness as a badge of honor, a crucial mark of high standing and good reputation. He sees such attunement to wastefulness reaching a furious pitch under the kind of economic and social conditions characteristic of late 19th-century life in parts of the United States, Europe, and Great Britain. At the same time, he treats that historical moment as merely one chapter in our complex and ever-evolving responses to the unmistakable demands on human existence for the provision of basic subsistence and comfort and to the fact of our sociality, our being dependent on each other for the regard in which we are held and hold ourselves.

The aim here is not to decide whether Veblen's depiction of our romance with wastefulness provided an adequate explanation of the phenomena on which he focused, or to see whether it can offer sufficient insight into the nature of consumption, leisure, and waste today. Such questions about his views remain alive and well both despite and because of Veblen's current relative obscurity.[4] The point rather is that Veblen remains one of our most piercing portraitists of waste and wastefulness, and we have much to learn from his landscapes even if questions remain about how faithfully they presented the world he depicted or how prescient he was or could have been about the world we now inhabit.

None of this is to say that Veblen's use of "waste" was clear and uncontestable. But his very attempt to carve out what could be considered a non-normative, indeed non-derogatory use of the word

---

4. Interest in the various dimensions of Veblen's work has hardly disappeared. See, for example, Janet Knoedler and Anne Mayhew, "Thorstein Veblen and the Engineers: A Reinterpretation," *History of Political Economy* 31, no. 2 (1999): 255–272; Patrick Brantlinger and Richard Higgins, "Waste and Value: Thorstein Veblen and H. G. Wells," *Criticism* 48, no. 4 (Fall 2006): 453–475.

is instructive for any of us (which is to say almost all of us) who toss the word around as if its meaning were clear and its applicability straightforward. Moreover, even if one does not find Veblen's portraiture to be persuasive, it's hard to go away from a close and careful reading of *The Theory of the Leisure Class* and related work without wondering about what waste and wastefulness mean to us and about the beliefs concerning and practices shaping waste that individuals and communities take for granted—indeed, perhaps celebrate.

In light of the garbage-combing explored in Chapter 1, Veblen's work invites us to reflect on why on the one hand we don't think our trash reveals us at our best and yet on the other we—surely at least some of us, surely at least some of the time—appear to accept without question that the capacity to waste offers evidence of an enviable way of being in the world. It is, after all, on the face of it rather strange that while it is "uncivilized" behavior to paw through the trash of others in search of information about them they would prefer to keep private, according to some notions of "civilized" behavior it is important for the public to recognize you as having the capacity to produce lots of such stuff; it is curious that on the one hand, having to scavenge through trash detracts from one's human dignity, but on the other, being able to be wasteful adds to personal luster.

We turn now to some of the central features of Veblen's portrait of human communities that have a taste for waste. Quotations from Veblen's work, especially *The Theory of the Leisure Class*, are on the quite generous side, in the expectation that readers not familiar with his writing (or who might welcome some reminders about its themes and tenor) can gain a sense of his distinct style, and to illustrate how frequently, in what contexts and to what end Veblen invokes the concept of waste.

ON THE "INVIDIOUS DISTINCTION
ATTACHING TO WEALTH"

According to Veblen, when the institution of private property is well and broadly established in a society, this typically means that people (probably most people) have to fend for themselves to make a living, but it also means that people (at least some people) can accumulate wealth, can add to their private property without limit. For those in a position to keep putting more in their pot, meeting subsistence needs is hardly the aim: the "dominant incentive" of their pecuniary practices is "the invidious distinction attaching to wealth" (*Leisure*, 26). One's social status and "reputability" (*Leisure*, 30 and *passim*) depend on one's "pecuniary strength" (*Leisure*, 31) relative to that of others. The shuffling and wrangling does not end:

> So long as the comparison is distinctly unfavorable to himself, the normal, average individual will live in chronic dissatisfaction with his present lot; and when he has reached what may be called the normal pecuniary standard of the community, or of his class in the community, this chronic dissatisfaction will give place to a restless straining to place a wider and ever-widening pecuniary interval between himself and this average standard. (*Leisure*, 31)

The very advances in "industrial efficiency" that offer a guarantee that people's survival and comfort needs will be satisfied create at the same time the grounds of a goal that cannot be reached: "since the struggle is substantially a race for reputability on the basis of an invidious comparison, no approach to a definitive attainment is possible" (*Leisure*, 32). When you are engaged in such a struggle, the fact that you can rest easy about having enough food on the table, enough clothing on the body, and sturdy shelter for self and loved ones is irrelevant. It's not enough to have enough: the central function of the accumulation of wealth is to rank you ahead of others, mark a clear line of discrimination between you and them.

WHY YOUR WEALTH HAS TO BE KNOWN TO OTHERS AND HOW THIS CAN HAPPEN

If the overweening reason for the accumulation of wealth is to indicate your rank relative to others, those others have to be made aware of your wealth. This puts considerable constraints on how and where you put your wealth to use. If you put most of it in a savings account and don't spend any more than you need for basic upkeep, it's going to be unnecessarily difficult for others to know how much you have. The proof of the wealth is in its spending, not in its saving. You must make it conspicuous—put it on show, in a way that will be readily intelligible to others. Otherwise your wealth will have been wasted, insofar as it has not been put to the use for which it is so well suited. That is, for the purpose of invidious comparison, there's no point in having wealth unless you spend it, no point in spending it unless others can tell—without guessing or hunting or spying—that you spend it and that you know how to spend it. You must offer incontrovertible evidence that you have more than enough to provide more than you need. In the endless battle of invidious comparison, there is no place for any obvious signs of thrift, penny pinching, voluntary or involuntary budgetary constraint. There is to be no doubt that you enjoy an indefinite abundance of goods made possible by an indefinite abundance of pecuniary resources.

Convincing proof of such wealth in the court of public opinion[5] requires of the one to be judged that he "not only consumes of the staff of life beyond the minimum required for subsistence and physical efficiency," but that

> he consumes freely and of the best, in food, drink, narcotics, shelter, services, ornaments, apparel, weapons and accoutrements, amusements, amulets, and idols or divinities. (*Leisure*, 73)

What you want far from public view, on the other hand, is any activity hinting at "productive labor," a sure "mark of poverty and subjection" (*Leisure*, 38). A life of leisure—of "exemption from contact with such industrial processes as serve the immediate everyday purposes of human life"—has been extolled "from the days of the Greek philosophers to the present" as a "prerequisite to a worthy or beautiful, or even a blameless, life" (*Leisure*, 37–38). Since even the wealthy have to attend somehow to their own everyday needs but shouldn't be seen doing so themselves, the clear presence of servants is called for; since the accumulation of wealth has something to do with indecorous "productive labor" (someone else's if not one's own), one's own relation to such labor must be distant. One must display one's wealth but in a manner that indicates that one had no hand— quite literally—in actually producing the goods and services it provides.

Conspicuous leisure and conspicuous consumption thus complement each other as intelligible insignia of reputability, though

---

5. It may be useful to underscore here that while Veblen seemed to have in mind especially the wealthy classes of the late 19th-century United States and Britain, he also thought that on the whole other classes strove to emulate those in the classes above them.

the relative usefulness of one or the other is likely to vary in accordance with specific circumstances (for example, in the anonymity of cities, Veblen suggests, conspicuous consumption is more likely than conspicuous leisure to perform the requisite work of publicity [*Leisure*, 86]).

Putting and keeping one's "opulence in evidence" (*Leisure*, 75) takes no little effort on the part of those who at the same time cannot be known to engage in any kind of labor considered of practical use. It is of enormous benefit to their project of keeping their consumption and leisure conspicuous to surround themselves with a large retinue of family members and servants who can engage in vicarious consumption and vicarious leisure, that is, whose apparent enjoyment of a bottomless cornucopia of goods and freedom from productive work is for the benefit of their employers and not themselves.[6] The show must go on, and if the main player—the man of the house—can't always be on the stage, others can be employed to sustain the desired impression.

Leading a life characterized by conspicuous consumption and conspicuous leisure, then, is a considerable undertaking, and mounting and sustaining it requires no small amount of effort. One

6. "Vicarious" appears to be ambiguous in this context. It could suggest that the household retinue imagine having but do not actually experience the social standing of those for whom they work. But Veblen seems to have in mind that the consumption and leisure are vicarious in the sense that they are meant to bring to mind that of the male head of household. When services are "performed by others than the economically free and self-directing head of the establishment, they are to be classed as vicarious leisure" (*Leisure*, 59). Far from being actual leisure, the "vicarious leisure performed by housewives and menials . . . may frequently develop into drudgery," perhaps better described as "wasted effort" than "vicarious leisure" (*Leisure*, 59). Indeed, "the leisure of the servant is not his own leisure" (*Leisure*, 60). The point then seems to be not that the housewife and male and female servants vicariously experience the leisure of the master—their own experience makes clear to them that they are hardly at leisure. They are not imagining themselves enjoying being like a man of leisure. They are laboring in a way so as to allow others to imagine what the master enjoys.

who hopes to display such abundance of goods and unclaimed time has to go to the trouble of knowing just what to consume and just how to consume it. One must learn manners: "refined tastes, manners, and habits of life are a useful evidence of gentility, because good breeding requires time, application, and expense, and can therefore not be compassed by those whose time and energy are taken up by work" (*Leisure*, 49). Family members—especially wives—and servants have to be decked out appropriately and trained correctly: "the servant should show not only an attitude of subservience, but also the effects of special training and practice in subservience" (*Leisure*, 60).

MUTING THE "INSTINCT OF WORKMANSHIP"

Though those involved in maintaining a life of conspicuous consumption and leisure are engaged in arduous and demanding activity, they must give up whatever allegiance they might otherwise have to the idea that there are better ends to which to put their time and effort; they have to mute or dampen what Veblen called the "instinct of workmanship," which along with "parental bent" underwrites an "approval of economy and efficiency for the common good and a disapproval of wasteful and useless living."[7] They must put aside any interest in or preference for work serving the ends of efficiency and utility because conspicuous consumption and conspicuous leisure are deeply and profoundly *wasteful*. The successful staging of such display is not possible apart from close adherence to a principle of

7. Thorstein Veblen, *The Instinct of Workmanship and the State of the Industrial Arts*, with an introduction by Dr. Joseph Dorfman (New York: Sentry Press, 1964 [1914]), 27. Hereafter referred to as *Instinct*.

conspicuous waste: conspicuous consumption involves "a waste of goods," conspicuous leisure a "waste of time and effort" (*Leisure*, 85). The point of these forms of conspicuous display, recall, is to create and sustain one's "good repute," one's "good name," in terms of "pecuniary strength" (*Leisure*, 84). The more one can afford to waste, the more wealth one must have. I don't just have some money to spend; I have so much that I can waste it. I can use it to purchase goods and engage the labor of others beyond what I possibly could be said to need in order to survive and enjoy the basic comforts of life.

VEBLEN'S CONCEPT OF WASTE

Veblen was fully aware that "wasteful" is likely to be heard as a derogatory term. "In the speech of everyday life," he acknowledged in a characteristic understatement, it no doubt "carries an undertone of deprecation," an implication of "an illegitimate expenditure of human products or of human life" (*Leisure*, 97). He acknowledges that from the perspective of those engaged in conspicuous consumption and leisure, such expenditures of goods and time and effort are not wasteful, are not misdirected (*Leisure*, 98). Indeed they are regarded as indispensable (*Leisure*, 99). Moreover, economic theory as he understood it refrains from ranking expenditures in terms of their relative legitimacy (*Leisure*, 97).[8]

---

8. Veblen was hardly an enthusiast of the tradition of economic theory taking such a position. In his introduction to *The Portable Veblen* (New York: Viking Press, 1948), 30, editor Max Lerner comments that Veblen devoted some of "his hardest and most painstaking work" to destroying "orthodox economics. He did not want economics to remain an apology for differential income inside a system of arbitrary and functionless ownership." Veblen's analyses of Adam Smith and Karl Marx first appeared in print in the *Quarterly Journal of Economics* in 1899 and 1906 and were reprinted in *The Place of Science in Modern Civilisation and Other Essays* (New York: B. W. Huebsch, 1919), 114–147 and 409–456.

Why then does Veblen nevertheless use "waste," and what does he mean by it? "Waste" aptly describes such expenditures, he says, insofar as they do "not serve human life or human well being on the whole" (*Leisure*, 97). From the perspective of the instinct of workmanship, that other principle of human activity that is constantly in tension with and mostly having lost ground to the principle of conspicuous waste, "any economic fact must approve itself under the test of impersonal usefulness—usefulness as seen from the point of view of the generically human" (*Leisure*, 98); it must "further the life process taken impersonally" (*Leisure*, 99), "human life on the whole," that is, apart from the prospective pecuniary gain of any particular individual, "the invidious or predatory interest of one as against another."[9] Indeed, Veblen argues, *Homo sapiens* could not have survived had it not developed "facility in shaping things and situations for human use" (*Irksome*, 87).[10] Unless self-interest had been put aside (*Irksome*, 87), the group and thus all the individuals within it could not have adapted to environmental demands. When the sense of solidarity central to the instinct of workmanship is strong, "efficiency, serviceability, commends itself, and inefficiency or futility is odious" (*Irksome*, 87).

The degree to which conspicuous waste is not seen as such by those engaged in it (which is most of us, no matter how rich or how poor, he says), the extent to which it has become "customary and prescriptive" is simply a measure of the relative though

---

9. Veblen, "The Instinct of Workmanship and the Irksomeness of Labor," in *Essays in Our Changing Order*, edited by Leon Ardzrooni (New York: Viking Press, 1945), 84 (reprinted from the *American Journal of Sociology* 4 [September 1898]). Hereafter referred to as *Irksome*.

10. Veblen takes what he calls "instincts" to be "proclivities" or "predispositions" distinct from automatic reflexes. Both instincts and reflexes are teleological, but acting on instinct, unlike being triggered by reflex, involves the conscious pursuit of particular ends with the aid of intelligence. See *Instinct*, especially 1–37.

not complete triumph of the "principle of pecuniary reputability or relative economic success" (*Leisure*, 100) over the instinct of workmanship. From the perspective of those motivated by no more unusual a desire than "to conform to established usage, to avoid unfavorable notice and comment, to live up to the accepted canons of decency in the kind, amount, and grade of goods consumed, as well as in the decorous employment of his time and effort" (*Leisure*, 115), conspicuous waste is unmistakably useful, however "odious" in light of the instinct of workmanship.

But if conspicuous waste is in fact useful from the perspective of acquiring and maintaining social status, why doesn't such wastefulness count as falling under the instinct of workmanship? After all, Veblen allows that this instinct is instrumental, oriented toward means rather than ends, whatever such ends might be (*Instinct*, 31). However, as just noted, Veblen also hypothesizes that the instinct first emerged at a time in which humans were "unremittingly dependent for their daily life on the workmanlike efficiency of all the members of the group," when "the prime requisite for survival . . . would be a propensity unselfishly and impersonally to make the most of the material means at hand and a penchant for turning all resources of knowledge and material to account to sustain the life of the group" (*Instinct*, 36–37). Hence the "efficient use of the means at hand and adequate management of the resources available for the purposes of life" have a history of appearing as themselves "an end of endeavor, and accomplishment of this kind is a source of gratification" (*Instinct*, 32). As such an end it would seem to ground strong disapproval of activities and undertakings that appear to be futile or wasteful (*Leisure*, 15).

However, by the time human habits and institutions have evolved to underwrite the reign of the "leisure class regime," the instinct of workmanship has come to serve ends "that have little traceable bearing on the means of subsistence" (*Instinct*, 37). As we've seen, it's not as if conspicuous consumption and leisure are not useful; it's not, then, as if the conspicuous waste underlying them is not useful, however incoherent such a claim may seem at first glance. Veblen makes very clear how useful they are for a way of life in which the preeminent, widely shared, and taken-for-granted goal is to establish superior economic and social position. Anyone embracing such a goal could find much in the details of Veblen's analysis to build a case for the efficiency and proficiency of a kind of waste management at the heart of such striving. Conspicuous consumption and conspicuous leisure appear to offer highly practical and useful tools for the purposes of invidious comparison. Indeed, to those who regard them as good instruments in the attainment of such an end, not using them for that purpose would seem a major waste of resources.

ALL-PERVADING WASTEFULNESS

One measure of how slight a hold the instinct of workmanship has come to have on industrial society (except insofar as it has been hijacked for purposes that do not serve "humanity in general"), in Veblen's account, is the degree to which wastefulness is central to all dimensions of social and economic life. Just as generating bodily waste is a biological imperative, so being wasteful becomes, under particular circumstances, a social and economic imperative. Indeed, according to Veblen it pervades every dimension of human life— aesthetic, religious, educational, legal, moral, and commercial.

The principle of conspicuous waste animating the household finds support—indeed at the very least would have to not be seriously countermanded—elsewhere in the society. Attunement to

wastefulness reaches broadly and deeply into the habits and practices of people living in societies based on industrial technology
and private property and across all the other major social institutions that give stitch and starch to their lives.

We can perhaps see this most easily by reflecting on what
Veblen describes as the signs of taste and good breeding that must
be in evidence in the items of consumption and performance of
leisure in the household—a demonstration of "discrimination as
to what articles of consumption are decorous and what are the
decorous methods of consuming them," the test of which "is the
requirement of a substantial and patent waste of time" (*Leisure*,
50–51). It would be difficult for conspicuous waste to do the social
work Veblen claims it does[11] if these marks of taste and good
breeding on display in the household did not also find expression
and support in the social fabric of which the household is simply
one inseparable piece.

The household announces ownership of private property. But
its being *private*, in the sense of being owned by a particular party,
doesn't necessarily mean that what goes on in it is private in the
sense of not known to the public. After all, the display one puts on
through one's private property is for the public—there is no point
in having it unless one puts it on display. The privacy of the household is not at odds with but the necessary condition of the display
it puts forth for the public audience. And the display has to be
understood by others—one's standards cannot be peculiar, cannot be illegible or unintelligible to the public one is addressing. In
order not to be considered bizarre or unacceptable, they have to be

11. According to some of Veblen's critics, he was not attentive enough to whether and
how such work is accomplished. See, for example, Colin Campbell, "Conspicuous
Confusion? A Critique of Veblen's Theory of Conspicuous Consumption," *Sociological
Theory* 13, no. 1 (March 1995): 37–47.

supported by something other than the personal taste of the members of the household. Hence Veblen's frequent use of the words "canon" and "principle" in connection with the regulative status of conspicuous waste, signaling its institutional strength even while focusing a great deal on the effects of its devout application within the household.

The display of conspicuous waste in matters of dress is particularly well suited to the job of mounting evidence of one's wealth: "our apparel is always in evidence and affords an indication of our pecuniary standing to all observers at the first glance" (*Leisure*, 167). The more expensive it is and the more clear its signal that the wearer is not working, the greater success it is likely to have in so functioning. Among Veblen's examples are items such as women's skirts, about which he goes into grand detail in his pre-*Leisure* essay "The Economic Theory of Women's Dress." While clothing has to do with physical comfort, dress is all about "adornment," and adornment serves as an "index of the wealth of the economic unit that the wearer represents."[12] Here and elsewhere, Veblen is careful to note the difference between the actual owner of the displayed item (and of everything else within his household) and the female wearer of said item: "even today [1894], in spite of the nominal and somewhat celebrated demise of the patriarchal idea, there is that about the dress of women which . . . quite plainly involves the implication that the woman is a chattel" (*Dress*, 67). So crucial has such a role for women and their dress become, Veblen urges, that "the great, peculiar, and almost the sole function of woman in the social system [is] to put in evidence her

---

12. Veblen, "The Economic Theory of Women's Dress," in *Essays in Our Changing Order*, 66–67 (reprinted from *Popular Science Monthly* 46 [November 1894]). Hereafter referred to as *Dress*.

economic unit's ability to pay," to "consume unproductively . . . costly goods that afford no return to their owner, either in comfort or in gain" (*Dress*, 68). And it is not enough to own and display dress; the wearer of such dress must exhibit "manners, breeding, and accomplishments" of a sort that could not have been acquired without the kind of leisure that bespeaks wealth (*Dress*, 69), nor worn by anyone actually engaging in labor (skirts are among Veblen's favorite examples) (*Dress*, 73).

In this essay Veblen mentions that the purchasers of "wasteful goods" for display don't really "desire the waste" but only its appearance (*Dress*, 70). That is, they are perfectly content with getting a bargain, but they don't want what they wear to look cheap or suggest lack of knowledge of quality. It's not enough to indicate how much wealth you have; you must also exhibit good taste and thereby adequate evidence of being able to have had the leisure to develop it (*Dress*, 70–71).

The principle of conspicuous waste also pervades judgments of taste and beauty more broadly. The hand-wrought filigreed silver spoon is no more, in fact perhaps less "serviceable" than its machine-produced aluminum cousin, and more expensive. Why then would anyone needing a spoon prefer the former to the latter? Ah, the reply might go, it's because the one far exceeds the other in beauty. *Really*, asks Veblen? Or it could be a case of "a gratification of our sense of costliness masquerading under the name of beauty" (*Leisure*, 128). Veblen does not go so far as to insist that judgments of beauty are based entirely on "the requirement of conspicuous waste" (*Leisure*, 128) and have no meaning or function apart from that principle. Still, the principle is so powerful "as to inextricably blend the marks of expensiveness, in our appreciation, with the beautiful features of the object, and to subsume the resultant effect under the head of an appreciation of beauty simply" (*Leisure*, 131).

Veblen's analysis of aesthetic experience and judgment underscores the fact that he does not think that in its actual application the canon of conspicuous waste is understood as such by those adhering to it. Veblen is not claiming that the person judging the silver spoon to be more beautiful than the aluminum one is surreptitiously or underhandedly importing into her claim a judgment that the silver spoon is more expensive—as if she has consciously deliberated, but will not admit, that because its production and care are wasteful of time and effort it deserves to be described as beautiful. Veblen's view appears to be that any importation of wasteful expensiveness has long been tucked into the meaning of "beautiful" without it occurring to those making use of the term that its applicability turns in part on the cost of the object so described. In this connection, one measure of the social reach and depth of the canon of conspicuous waste is its impersonal operation in the language of aesthetic apprehension and appreciation. Its operation need not depend, in fact cannot depend, on such conscious invocation.

Further evidence of the pervasive reach of the principle of conspicuous waste is its influence on "the sense of devotional or ritualistic fitness" (*Leisure*, 116). Houses of worship "are constructed and decorated with some view to a reputable degree of wasteful expenditure" (*Leisure*, 119). The point of the expense is not the physical comfort of the worshippers; even those whose own dwellings are quite modest are likely to find much more comfort at home. Indeed the expense involved in decking out the house of worship could not be understood as being for the comfort of the worshippers without undermining the spirit of wastefulness. "Devout consumption," a variation on vicarious consumption within the private household, enhances "not the fullness of life of the consumer, but the pecuniary repute of the master [the object of worship] for whose

behoof [behalf] the consumption takes place" (*Leisure*, 120–121).
Requisite waste of time and effort also is on display, in the per-
functory rituals of the religious service and the unproductive and
unnecessary performance of the "unprofitable servants" engaging in it—"the master for whom it is performed is exalted above
the vulgar need of actually proficuous [useful] service on the part
of his servants" (*Leisure*, 123). Moreover, "through its pervading
men's habits of thought, the principle of conspicuous waste has
colored the worshippers' notions of the divinity and of the relation in which the human subject stands to him" (*Leisure*, 123):
the divinity "must be of a peculiarly serene and leisurely habit
of life" (*Leisure*, 124–125);[13] in the presence of the divine neither
priests nor worshippers are to betray, in their activity or dress, any
sign of productive labor (*Leisure*, 126).

Providing further details of the pervasiveness of the principle
of conspicuous waste, Veblen turns to the canons of reputability in education: on the one hand, time and effort spent thinking and learning can be directed toward practical ends: that is,
toward promoting "the industrial efficiency of the community"
(*Leisure*, 382), acquiring "knowledge of facts that are vulgarly useful" (*Leisure*, 384), and gaining "familiarity with the everyday life
and the knowledge and aspirations of commonplace humanity in
a modern community" (*Leisure*, 391). On the other hand, such time
and effort can be "diverted to fields of speculation or investigation
which are reputable and futile" (*Leisure*, 384), guided by "a scheme
of contemplation and enjoyment of the true, the beautiful, and the
good, according to a conventional standard of propriety and excellence, the salient feature of which is leisure" (*Leisure*, 390–391),

---

13. In this connection perhaps it is of relevance that though Jesus was a carpenter,
Christianity's God apparently is not.

evincing thereby "an habitual aversion to what is merely useful, as contrasted with what is merely honorific in learning" and a strong taste for "such exercise of the intellect as normally results in no industrial or social gain" (*Leisure*, 394). Indeed "classical learning acts to derange the learner's workmanlike aptitudes" (*Leisure*, 395). In short,

> the conventional insistence on a modicum of conspicuous waste as an incident of all reputable scholarship has affected our canons of taste and of serviceability in matters of scholarship in much the same way as the same principle has influenced our judgment of the serviceability of manufactured goods.
>
> (*Leisure*, 396)

The point is not that the Classics, for example, are utterly without use; on the contrary, "it is their utility as evidence of wasted time and effort, and hence of the pecuniary strength necessary in order to afford this waste" that led them to being "esteemed the most honorific of all learning" (*Leisure*, 397).[14]

Exquisitely sensitive to signs of waste and the dimming of the instinct of workmanship, Veblen paid close attention not only to principles and habits governing consumption but also to those undergirding production. Indeed, as an economist and social critic, he had an abiding interest in and wrote at length about business

---

14. The fact that Veblen described science as involving "idle curiosity" might suggest at first glance that he considered it to be as wasteful as the Classics or language acquisition. But in fact he sang its praises: "Human curiosity is doubtless an 'idle' propensity, in the sense that no utilitarian aim enters in its habitual exercise; but the material information which is by this means drawn into the agent's available knowledge may none the less come to serve the ends of workmanship" (*Instinct*, 88). Indeed it is to idle curiosity that we owe "the most substantial achievements of the race—its systematized knowledge and quasi-knowledge of things" (*Instinct*, 87).

and industry. The former he found to be committed above all to the creation of wealth for the owning, the "kept" classes. In the latter he thought, or hoped, one might hear at least the faint heartbeat of workmanship, of productive efforts undertaken for the well-being of the whole community. While businessmen counted on waste of machinery and materials and labor to guarantee handsome profits for themselves, engineers—at least some of them—abjured such waste and were guided by an understanding of production aimed at taking care of people's material needs and physical comfort.

Business effectively controls industry, Veblen argued, and in consequence "various kinds and lines of waste . . . are necessarily involved."[15] Such waste includes both the underuse of equipment and labor (in order to increase profits by making sure the market is not glutted with goods), and yet also their inefficient overuse, in the "duplication of work, personnel, equipment, and traffic" characteristic of the "simple and obvious waste" of competition with other businesses.[16]

But why, according to Veblen, do the "captains of industry"—a term that Veblen wants us to understand actually refers to owners of business, who lack the knowledge, training, and aims of experienced industrial technicians (*Engineers*, 133) for whom such inefficiencies would be problematic—allow for such waste? Their foremost aim, Veblen urges, is to make a generous profit and to do so for themselves. If the waste of material and human labor is necessary in the achievement of such a goal, so be it. Indeed by the time Veblen published *Absentee Ownership and Business Enterprise*

15. Veblen, *The Engineers and the Price System* (New York: Viking Press, 1954 [1921]), 152. Hereafter cited as *Engineers*.
16. Veblen, *Absentee Ownership and Business Enterprise in Recent Times: The Case of America* (New York: B. W. Huebsch, 1923), 146. Hereafter cited as *Business*.

in Recent Times: The Case of America, in 1923, he proposed that "the most engrossing care that habitually engages the vigilance of the business executive" was to "administer a salutary running margin of sabotage on production, at the cost of the underlying population" (*Business,* 112–113). Waste was not excluded by such a program; it was necessitated by it.

Veblen traced the ascendancy of business over industry as emerging from an already existing distinction between "pecuniary or business" and "industrial or mechanical employments."[17] As production was aimed more and more toward larger markets, labor came to be more explicitly divided between those in sales and marketing and those attending to "the mechanical processes involved in this production for a market" (*Enterprise,* 314). Such narrowing of focus had far-reaching consequences for those on both the business and industrial side, in terms of the kinds of skills they developed, the nature of the arguments they thought were relevant, and the facts to which they paid attention (*Enterprise,* 320–321).

For example, while those on the business side need to become good judges of "what persons will do in the face of given pecuniary circumstances," those on the technical side have to hone their understanding of "what inanimate things will do under given mechanical conditions."[18] To direct and justify their actions, those in business turn to moral and legal conventions, in particular those having to do with the rights of property owners. Those people in "industrial operations"—at least unless they become captivated

17. Veblen, *The Theory of Business Enterprise,* with a New Introduction by Douglas Dowd (New Brunswick, NJ: Transaction Books, 1978 [1904]), 314. Hereafter cited as *Enterprise.*
18. Veblen, "Mr. Cummings's Strictures on 'The Theory of the Leisure Class,'" in *Essays in Our Changing Order,* 28 (reprinted from *the Journal of Political Economy* 8 [December 1899]).

by the siren call of business—perforce occupy themselves with "mechanical sequence or causation" (*Enterprise*, 318), with matters of cause and effect rather than the validity of claims to entitlement, with mechanical efficiency rather than the "'practical' efficiency" employed to further pecuniary ends (*Enterprise*, 320). Employing a technology that is "impersonal and dispassionate," they deal closely with the material world in order to "serve human needs" (*Engineers*, 132) and to carry out the "responsibilities of workmanship" (*Business*, 107). It would be entirely at odds with the "deprecation of waste" at the heart of the instinct of workmanship (*Irksome*, 81) to join efforts to ensure the profits of the "Vested Interests" (a term that occurs regularly in much of the Veblen opera), to work for the "gain of the businessman at the cost of the community," or to acquire "arts of bargaining, effrontery, salesmanship, make believe" (*Business*, 107).

Try as he might to at least appear to remain "dispassionate" himself, Veblen can't hide his contempt for businessmen or his worry about what their social and political ascendancy bodes for the well-being of the rest of society and for the health of democracy, namely,

> a régime of continued and increasing shame and confusion, hardship and dissension, unemployment and privation, waste and insecurity of person and property. (*Engineers*, 134)

Veblen doesn't think that his view of these matters is widely shared among his fellow citizens. The very people who come into "possession of an unearned increase of wealth" are counted as "substantial citizen[s]," while anyone who "falls short in this pursuit of something for nothing, and so fails to avoid work in some useful occupation, is a shiftless ne'er-do-well; he loses self-respect as well as the respect of his neighbors and is in a fair way to be rated as an undesirable citizen" (*Business*, 12–13). Having succumbed to the illusion that the common good depends on business practices that in fact serve only the "captains of solvency," the "loyal citizens of the Christian nations" revere members of the "kept classes" for their "moral excellence" and contribution to "public utility" (*Business*, 113–115). The latter gain in "deference" and "merit" in proportion to how much of the wealth of the community they commandeer (*Business*, 118). In America—surely, Veblen adds wryly, of democracies "the most democratic of them all"—the "pecuniary personage" shines out as the "standard container of the civic virtues" (*Business*, 118).

Such enshrinement of business virtues, Veblen comments with considerable chagrin, is in fact entrenchment of waste and a travesty of democracy. Veblen would not despair over such a state of affairs if he could be more certain that technicians with a strongly developed instinct of workmanship were ready and authorized to take care of "the country's productive industry" (*Engineers*, 133)—to eliminate unnecessary waste and, with the "support of the industrial rank and file" (*Engineers*, 166), provide means for "the people's material welfare" (*Engineers*, 134) instead of the unearned income of the "kept classes." But he thinks the chances of such change coming about are quite slim, not least because "the technicians, the engineers and industrial experts" capable of effecting salubrious reform tend to be "a harmless and docile sort" who are comfortable and content under the present dispensation (*Engineers*, 135). And from Veblen's perspective there is no "third party" (*Engineers*, 134) positioned to propel the necessary re-orientation of industry. Although technicians would have no claim to constitute the industrial directorate in the absence of the consent of the "industrial rank and file," members of that larger population lack the aptitude, knowledge, and training in virtue of which they could lay claim to or be called upon to steer the industrial ship of state.

Veblen's extensive writings about business and industry in a sense complete the portrait of wealthy heads of household in *The Theory of the Leisure Class*. *Leisure* tells us that such households not only have wealth far beyond what they need to live comfortably; they broadcast their possession of such wealth through the trumpeting of wastefulness in conspicuous consumption and leisure. But *Leisure* doesn't tell us much about where that wealth comes from, though it does report that such wealth mustn't be seen as based on or associated in any way with the kind of useful productive labor characteristic of the instinct of workmanship. Veblen offered depictions of the means by which such wealth is generated in works such as *The Theory of Business Enterprise* (1904), *The Engineers and the Price System* (1921), and *Absentee Ownership and Business Enterprise in Recent Times: The Case of America* (1923). The wealth supporting the conspicuously wasteful household depends in no small measure on waste created through industrial processes under the direction of business. According to Veblen, business uses industry to build and bolster the wealth of the owners, never hesitating along the way to waste the capacities of equipment, technicians, and laborers through the sabotage of underuse or the obvious inefficiency of overuse accompanying competition.

The complementary portraits that emerge from these parts of Veblen's ouevre offer us, then, images of the captain of industry overseeing (or having others oversee) waste-producing activities geared to produce handsome income for himself and his ilk, and then making sure that others recognize his possession of such wealth in the patent wastefulness of his household's conspicuous consumption and conspicuous leisure. The household display of wealth through the exhibition of wastefulness depends on and is echoed at the industrial workplace in the creation of the waste used to generate the very wealth on exhibit at home. Make waste at work in order to afford wastefulness at home. Managing waste—arranging for its production—is a full-time job for wealth-producing businessmen/heads of household: they depend on the creation of waste to generate income, income they then can use for the shows of wastefulness necessary for providing proof of such income.

A PUZZLE ABOUT WASTEFULNESS

Though wastefulness, in Veblen's account, is spread everywhere across the economic, social, religious, educational, and commercial landscape, there remain some outcroppings of "disapproval of futility in human life," some evidence of the "decay of the sense of status" (*Leisure*, 361). Indeed, "a weakness for crudely serviceable contrivances that pointedly suggest immediate and wasteless use is present even in the middle-class tastes." But it is "kept well in hand under the unbroken dominance of the canon of reputable futility" (*Leisure*, 137), and overall the "requirements of waste absorb the surplus energy of the population in an invidious struggle and leave no margin for the non-invidious expression of life" (*Leisure*, 362). Humans on the whole—at least those in industrial society—have come to regard wastefulness as too useful to let go to waste.

But why? Why should *wastefulness* enjoy such an elevated position? After all, as Veblen points out, the instinct of workmanship may fade but it never disappears from human life, and pride in useful, efficient, and painstaking labor is not nonexistent. And yet, beginning at an early stage in human culture, "labor comes to be associated in men's habits of thought with weakness and sub-jection" (*Leisure*, 36), the default position of those who, lacking wealth or the power to dominate or some combination thereof, cannot force or otherwise convince others to perform such labor. But to say this only pushes the question back further: why would you want others to do that for you, especially since it is hardly unknown for people to take pride in engaging in such labor and in doing a fine job of it—that is, in acting in accordance with the instinct of workmanship? Veblen suggests at least three closely related reasons: the work tends to be taxing, dirty, and at odds "with life on a satisfactory spiritual plane—with 'high thinking'" (*Leisure*, 37), as reflected in the inheritance of those "Greek philosophers" mentioned earlier. Freedom from such labor comes to be regarded as a necessary condition of a life of beauty, nobility, and dignity.

At this point Veblen comes close to articulating another reason for disdaining labor that finds expression in some of the Greek philosophers he seems to have had in mind (e.g., Plato, Aristotle): as embodied beings, in order to survive and reproduce the species, we have to provide, one way or another, sustenance and protection from threatening aspects of our environments. But we aren't content with the idea that this is all human life is about or is for. The very necessity of attending to bodily needs and the relent-lessness of the body's demands are the cause of some resentment, however irrational or unreasonable that may seem, considering that whether or not there is life after death, life before death is impossible without a body. The best solution—short of continuing on, immortally, in non-bodily form—would seem to be a life in which bodily needs are taken care of, but without such care being the focus of one's attention or supplying the only grounds for the worth and meaningfulness of one's life.

In short, if the instinct of workmanship is an expression of a sense that time and effort not devoted to useful and efficient labor are futile, the desire for a life of leisure removed from such labor can be an expression of a sense that a life consisting of eating to work and working to eat is one of futility and meaninglessness. (Veblen recognizes that from the perspective of those fully committed to the "leisure class regime," it is not wasteful but crucial to have a life of what from another perspective is "conspicuous waste.")

Moreover, the very usefulness of objects and of people's time and energy of which the instinct of workmanship approves is at the same time a reminder of the unrelenting demands of bodily existence. For if the case for the preeminence of their usefulness depends on their appeasing the unending neediness of the body, there is on the contrary a kind of triumph over the body in the exhibition that if the conditions are right its demands can easily be taken care of, that it need not be engaged in laborious effort but can serve ever so nicely as a hanger for work-prohibitive clothing and as the medium of non-productive performances. Of course, one is still using the body, but in ways that show one is not catering to its insistent demands.

What I've just described veers away from Veblen's emphasis on conspicuous waste as currency in the never-ending jockeying for status vis-à-vis our neighbors. The battle I've referred to has more to do with a kind of struggle between humans and their bodies than with one among humans for social and economic bragging rights. But the two are not unrelated: if it is "the human condition" to be embodied and have to figure out how each day to attend to the requirements of and demands on embodiment (indeed doing so is, as Veblen comments, a condition of the survival of individuals and the species of which they are a part), then one kind of difference among humans will be how well they meet or exceed those requirements. If I don't have to budget my attention and time and effort on them, or anyway not nearly as much or as directly as you do, well take that, oh social inferior!

In this connection, Veblen's attention to the condition of women and their various roles in conspicuous consumption and conspicuous leisure is pertinent. Veblen made clear that he did not regard women, even those of the leisure class of his own period, as direct beneficiaries of the status awarded those able to display conspicuous waste. Conscripts in the requisite performances of wastefulness, the wives in such households, along with the male and female servants, were to enjoy extravagant consumption and leisure not for their own sakes but vicariously, for the benefit of the master of the house. And long before the institutions of private property and accumulated wealth as we know them took hold, Veblen claims, the only readily available basis of distinction between members of "an honorable superior class" on the one hand and "a base inferior class" on the other was between men and women, or more precisely, between those who consume what the others produce and do so for "their own comfort and fullness of life," and those who consume what they themselves produce and then only as a "means to their continued labor" (*Leisure*, 69). One way or another, as many feminists have pointed out, the association of women with the bodily for the most part tends to be tighter than that of men of their own social and economic classes, echoing an ancient sense, Veblen says, that woman's work involves simply "uneventful diligence" (*Leisure*, 5), however useful that is.

Moreover, Veblen regards the vestiges of the instinct for workmanship as in general stronger among women than men (though he suggests that this is not evenly distributed across the different economic and social classes of women). As we saw, he thinks dress is a particularly apt place for the display of wastefulness. Yet in discussing this he nevertheless treats as a "psychological law" that "all wastefulness is offensive to native taste," that is, to the instinct of workmanship that is never fully expunged: "all men—and women perhaps even in higher degree—abhor futility, whether of effort or of expenditure" (*Leisure*, 176). Hence even in what might seem a particularly extravagant display of wastefulness in fashionable dress, there is some hint of "ostensible use," however badly disguised (*Leisure*, 177). Moreover, though he judges the position of women "in the modern economic scheme" to present more of an affront to the instinct of workmanship than that of the men of their same class, he also thinks it "apparently true that the woman's temperament includes a larger share of this instinct that approves peace and disapproves futility" (*Leisure*, 353), an instinct according to which "the futility of life or of expenditure is obnoxious" (*Leisure*, 358). In commenting on the " 'New-Woman' movement" of his era he observes that demands cast in terms of emancipation and work come mainly "from that portion of womankind which is excluded by the canons of good repute from all effectual work, and which is closely reserved for a life of leisure and conspicuous consumption" (*Leisure*, 357). This leads him to remark that the vicarious activity required of such women, as evidence of their freedom from "purposeful activity," in fact provides "conventional marks of the un-free" (*Leisure*, 358).

Such remarks are perhaps the closest Veblen comes to commenting on the extent to which those playing non-starring roles in grand performances of consumption and leisure have doubts about the worth of what they are called upon to do. True, much about the situation of wives keeps them from seeing that what they understand to be a "personal relation" is in fact "an economic relation conceived in personal terms" (*Leisure*, 342). "Women of the well-to-do classes" in particular, along with the clergy, Veblen says, "are so inhibited by the canons of decency from the ceremonially unclean processes of the lucrative or productive occupations as to make participation in the industrial process of to-day a moral impossibility for them" (*Leisure*, 342). Yet, as we've seen, he thinks that at the same time the instinct of workmanship still rumbles loudly enough in some of them to provide an inkling that removal from such occupations is a mark not of freedom but its opposite.

Just as distaste for wastefulness can bubble up among members of the leisure class, so also enthusiasm for conspicuous consumption and conspicuous leisure is to be found among those in the "productive" laboring class. Indeed, Veblen took it pretty much as a matter of course not only that invidious discrimination was robust within all socioeconomic classes but also that those not in the leisure class emulated that class's habits and patterns of living. In the case of the "middle and lower classes," he says, "the leisure-class scheme of life . . . comes to an expression at the second remove" (*Leisure*, 83–84). And in fact "no class of society, not even the most abjectly poor, foregoes all customary conspicuous consumption. . . . Very much of squalor and discomfort will be endured before the last trinket or the last pretence of pecuniary decency is put away" (*Leisure*, 85).

AT THE WORKPLACE

It's difficult to avoid the conclusion that Veblen would have more happily embraced what he saw the industrial world coming to if individual habits and social institutions had jointly evolved to listen more to the bidding of the instinct of workmanship and less to the beckoning of pecuniary emulation. One of his admirers, Max Lerner, marveled that despite his depiction of industrial society as saturated with appalling wastefulness, Veblen seemed to maintain a kind of faith in human beings[19]—a faith, perhaps, in the power of the instinct of workmanship to reassert itself and prune back rampant wastefulness. Still, it's hard not to pick up a sense of profound regret over the fading away of productive labor—of life based on the instinct of workmanship and a robust distaste for futility and the waste of goods and effort.

However, such regret does not seem to have been tempered or troubled by concern about possible abuses to which a celebration of workmanship might lend itself. According to Veblen, when the instinct of workmanship recedes or is forced into the background, the fruits of labor are not aimed at serving the well-being of "humanity in general." We've seen to some extent what he thinks this means for those playing subservient roles in the leisure class household: because "the leisure-class canon demands strict and comprehensive futility" (*Leisure*, 259), the performances of the woman of the house and the male and female servants are aimed at securing and sustaining the status of the owner, no matter how well or willingly they carry out their tasks. Their consumption and leisure are at best vicarious, something not for their benefit but for the reputation and standing of the head of household. Veblen does not seem to have commented much on what it might mean to those in such subservient roles to be so employed. His writings do provide an analysis that aims to clarify the actual conditions under which they are working, though his laments over the dampening of the instinct of

19. Lerner, *The Portable Veblen*, 42.

workmanship in their endeavors seem to be more about what the society is losing than what they make of the work they do and the ends it serves. This is perhaps especially clear in an essay he published in 1918 entitled "Menial Servants during the Period of the War."[20] The "untrammeled consumption of superfluities by persons whose craving for social prestige can be gratified by a conspicuous waste of goods and man power" stands out particularly vividly in a time of war, when it certainly ought to be clear that "the nation's war need" trumps this alleged "good and righteous exercise of personal liberty" (*Menial*, 269). Veblen here decries the use of "menial servants" in both "domestic and public establishments" (*Menial*, 269) not so much on account of what it is like for them to be engaged in such wasteful work, but because unattractive as it is during peacetime, such ill-aimed labor is clearly at odds with the needs of the nation in wartime.

What about those working not within the household but for the captains of industry, that is, the captains of business enterprise? We've noted the dashing of Veblen's hopes that people whose aptitudes, training, and knowledge embrace and express the instinct of workmanship might come to prevail over the captains of business enterprise and begin to eliminate the abundantly wasteful practices of industry. But what are the conditions under which people labor even if the instinct of workmanship is guiding their work?

Veblen tells us that when the instinct of workmanship is allowed to be very much in play, work is performed for the benefit not of the predatory few but for humanity as a whole. But does that mean that the conditions of labor are any different from or

20. Veblen, "Menial Servants during the Period of the War," *The Public* 21 (May 11, 1918). Reprinted in *Essays* 267–278. Hereafter cited as *Menial*.

better than those when the work benefits the few? That is, what about those who are engaged in "productive labor"? On the one hand, such labor may satisfy the "instinct of workmanship," but what about the extent of the laborers' control over their work? Looking only at what they produce and its usefulness for humanity impersonally regarded may well invite one verdict; but examination of the conditions under which they produce such goods may well lead to another. Isn't it quite possible to be engaged in useful, productive labor that benefits "humanity in general" and yet work in conditions that may be harmful or otherwise undesirable? Is there anything about labor conducted in accordance with the instinct of workmanship that rules out exploitation or oppression? Can human lives be laid waste on the road to eliminating wasteful labor?

Recall how Veblen described the difference between a handmade silver spoon and a machine-produced aluminum one. The silver spoon has waste written all over it: in meeting the standards of beauty and in its evident disregard of "serviceability," it succeeds in exhibiting the waste of its producer's time, effort, and skills as well as of those who keep it in tiptop shape and shine and those who have learned how to use it properly. The aluminum spoon seems, on the contrary, to be the forthright and obvious expression of the instinct of workmanship, in its unabashed "serviceability" for the function it is meant to serve, the relative efficiency with which it has been produced, the relative ease with which it can be taken care of.[21] The workers involved in its production have not wasted their time and effort;

---

21. However, "Even in articles which appear at first glance to serve for pure ostentation only, it is always possible to detect the presence of some, at least ostensible, useful purpose," and vice versa. *Leisure*, 100–101.

they've helped create something undeniably of use for people's everyday needs.

How is such efficiency in the production process achieved—how is the elimination of wasted time and effort brought about? What does it require of those involved in the production?

One celebrated means of eliminating waste of workers' time, effort, and skill is the division of labor. Adam Smith begins *The Wealth of Nations* with this remark:

> The greatest improvement in the productive powers of labor, and the greater part of the skill, dexterity, and judgment with which it is any where [*sic*] directed, or applied, seem to have been the effects of the division of labor.[22]

The contrast he draws between the productivity and efficiency of a pin-making factory and a single pin-maker is no less famous for being homely: when "the important business of making a pin is . . . divided into about eighteen distinct operations" performed by different people (one "draws out the wire, another straights it, a third cuts it, a fourth points it, a fifth grinds it at the top for receiving the head . . . "), it turns out that a number of persons working together in such fashion can produce thousands and thousands more pins per day than the same number of persons each carrying out all the tasks (*Wealth*, 8–9). Specialization of task creates greater dexterity, and dexterity improves quantity. It also decreases the waste of time, Smith adds, as can be seen by comparing the joint synchronized efforts of pin-makers to the series of tasks taken on by a "country weaver":

22. Adam Smith, *An Inquiry into the Nature and Causes of the Wealth of Nations*, ed. Edward Cannan (Chicago: University of Chicago Press, 1976 [1789]), 7. Hereafter cited as *Wealth*.

The habit of sauntering and of indolent careless application, which is naturally, or rather necessarily acquired by every country workman who is obliged to change his work and his tools every half hour and to apply his hand in twenty different ways almost every day of his life, renders him almost always slothful and lazy, and incapable of any vigorous application even on the most pressing occasions. (*Wealth*, 12)

Such elimination of waste is also what "scientific management" is supposed to ensure. The kinds of schemes for eliminating "waste" and increasing efficiency for which Frederick Winslow Taylor gained notoriety in the decades not long after the publication of Veblen's *The Theory of the Leisure Class* were nothing new in the annals of industry. In 18th-century England, according to the historian Neil McKendrick, Josiah Wedgwood's pottery works offered a paradigm of factory discipline.[23] Wedgwood undertook to change the habits and attitudes of workers who "regarded the dirt, the inefficiency and the inevitable waste, which their methods involved, as the natural companions to pot-making" (McKendrick, 38). To do so, Wedgwood had, in his own words, " 'to make Artists ... (of) ... mere men', and second, to 'make such machines of the Men as cannot err' " (McKendrick, 34). In McKendrick's estimation, Wedgwood succeeded: "He never made 'such Machines of the Men as cannot Err,' but he certainly produced a team of workmen who were cleaner, soberer, healthier, more careful, more punctual, more skilled and less wasteful than any other potter had produced before" (McKendrick, 46).

23. Neil McKendrick, "Josiah Wedgwood and Factory Discipline," *Historical Journal* 4, no. 1 (1961): 30–55.

Wedgwood pottery is just the kind of item a "leisure class" household Veblen had in mind would treasure. While wastefulness may reign in the consumption of Wedgwood's pottery, he was determined that rigorous work habits were to rule in its production, regardless of whether Wedgwood's workers liked it (Wedgwood was convinced that he knew better than they did what was good for them as workers and what was good for the society in which they lived). The struggle between Wedgwood and his workers brings vividly to the fore the question of whether some people know better than others what actually is useful, what actually is wasteful—or rather know better the aims and considerations in light of which such judgments are to be made. And whether or not some people know better, some people are in a strong position to put their judgments into effect: Wedgwood prevailed. Not surprisingly, his efforts met with considerable resistance. But he persevered, convinced that the men and women who worked for him had capacities they weren't aware of, and that the discipline in force at his pottery allowed them to realize this and thereby made it possible for them not to have wasted their lives engaged in inefficient wasteful activity.

Among Veblen's reflections on being trained "in the ways and means of productive industry," with its intensive and "dispassionate" focus on inanimate material and the laws of cause and effect governing it, we find comments on what he calls "the discipline of the machine" and its effect on "the human material" (*Enterprise*, 306). Along with controlling the motions of the worker, the machine demands a standardization of attention parallel to the standardization of "gauge and grade" (*Enterprise*, 308). This narrows the focus of the worker's actions and thoughts, but it does not, Veblen insists, necessarily degrade his intelligence; in fact, the worker "is a more efficient workman the more intelligent he is, and the discipline of the machine process ordinarily increases his efficiency even for work in a different line from that by which the discipline is given" (*Enterprise*, 308). Not all workers are affected in exactly the same way. Those who "serve merely as mechanical auxiliaries of the machine process" are not likely to acquire or strengthen the ability to "comprehend and guide" (*Enterprise*, 312) the processes under which they are working. But more skilled mechanics, and those with the knowledge and training necessary to supervise such processes, develop and sharpen the habits of thought and patterns of attention that Veblen considered necessary to countermand the pernicious influence of predatory business executives. And so, according to Veblen, not only does working closely with good machinery not have the bad effects long thought to be associated with its discipline; it has highly salutary effects in the ways it shapes those who know how it works and how it should be employed. That is, the discipline of the machine, contrary to "something more than a hundred years" of bad press, does not numb workers' minds or weaken their intelligence (*Enterprise*, 313); moreover, it actually helps to develop just those habits of thought and behavior that can shape industry to serve the common good rather than that of the "kept classes."

Veblen did not appear to share Adam Smith's concern about the dulling of mind and body brought on by being tied to a machine,[24] or Karl Marx's sense of the inevitable alienation of

---

24. Smith recognized that the very improvement in dexterity vaunted in his celebration of the division of labor "seems . . . to be acquired at the expense of [the worker's] intellectual, social, and martial virtues. But in every improved and civilized society this is the state into which the laboring poor, that is the great body of the people, must necessarily fall, unless government takes some pains to prevent it" (*Wealth*, vol. 2, 303)—for example, through education.

workers from the fruits of their labor—at least as long as the workplace was governed by the instinct of workmanship and not dictated simply or mainly for the profit of owners. Indeed he thought there was a definite upside to their being subject to the "discipline of the machine." His despair over the receding instinct of workmanship and the growing waste and inefficiency of business-governed industry perhaps occluded and in any event seems to have taken up much more of his attention than questions about whether the instinct of workmanship is or is not incompatible with all too familiar forms of exploitation. In short, Veblen does not appear to have considered the possibility that schemes to eliminate the waste of people's time and effort can make waste of those same people, can be a way of treating them as disposable beings: people with capacities that perhaps could be more fully utilized, but at the same time who can be discarded once their capacities are spent, or who don't want their capacities to be utilized in behalf of goals they had no part in setting. Exploiting the usefulness of people, not letting their capacity for work go to waste, can be a way of treating them like trash-in-waiting.

According to Veblen scholar Doug Brown, the "real problem of capitalism" in Veblen's eyes was "not exploitation but the observable waste of resources and energy that result from an economic system driven by the manic desire for status."[25] Veblen certainly was interested in labor, in particular in the various ends it can serve and human instincts of which it can be an expression. But while he noted that those not participating in useful work might come to

<hr/>

25. Doug Brown, "Editor's Introduction," in *Thorstein Veblen in the Twenty-First Century: A Commemoration of* The Theory of the Leisure Class (1899–1999), ed. Doug Brown (Cheltenham, UK: Edward Elgar, 1998), xvi.

see that this was at odds with rather than proof of their enjoying a significant form of freedom, he seems to have ignored the possibility that those engaging in useful work might not thereby be free from coercive and unjust conditions of labor.

It is true, however, that he does remark on ways in which manifestly useful work, and those who perform it, are not properly valued: recall his comments on the strength of contempt for the "uneventful diligence" (*Leisure*, 5) of "women's work" and of scorn for the "shiftless ne'-er-do-wells" (*Business*, 13) who, unlike those in the "kept classes," haven't managed to escape from doing useful work. In a moment we shall take this as an invitation to reflect on a clear example of employment that is unmistakably useful to human communities and yet almost invariably regarded as undesirable—indeed, in a phrase used by Veblen, as "ceremonially unclean" (*Leisure*, 342): taking out the trash. But now, a final glance at Veblen's contribution to our understanding of how and why it is that we maintain a surprisingly intimate connection with waste.

In Chapter 1 we explored the use of rejectamenta to reveal intimate details of people's lives—in particular, facts about their habits and activities that they may wish not to be known to others nor even to themselves. Veblen's work suggests that however resistant we may be to others pawing through our trash, there is something about the nature of human existence that makes the capacity to be wasteful very attractive—indeed, paradoxical as it seems, to be very useful. For if the penury of the condition of *Homo sapiens* unadorned has made it necessary for us to be wary of wasting our resources, it also thereby has provided a ready means by which invidious distinctions among us can be articulated: some of us acquire enough power and wealth to be able to waste goods, time, and labor with impunity; others just dream of doing so, and in fact may be recruited to be performers in but not beneficiaries of the grand spectacles of the spendthrifts.

In Veblen's account, our capacity for and investment in wastefulness cuts close to the bone of our being: for him, the history of humanity reflects the endless strife between the urge to possess, display, and expend an excess of resources, on the one hand, and on the other, an "instinct for workmanship" in virtue of which we repudiate and try to avoid the futile waste in such expenditure. We can appreciate the attention Veblen brings to the wastefulness at the core of "conspicuous consumption" and "conspicuous leisure" without committing ourselves to his views about basic human instincts or about the vectors through which the broad direction of the history of humanity is given shape. For there can be little doubt about the constancy and ubiquity of the efforts of humans to create and maintain a leg up on others of the species.[26] Veblen allows us to see why it is not surprising that conspicuous wastefulness has been and continues to be such a useful prop in displays of this alleged superiority: we are all alike in our need for enough food and sufficiently adequate shelter in order to remain alive, and in our dependence upon our labor or that of others to procure and protect those necessities. If by hook or by crook I do a better job than you in responding to such need and dependence, accumulating much more than required, I have ready at hand a means by which to display my superiority in this regard. And I can underscore this invidious distinction by having you do the work it otherwise would be incumbent upon me to do.

By the way, please be sure to take out the trash as you leave.

---

26. Not to mention, of course, other species.

Chapter 3

On Taking Out the Trash

Humans are prodigious producers of trash and garbage and rubbish and waste. Some of us also are removers or haulers of all that rejectamenta. Despite how important such labor is for households and communities, it usually is not highly valued as a family chore or paid job. Indeed those who do it typically gain attention only as recipients of complaints about failure to carry out their task well.[1] At the same time there is a surprising amount of speculation about people based on their designation as handlers of trash and waste. In particular, they may become vulnerable to charges of being contaminated. The contamination in question is not the obdurate stench familiar to and often remarked on by sanitation workers. The imputed condition is deeper, suffusing a person's moral character or very being, and in some cases it appears to be ineradicable. As shown by close attention to three rather distinct examples, there can be a lot at stake in being able to establish the "right" relation to trash and waste.

---

1. For a recent example, see Robin Nagle, *Picking Up: On the Streets and Behind the Trucks with the Sanitation Workers of New York City* (New York: Farrar, Straus and Giroux, 2013).

We turn first to *A Fairly Honourable Defeat*,[2] a relatively early work of the philosopher-turned-novelist Iris Murdoch. The character Tallis Browne is introduced through the critical eyes of Hilda, the sister of Tallis's estranged wife, Morgan. It was really no surprise to Hilda when Morgan abruptly left Tallis for the brainier, crisper, smoother Julius King. Tallis is all too serious ("too serious to read the evening paper" [13]) and yet at the same time apparently utterly without accomplishment—he's been poking along forever with a book on Marx and de Tocqueville, spends what appears to be his working time in "all that bitty adult education and dribs and drabs of social work and nothing ever achieved or finished" (20); he's "still giving those lectures on the trade-union movement, and he works part-time for the Notting Hill housing department and he's involved in some committee on race relations and of course there's the Labour Party and he does a lot of other odd jobs" (51). In Hilda's estimation he is "spiritless" and a "muddler"; he "never seems to know what he can manage and what he can't" (21). After Morgan left him he moved to a rental flat and took in his elderly and slightly demented father; moreover, Peter, the son of Hilda and her husband Rupert, has been living at Tallis's while he figures out whether he wishes to return to his studies at Cambridge.

Tallis's house, according to Hilda, is "never cleaned. It's littered with filthy junk of every sort. It smells like the zoo. And the father making messes in corners. I wouldn't be surprised if there were lice, only of course Tallis would never notice" (19). On one of her visits,

---

2. Iris Murdoch, *A Fairly Honourable Defeat* (Greenwich, CT: Fawcett, 1970). Further page references appear in parentheses.

Hilda inspected the kitchen. It looked much as usual. The familiar group of empty beer bottles growing cobwebs. About twenty more unwashed milk bottles yellow with varying quantities of sour milk. A sagging wickerwork chair and two upright chairs with very slippery grey upholstered seats. The window, which gave onto a brick wall, was spotty with grime, admitting light but concealing the weather and the time of day. The sink was piled with leaning towers of dirty dishes. The draining board was littered with empty tins and open pots of jam full of dead or dying wasps. A bin, crammed to overflowing, stood open to reveal a rotting coagulated mass of organic material crawling with flies. The dresser was covered in a layer, about a foot high, of miscellaneous oddments: books, papers, string, letters, knives, scissors, elastic bands, blunt pencils, broken Biros, empty ink bottles, empty cigarette packets, and lumps of old hard stale cheese. The floor was not only filthy but greasy and sticky and made a sucking sound as Hilda lifted her feet. (61)

Hilda takes the state of Tallis's living quarters to be emblematic of his incompetence and confusion. She owns that she "always took it as a bad sign" that the house Morgan and Tallis had shared was a mess: "If people love each other they keep things neat" (19). She worries that her son Peter's "living on that stinking rubbish heap can't be good for his mind"—he needs "discipline and order" (19). Her husband Rupert is less militant than she about such matters but appears to share at least some of her views about the significance of tidiness: at his government office, his papers are always "set in neat piles. Neat piles calm the mind" (213). Julius, the highly accomplished scientist for whom Morgan left Tallis, also describes himself as someone with "a passion for cleanliness and order," though he insists that "it does me no credit" (363).

At least three of the major characters, then, don't hesitate to draw (or to comment on not drawing) inferences based on the degree of care one takes to not be surrounded by ordinary waste and trash and rubbish. A kind of case is made against Tallis, who seems not only to live, as Hilda puts it, in a "stinking rubbish heap," but not to be concerned about that fact; unlike the others, he isn't busy making or blocking inferences about his own or other people's character on the basis of their relation to their own rubbish.

There's no doubt that Murdoch is encouraging us to think that there is something significant about Tallis's relation to garbage and about Hilda's being certain what that relation means. But Murdoch does not give the novel a distinct point of view about the soundness of the rather tidy inferences Hilda and Rupert make and Julius in his own way tries to block (his own orderliness "does me no credit"). Murdoch does remind us how common such inferences are, implicitly inviting us to examine what grounds could support them.

What might Tallis's lack of attention to the state of his physical surroundings indicate? Does it perhaps signal his womanlessness— his need for someone, a female someone, to pick up after him, that he can't do it himself? (But then Hilda claims that even when Tallis was living with Morgan things were a mess.) Are we to read his obliviousness as a measure of how distraught and distracted he is? Is it that he sees the world ordered differently than the other, more "bourgeois," characters? Perhaps, since Tallis is portrayed as taking care of society's rejects, including his father, his tolerance for messiness might be indicative of an openness for those treated more or less as disposable people by the society around him.

Murdoch does make fairly clear, in a scene involving Tallis's directly confronting a small posse of racist thugs, that however much a "muddler" Tallis is in some ways, he is a fierce and thoroughly clear-headed defender of the dignity of those subject to grinding everyday cruelty. Meanwhile the super-tidy Julius, though in no way a "muddler," turns out to be a meddler, in fact a world-class, gratuitously cruel meddler, who throws into utter disarray the relationships of most of those around him and does so more or less for the fun of it. But Murdoch declines to endorse close associations commonly and unthinkingly drawn between people's treatment of their own rubbish and their repertoire of strengths and weaknesses, virtues and vices.[3] The book tacitly suggests that we look before we leap to facile though hardly uncommon conclusions such as (a) people who live in rubbishy surroundings are psychologically and emotionally a mess, while people who stay well on top of their rubbish are in psychological and emotional good health; or, something like an opposite view, (b) people who worry a lot about the tidiness of their own and others' surroundings are control freaks and probably proto-fascists, whereas those who don't worry so much are free of bourgeois concerns about neatness and order and are more likely to be engaged in truly meaningful projects.

3. There have been rather frequent references in biographical works on Murdoch, especially after her death, to the housekeeping and related personal habits of Murdoch and her husband John Bayley. The interior of their home has been described as having been not only very messy and dusty but in fact as decidedly unhygienic. See, for example, "Age Will Win," Martin Amis's review of the 2001 film *Iris* directed by John Eyre, http://www.theguardian.com/film/2001/dec/21/artsfeatures.fiction. Amis also reported that at a cocktail party John Bayley produced a long-abandoned and quite furry olive on a toothpick out of the deep recess of his jacket pocket and popped it without hesitation into his mouth. "Remembering Iris Murdoch," http://www.martinamisweb.com/commentary_files/ma_irismurdoch.doc.

Rendering judgment on the moral or psychological significance of household tidiness was not within the ambit of Murdoch's work as philosopher or novelist. And it may well seem as if there's really nothing much to reflect on. Households create waste. Standards for efficiency and thoroughness in dealing with it and taking it out vary among households—and, notoriously, within them (variations in accordance with age and gender are widely and commonly alleged).[4] It is perhaps not surprising, then, that household negotiations over rubbish responsibility can serve up excellent fodder for sitcoms and provide fine opportunities for the Self-Help and Do-It-Yourself industries. But on the whole it seems safe to assume that however much disagreement there is about just who is going to take out the trash, and how and when they are going to do it, there is agreement that the job is a nuisance (Murdoch's novel does nothing to disabuse us of this assumption). Indeed, its being considered a disagreeable chore surely is a large part of the explanation of the rancor connected with assignment of the task. If we try to escape responsibility for the job, it may well be simply because we don't like it, not because we think our or anybody else's character will be revealed by how we handle it. But that may turn out to be a rather provincial view.

Not everyone who deals with homely household trash treats it as an unpleasant and unwelcome chore. In the short essay "La Poubelle Agréée,"[5] drawing on his experiences as chief rubbish handler for

---

4. For a recent example, see Stephen Marche, "The Case for Filth," *New York Times*, December 7, 2013, http://www.nytimes.com/2013/12/08/opinion/sunday/the-case-for-filth.html.

5. Italo Calvino, "La Poubelle Agréée," in *The Road to San Giovanni* (New York: Vintage, 1994), 93–126. Further page references appear in parentheses.

his own household, the celebrated writer and famous fabulist Italo Calvino offers an extended meditation on the ritual of filling the garbage pail and preparing it for pickup by the trash collector.[6]

Poubelle is a French word for dustbin, so named in honor of one M. Eugène-René Poubelle, whose efforts to clean up the streets of Paris in the late 19th century are forever sung in a common term for rubbish containers small and large. *Agrée* means something like pleasing, in the special sense, Calvino says, of being in accordance with the appropriate regulations (97). Calvino's essay dates from a period in the 1970s when he and his family were living in Paris.

Insisting that he is not one to shun chores, this man of the house declares at the outset:

> When it comes to housework, the only task I can perform with a certain amount of competence and satisfaction is that of taking out the rubbish. (93)

The satisfaction he takes has nothing to do with pride in being willing and able to carry out a necessary but distasteful chore. On the contrary, every stage of the daily ritual—from scraping off what remains on the dinner plates into the small kitchen *poubelle*, to carefully transporting its contents to the larger container outside, to lining the inside of the *poubelle* once again in preparation for the next batch of assorted post-consumption food scraps and cigarette ashes—is described with the calm relish of a connoisseur. The repetitiveness of his task underscores its usefulness within

6. Gay Hawkins draws attention to Calvino's essay in her lively *The Ethics of Waste: How We Relate to Rubbish* (Lanham, MD: Rowman and Littlefield, 2006), 39–41. The more extensive analysis offered here echoes some of the broad points made by Hawkins but does not share Hawkins's particular focus on the absence of guilt in Calvino's description of his producing and disposing of trash.

the family fold, and provides reliable evidence of the household's adherence to the crucial if precarious social contract between private generators of waste and public agencies governing the proper disposal of it. The very familiarity of the routine produces neither boredom nor impatience but the chance for reflection on grand themes, for, far from being a waste of one's precious time, taking out the trash offers rich food for thought, an opportunity for meditation:

> Carrying out the *poubelle agréée* is not something I do without thinking, but something that needs to be thought about and that awakes the special satisfaction I get from thinking. (101)

I take out the rubbish, therewith I think . . . but about what? About how much it stinks? About why I of all people have this chore? About why little Leo barely touched his tofu? When Calvino takes out the rubbish, he thinks about such ponderables as the meaning of the rite of purification *á la poubelle*; the significance of what we throw away for our sense of who we are; writing as an inevitably dross-producing activity; the adumbration of death in detritus; and the manner in which rubbish mediates relations between those who toss it out and those who haul it away.

Among the matters about which Calvino is prompted to think, then, is what we might call *exfoliating purification*. The city of Paris, like most other municipalities, is interested in its inhabitants' trash and garbage for one main reason: that stuff's well-established role in the creation of decidedly unhygienic conditions. (Such official bodies are likely to look unfavorably on what the majority decision in *Greenwood* referred to as "animals, children, scavengers, snoops, and other members of the public," who seem to have no regard for the sanitation problems caused by their nosing about in others' garbage.)[7] Calvino acknowledges the hygienic aspect of his *poubellian* activity, but focuses on purification in another sense. Having filled the *poubelle* in the evening, he says, we may "begin the new day without having to touch what the evening before we cast off from ourselves forever" (102). We're finished with it. To let it still linger in our midst is to blur the line we need in order to get to the "substance" (103) of ourselves. Throwing things out enables us to know what that substance is, pick it out from among all the things we are, all the things we have:

> Only by throwing something away can I be sure that something of myself has not yet been thrown away and perhaps need not be thrown away now or in the future. (103)

Like defecation, Calvino remarks, such acts of unburdening satisfy a need to mark the difference between "what I am and what is unalterably alien" (103). (Calvino here echoes anthropologist Mary Douglas's broader view about the centrality of notions of dirt or filth or uncleanliness in creating and maintaining patterns of order; for example, stickiness in a thing "attacks the boundary between myself and it.")[8] My trash reveals who I am, but not, as A. J. Weberman, the Tokyo Trash Baby, and Justice Brennan thought, because I can in some sense be found in my rubbish, but because the "real" I is what remains of me in the wake of my rubbishing.

Writing, Thinking, Waste-producing. If handling the *poubelle* "awakes the special satisfaction" Calvino gets from thinking (101),

---

7. See Chapter 1 this volume.
8. Mary Douglas, *Purity and Danger: An Analysis of Concepts of Pollution and Taboo* (London: Routledge, 2007), 47.

the process of thinking, he adds, is waste-producing. Waste stimu-
lates thinking, but so also, thinking produces waste:

> these thoughts of mine that you are reading [are] all that has
> been salvaged from the scores of sheets of paper now crumpled
> up in the bin. (105)

To reach my considered judgment, the thoughts I am willing to
keep and endorse, I go through a process involving "dispossession"
(125), the visible expression of which has me "pushing away from
myself a heap of crumpled-up paper and a pile of paper written
all over, neither of the two being any longer mine, but deposited,
expelled" (125). Calvino doesn't note but certainly doesn't exclude
the fact of our having had thoughts we have entertained and discarded but never written down. And of course explorers of the dimmer recesses of the human psyche have posited the existence of
great reservoirs of rejected thoughts and feelings, many of which we
remain unaware of having had or ever noticed having entertained.

Detritus and Death. Calvino's *poubellian* meditations include
the thought that separating ourselves from our rubbish has something to do with death. As he sees it, getting rid of the trash isn't
only about adhering to the rules of the local sanitation department
or about peeling away the dross of non-self from the golden substance of self; it is, closely in tandem with the latter, being able to
exhibit, for yet again one more moment, the difference between
being a producer of detritus and being an instance of it: getting rid
of one's rubbish "is meant first and foremost to put off [one's] own
personal funeral, to postpone it if only for a little while" (104).

The Garbagio Connection. Whatever tossing out the trash
achieves, or at least promises to achieve, by way of clarifying a boundary between self and non-self, as well as between

alive-and-still-making-rubbish and deceased-and-now-part-of-the-rubbish, there is of course more to the removal of trash than the opportunity it presents for reflecting on the meaning of life and of death. As handler-in-chief of the household *poubelle*, Calvino is vividly aware of how dependent he and his family are on the people who come to pick up and haul away "life's leftovers" (120). He's keenly attuned to the fact that it is highly unlikely that the "dustbin men" (109) will have anything like the relationship to the contents of his *poubelle* that he and his family do.[9] His own "relationship with the *poubelle* is that of the man for whom throwing something away completes or confirms its appropriation, my contemplation of the heap of peels, shells, packaging and plastic containers brings with it the satisfaction of having consumed their contents" (110). But the dustbin men, he notes, are likely to read his rubbish quite differently. They have before them "a rich source of information indeed if anyone chose to consider them day by day: the empty bottles after party evenings, the wrapping paper from the shops where we've bought things, the pages full of crossings-out where a writer has racked his brains over his essay on *poubelles*" (109).

While A. J. Weberman, the Tokyo Trash Baby, and the Laguna Beach narcotics team investigated people's trash in hopes of getting what they thought to be important information about the producers of the trash, the dustbin men of Paris, Calvino postulates, read their own futures as consumers in the throwaways of the more well-to-do. What they tip into the "rotating crater" of their carts or trucks "offers only an idea of the amount of goods which are denied to [them], which reach [them] only as useless detritus" (110). Calvino notes

---

9. In her illuminating *The Cultural Promise of the Aesthetic* (London: Bloomsbury, 2014), Monique Roelofs explores, under the rubric of "relationality," the broad range of ways in which relations among humans are mediated by our relations to things and vice versa.

that in many countries picking up the trash is not uncommonly the first job an immigrant has; perhaps, he says of the immigrant,

> his having been taken on as a dustbin man is the first step up a social ladder that will eventually make today's pariah another member of the consumer society and like everybody else a producer of refuse, while others escaping from the deserts of the "developing countries" will take his place loading and unloading the bins. (110)

Calvino is under no illusion about the pressure on recent immigrants being "obliged to accept the lowliest and heaviest of jobs," and in many countries doing so "without proper contracts" (107–108). He's fully aware that "the dustcart isn't just grinding refuse, but human lives" (109), and he brings attention to the fact that though his position allows him to meditate on the charms of dealing with his own household's waste, the position of the dustbin men puts them in quite a different relation to his discards. The dustbin men may well wish to produce trash of the same kind and quality as Calvino's, but Calvino is far from suggesting that he finds treating his own trash so engaging that he'd like to make a living as a dustbin man himself. They may wish to be in his place, but he expresses no desire to be in theirs.

Not just willing but happy to have the job of garbage-tender-in-chief in his own household, Calvino creates a relation to trash quite different from that struck by Tallis. His very attention to the rubbish and garbage he and the rest of his household create makes him both closer to and farther away from waste than is the case with Tallis. Tallis's apparent lack of attention to or concern about the general stickiness and gooeyness and dust and dirt around him appears to Hilda to offer grounds for thinking that there is something rubbishy and disordered about his mind, his spirit, that there is no hope that Tallis could clean up his house, clean up his life. The less he bothers to notice the filth, the more it seems—to Hilda, anyway—to permeate his being, to define his character. Calvino, on the other hand, becomes distinct from his garbage in his acts of dealing with it. His appreciative, fond approach to his daily task—there is no hint of neurotic, obsessively hygienic habits—involves handling the rubbish, lingering over it; he's close enough to it to identify it as a crucial source of thinking, but the very process of his thinking about it keeps him from being identified with it or by it.

The anomaly of Calvino's cherishing his household duty for its rich lode of insight does nothing, of course, to change the other conditions to which he brings our attention. His direct responsibility for the disposition of the rubbish stops at his own curbside. Beyond that it is the municipality or community, not the household, where negotiations take place over what is going to happen to the trash, who is going to take care of it, the conditions under which they will be working, and what their wages and benefits, if any, are to be. Calvino is not ignorant of the fact that his own attitude about garbage and rubbish is atypical—indeed his highly unusual take on his job is no doubt a powerful incentive for writing about it. The refuse haulers may envy the ability of households like Calvino's to consume goods the remains of which show up in the *poubelle*, but Calvino is under no illusions about the close connection between their work as dustbin men and their economic, social, and political standing in the community.

As Calvino suggests, what it means to have a career (in the broadest sense) in trash varies across class, culture, and historical moment. Though we won't here be exploring such variation at length,

Calvino's musings certainly provide a striking contrast to the vast literature (some of it autobiographical) on the lives of those formerly called "untouchables" in India, whose appointed duties as cleaners of latrines and sweepers of waste and rubbish have been held to be the appropriate match for their inescapably polluted and impure nature. Unlike Tallis, their being treated as tainted by their association with waste and rubbish is a sign not of an individual personality quirk but of the low standing of the hereditary communities into which they are born; unlike Calvino, they cannot think of rubbish as something from which they can establish a purifying distance. Indeed, they are "untouchable" in the eyes of those in higher castes who regard being touched by them or having contact with items touched by them as defiling and requiring ritual purification.

A brief word about appellations: Part of Gandhi's campaign to better the situation of untouchables (a campaign that was contested by some of its intended beneficiaries) was to refer to those who had been known as untouchables as the "Harijan" or God's children. Under the influence of Dr. B. R. Ambedkar, a powerful leader and co-drafter of the Indian Constitution who, unlike Gandhi, was himself an untouchable, many in the untouchable castes came to prefer the term "Dalit," which means something like "ground down," "broken into pieces." Though there is still debate over which term is preferred by those to whom such terms (including the legal designator "Scheduled Castes") are meant to refer, Dalit certainly seems the one most commonly used in recent literature by and about this community (more accurately, collection of communities), and is the term used here.

A look back at our earlier examples of people closely entwined with trash reveals various kinds of assumptions at work in the judgments made about the meaning of such associations. In the case of Murdoch's Tallis, there appears to be an allegedly common-sense connection drawn between the rubbishy condition of his household and his foggy state of mind, general incompetence, and inability to get on in the world. Murdoch, intentionally or not, certainly offers us the occasion to raise questions about the source of such "common-sense" thinking, to notice how ordinary and powerful it is, to wonder what might justify it. In the context of the novel, Hilda's views are not presented as being at all unusual or remarkable. The cultural influence of such assumptions is perhaps all the more powerful for not being clearly articulated and not being given any clear roots in the religious or medical or other major institutions of the society.[10] When Calvino reflects on the high proportion of new immigrants in urban sanitation departments, especially among those immigrants whose social and economic condition is precarious, he doesn't seem to be making statements we expect to be contradicted by labor economists, for example, or students of the labor market and its relation to other dimensions of the society. Hilda may be a fictional being, but her assumptions about the relation between a person's character and the level of his concern for basic cleanliness resonate with assumptions alive and well in the world of the author who created her and that author's audience. Calvino may not be a sociologist or economist or specialist in immigration, but his comments on the link between immigration status and occupation are not presented as if they are likely to be open to much question.

---

10. Perhaps a look at instruction books for children, or manuals on housework or personal hygiene, would prove to be illuminating, à la Norbert Elias's searches through works on childrearing and etiquette in *The Civilizing Process: The History of Manners*, translated by Edmund Jephcott (New York: Urizen Books, 1978).

But the case of the Dalits appears to introduce a factor not present in those other examples for it seems to involve a much stronger claim, to the effect that there is an ironclad link between assignment to a particular kind of task and membership in a particular kind of group: if that kind of task needs to be done, it must be done by someone in that group; if someone in that group is going to be involved in labor, it must be that kind of labor. If waste and rubbish are to be swept, latrines cleaned, and leather treated, Dalits are the best ones, really the only ones, to do it; if Dalits are going to be employed, it must be in that line of work or other tasks considered dirty and polluting (though in practice most Dalits, despite their alleged ritual impurity, in fact are not employed in occupations considered polluting).[11]

If something along the lines of a lay psychological theory underlies a view like Hilda's about Tallis, and something like social science data could be found to ground Calvino's comments about immigrant occupations, what shores up the view tying Dalits to waste?

The existence of waste is troubling to human beings—indeed, many are the kinds of trouble we think it brings our way. The disposition of waste and rubbish has played a role in the history of India in ways it has not in the worlds of Iris Murdoch and Italo Calvino. In India, the meaning of waste and rubbish, and the proper handling of them, has been addressed in the context of a rich and potent mix of a caste system; Hindu-based beliefs and rituals in connection with purity; British colonialism and its legacy; and well-entrenched social, political, and economic hierarchies

---

11. See, for example, Oliver Mendelsohn and Marika Vicziany, *The Untouchables: Subordination, Poverty and the State in Modern India* (Cambridge: Cambridge University Press, 1998), 7.

possessing many elements that remain untouched by the promised guarantees of a constitutional democracy. (This is not to say that the meaning of waste and rubbish and beliefs about how to handle them are not also deeply embedded in the history of other countries' institutions. See, for example, Carl Zimring's account of the history of widespread negative attitudes toward scrap and other waste dealers in the United States and Robin Nagle's recent portrayal of the social and medical perils to which sanitation workers in New York City are vulnerable.)[12]

I won't pretend to present a complete or definitive account of these factors. The literature about each of them is enormous, and controversies abound about the very meaning of caste, the extent of its influence, the difference between norms of purity and actual ritual practices, the distinction between ritual impurity and ritually unmarked uncleanliness,[13] the past and present significance of the colonial presence in India, and the strengths and weaknesses of the country's democracy. But it seems safe to say that the position of Dalits is affected by all of these and that the meaning and function of their work as handlers of waste and rubbish cannot begin to be understood without at least a brief sketch of them.

In a caste society, there are—or are supposed to be—rigid and non-permeable boundaries among subgroups of the population. One's caste membership is determined by one's birth family. Though one can be expelled from one's caste (Gandhi

12. Carl Zimring, "Dirty Work: How Hygiene and Xenophobia Marginalized the American Waste Trades, 1870–1930," *Environmental History* 9, no. 1 (January 2004): 80–101; Nagle, *Picking Up*.

13. For a sense of the richly detailed and complicated set of terms in connection with purity and pollution, see Susan S. Bean, "Toward a Semiotics of 'Purity' and 'Pollution' in India," *American Ethnologist* 8, no. 3 (August 1981): 575–595.

was outcasted), one cannot join another caste. There are powerful restrictions against marriage or sexual union across caste (and subcaste). Castes (as well as subcastes) are hierarchically ranked; one's caste membership is supposed to determine the relative respect and access to resources and occupations to which one is entitled. Such a description, however, doesn't necessarily provide the best picture of how caste has been and continues to be played out. As Vijay Prashad among others has noted, "Many factors influence the idea and practice of caste and routinely transform not only the immediate relationship between discrete castes, but also the regime of castes as such."[14] But as he and other scholars of the Dalit nevertheless point out, in the context of the Indian caste system Dalits are at the bottom—and by many accounts not included among the four principal castes (Brahmins [priests, scholars], Kshatriya [rulers, warriors], Vaishya [merchants, agriculturalists], and Sudras [menial laborers, servants]).

Collecting waste and rubbish is widely regarded as difficult, dirty, and potentially polluting work. Indeed, it's not unusual for garbage and trash collectors to comment on how hard it is to get rid of the smell of the stuff they handle even after long, hot, soapy showers and a change of clothing. In the context of Hindu beliefs and rites in connection with purity and pollution, however, it's not that sweepers can't get rid of the aroma of pollution; they can't get rid of the pollution that is said to characterize their very being, however scrubbed their bodies and clothing. (Meeting what might

---

14. Vijay Prashad, *Untouchable Freedom: A Social History of a Dalit Community* (New Delhi: Oxford University Press, 2000), xvi; see also Marc Galanter, *Competing Inequalities: Law and the Backward Classes in India* (Berkeley: University of California Press, 1984), 12.

be considered ordinary standards of cleanliness is neither a necessary nor a sufficient condition of being ritually pure: pollution of
the Ganges does not affect its ritual purity.[15] A clean Dalit remains
impure. It doesn't matter, as Gandhi pointed out, that Dalit latrines
may in fact be much cleaner than those of upper caste Hindus.)[16]
A crucial difference between Hindu deities and the people who
worship them is that the deities are pure and humanity is not.
Proper respect for the deities requires as much purity in the wor-
shipper as is possible for a human to have, and such purity can only
be attained or approximated by the constant and careful obser-
vance of rituals of purification. Such rituals abound—for example,
those governing menstruating women. But there are some people
who are impure not just at intervals or due to certain activities,
but inherently impure, on account of deeds they performed in an
earlier life. They are so impure that no matter what rites of purification they undertake, neither they nor the things they have
handled should come in contact with others, especially with the
priests charged with mediating the relationship between the deities and the rest of the community. Hence the history of restrictions that prohibit untouchables from entering temples or sharing
food, drink, utensils, or even using the same roads as higher caste
members.

Hindu beliefs about purity and pollution are not the same
thing as the Indian caste system and they do not map onto each
other entirely neatly. But the two institutions tend to be mutu-
ally reinforcing, and this tendency apparently was strengthened

15. See Kelly D. Alley, *On the Banks of the Ganga: When Wastewater Meets a Sacred River*
(Ann Arbor: University of Michigan Press, 2002).
16. See Tanika Sarkar, "Gandhi and Social Relations," in *The Cambridge Companion to
Gandhi*, edited by Judith M. Brown and Anthony Parel (Cambridge: Cambridge
University Press, 2011), 178.

by colonialists during British rule as well as by some members of the dominant castes.[17] So, for example, the British reserved jobs in the Delhi sanitation department for a Dalit group called the Balmikis on the grounds that this cohered with what was understood to be the occupation dictated by their caste standing and their relative degree of impurity—even though in their case there was no "living, historical tie with refuse removal" and Indians of the dominant castes knew this.[18] If the condition of the Dalits did not change appreciably under British rule, neither did it in the nationalist movement, which on the whole expected the needs and demands of the Dalits to fit with the political agenda of the dominant castes. (Though Gandhi did much to bring attention to the condition of the untouchables and to improve their lot, he apparently never gave up his belief in hereditary callings and urged those he referred to as Harijan to perform their prescribed duties, hoping that they and everyone else could recognize the great importance of the sweepers' work to the life of the community.)[19] It is true that after independence, untouchability was officially banished in Part III, Article 17 of the Constitution:[20]

"Untouchability" is abolished and its practice in any form is forbidden. The enforcement of any disability arising out of "Untouchability" shall be an offence punishable in accordance with law.

17. For an extended analysis of the extent to which British law in India weakened or strengthened caste hierarchy, see Marc Galanter, *Competing Inequalities*, and his "Untouchability and the Law," *Economic and Political Weekly* 4, no. 1/2 (January 1969): 131–170.
18. Prashad, *Untouchable Freedom*, xviii.
19. Prashad, *Untouchable Freedom*, 112, 120.
20. For the full text of the Constitution, see india.gov.in/my-government/constitution-india/constitution-india-full-text.

And Article 15 specified the following:

(1) The State shall not discriminate against any citizen on grounds only of religion, race, caste, sex, place of birth or any of them.

(2) No citizen shall, on grounds only of religion, race, caste, sex, place of birth or any of them, be subject to any disability, liability, restriction or condition with regard to—

   (a) access to shops, public restaurants, hotels and places of public entertainment; or

   (b) the use of wells, tanks, bathing ghats, roads and places of public resort maintained wholly or partly out of State funds or dedicated to the use of the general public.

However—and probably not surprising to anyone familiar with the history of legal attempts in the United States, for example, to bring about change in the absence of broader institutional and attitudinal transformations—discrimination against the Dalits is still widespread, especially in rural areas. Stories of rape and other forms of violence are not uncommon;[21] in practice, the Constitution does not protect untouchables against physical and sexual violence. During the humanitarian crisis following the 2004 tsunami affecting South India, for example, Dalits reportedly were kept out of relief camps and were refused provisions.[22] Untouchability continues apace in the form of "separate glasses at the tea shop, unequal access to 'common resources,' and a skewed agricultural resource base in which 'dominant castes' owned or controlled the productive land."[23]

21. See, for example, Bela Malik, "Untouchability and Women's Oppression," *Economic and Political Weekly* 34, no. 6 (February 6–12, 1999): 323.

22. Hugo Gorringe, "The Caste of the Nation: Untouchability and Citizenship in South India," *Contributions to Indian Sociology* (n.s.) 42, no. 1 (April 2008): 124.

23. Gorringe, "Untouchability," 137.

In short, the implacably intimate connection between one's occupation as a handler of waste and rubbish and the lowly and impure state of one's being is still alive, and on the whole the Dalits remain very much on the margins of Indian society (exceptions—including some gains encouraged by forms of affirmative action for Dalits, and legal efforts to prevent atrocities against them—only prove the rule). The point of bringing this up is not to point a finger at aspects of Indian society—finger-pointers from the United States, for example, have more than enough use for their digits right here at home—but to note a prominent location along the spectrum of positions about the relation between trash and the humans who handle it. The sweepers and haulers of waste and garbage who are treated as disposable are indispensable to the working of their societies. But like disposable razors, the usefulness of which fails to prevent their disposability, the necessity of some people's labor does not automatically stand in the way of their being put to the important task and then unceremoniously abandoned.

Of course, the Dalits don't necessarily accept the view of themselves and their work—a view on account of which they have been reviled, exploited, oppressed, and subjected to violence. As Sara Beth has pointed out, many Dalits continue the long fight "to assert their influence over how [their] identities are defined, who they include, and what they mean."[24] Insisting on talking about themselves rather than only being talked about by others, they have brought attention to the value of their labor in agriculture and the leather trades, and their work as cleaners, contrasting it to the "consuming, exploitative and unproductive" occupations of the

---

24. Sara Beth, "Hindi Dalit Autobiography: An Exploration of Identity," *Modern Asian Studies* 41, no. 3 (May 2007): 547.

upper castes.[25] Refusing to be vilified by association with the pigs that are central to their feasts, some Dalits embrace the pig as a traditional symbol in scarcity-defying celebrations of abundance.[26] Not all Dalits join in such redefining of the meaning of their work and their lives, and even those who do remain aware of the fine line they must tread between proudly affirming their cultural traditions and underwriting the harsh social, political, and economic conditions in which those traditions developed.[27]

If the case of the Dalits—along with those of Tallis and Calvino—reveals the complex ways in which our relations to each other are mediated by our connection to our own and others' trash, India's reputation as the world leader in open defecation is regarded by many inside and outside India as complicating its relation to the rest of the world. In a fact sheet issued jointly by the World Health Organization (WHO) and the United Nations Children's Fund (UNICEF) in 2012, India is reported to have almost 60% of the 1.1 billion people across the globe for whom open defecation is a regular practice, usually on account of a lack of sanitary facilities.[28] It is not just the Dalits within India who have faced scorn and contempt in connection with their close association with garbage and trash. As the historian Dipesh Chakrabarty among others has pointed out, in the eyes of critical

25. Beth, "Dalit Autobiography," 557.
26. Beth, "Dalit Autobiography," 555.
27. Moreover, Dalits are neither homogeneous nor immune to invidious hierarchies among themselves, including though not limited to the subordination of women within their communities.
28. World Health Organization, "Water Sanitation Health," http://www.who.int/water_sanitation_health/monitoring/jmp2012/fast_facts/en/. See also Aarti Dhar, "'India Will Achieve Sanitation Goals only by 2054,'" The Hindu, March 27, 2012, http://www.thehindu.com/news/national/india-will-achieve-sanitation-goals-only-by-2054/article3250852.ece.

observers both foreign and native to India, much of the open space of India appears dirty, stinky, and chaotic.[29] Recall for a moment Hilda's description of Tallis's house: it's filthy, sticky, smelly; there often is a pile of Tallis's father's poop in the corner. Such commentary on this private dwelling place echoes what according to Chakrabarty characterizes the history of much British and European writing about public space in India: streets and temples reek of human waste, refuse, and decomposing animal bodies (Chakrabarty, 541). Moreover, he points out, such views were reiterated in comments by Gandhi, who was disturbed that "we [Indians] do not hesitate to throw refuse out of our courtyard on to the street"; they appear in the work of expatriate Bengali intellectual Nirad Chaudhuri, baffled and annoyed by what he considered the very avoidable mess produced by the "non-cooperation between the domestic servants and the municipal sweepers," and the writer V. S. Naipaul (a Trinidadian whose grandfather had emigrated from India to the West Indies), who found it appalling that "Indians defecate everywhere" (Chakrabarty, 541).

Chakrabarty reads such responses as indicative not so much of a "western" point of view but a "modernist" one:

> What it speaks is the language of modernity, of civic consciousness and public health, of even certain ideas of beauty related to the management of public space and interests, an order of aesthetics from which the ideals of public health and hygiene cannot be separated. (Chakrabarty, 541)

---

29. Dipesh Chakrabarty, "Of Garbage, Modernity and the Citizen's Gaze," *Economic and Political Weekly* 27, no. 10/11 (March 7–14, 1992): 541–547. Reprinted in his *Habitations of Modernity: Essays in the Wake of Subaltern Studies* (Chicago: University of Chicago Press, 2002), 65–79.

The modern state, Chakrabarty urges—more particularly the modern capitalist state—needs "benign, regulated places, clean and healthy, incapable of producing either disease or disorder" (Chakrabarty, 544). It's not just that the British Indian army wanted to prevent infection of their own number but also that a "vigorously productive and efficient capitalism" requires "a healthy workforce and increased longevity" (Chakrabarty, 544). However, Chakrabarty suggests, to the chagrin of critics, many of the open spaces in India appear to be dirty, disorderly, and dangerous, and the exchanges within them, such as at the bazaar, are open to the ambiguities of esoteric negotiation and the disruptive and possibly polluting influence of strangers. Such open spaces are "public" in the sense of being opposed to the private and ritually protected space of domesticity, but not "public" in the sense of an arena in which habits of good citizenship and civic responsibility are nourished and rewarded. Even the most thoughtful and culturally sensitive ethnographers, Chakrabarty says, can't really fathom why the people they study don't see the clear advantages of "'long-life,' 'good health,' 'more money,' 'small families,' and 'modern science'" over the "'thrills' of the bazaar" (Chakrabarty, 544) and other open spaces, with all their rumors and risks, detritus and disorder. Indeed Chakrabarty reports that his own interest in reflecting on the significance of waste and trash in Indian open spaces was piqued by his memory of a somewhat testy exchange he had with a young boy on the streets of Calcutta (or Kolkata): to Chakrabarty's injunction that the boy shouldn't be throwing trash on the street, the boy retorted: "'Why not? . . . I suppose you like to think that we live in England, do you?'" (Chakrabarty, 545–546).

Though Chakrabarty doesn't invoke the concept of "civilized behavior" in his account, such a notion seems to be implicitly at play in all the examples we've explored above (and we might recall in this connection Justice Brennan's emphatically remarking that going through another's trash is "contrary to commonly accepted notions of civilized behavior").[30] Whatever else being "civilized" involves, it seems to include striking the "right" relationship to waste and trash and rubbish and garbage (of course that "right" relationship, and what counts as civilized and uncivilized, is subject to change over culture and time).[31] It's one thing for Tallis to be thought incapable of achieving anything, to bumble and muddle through life; but in the eyes of his anxious and appalled in-laws, it is his apparent lack of concern about his house having become a landfill, garbage dump, and open latrine that puts him beyond the pale, makes him someone too rough and unfinished for polite company. The reason Calvino succeeds in not suffering contamination from his intimate, indeed pleasure-inducing, relationship to garbage is that he links his *poubellian* work to unqualifiedly, perhaps quintessentially "civilized" activities of his time and place: keeping the house tidy; performing the civic duty of getting the trash to the proper place and in the proper container; taking seriously the social, political, and economic standing of those members of the community who pick up the trash; generously expending time and effort separating out his carefully considered thoughts from unproductive starts or hastily produced, unexamined outbursts.

To the extent to which it is the Dalits who are responsible for gathering and disposing of human and animal waste and the various forms of trash and rubbish, their work is necessary for

30. Chapter 1, this volume.
31. "In the West, since the onset of the early modern period, the archetypal rules, the earliest and most systematic of which the child is exposed and in which he is trained, are those governing the definition and control of wastes." Such exposure and training is thought to distinguish "the civilized from the savage." Stephen Greenblatt, "Filthy Rites," *Daedalus* 111, no. 3 (Summer 1982): 2.

establishing some of the basic conditions for what Chakrabarty presents as a kind of "keep it clean and orderly" commandment of modernity. At the same time, their efforts apparently do little to mitigate charges laid by British colonialists, nationalists such as Gandhi, critics such as Chaudhuri and Naipaul (themselves the subject of biting criticism),[32] and even earnestly sympathetic observers that Indian open spaces are literal and figurative cesspools. Chakrabarty suggests without saying it explicitly that from the perspective of such observers, on the whole India has yet to join the company of fully civilized humanity despite the shining examples it was offered in the persons and habits of British colonialists.[33] It is as if in the eyes of those to whom Chakrabarty brings our attention, no matter how much India has contributed to humanity's vast inventory of art, music, literature, and religious and philosophical traditions, it still hasn't gotten waste and garbage and trash right.

In this connection, it is illuminating to return to Calvino and the Paris in which he was living in the 1970s. What a happy, nay, civilized approach to taking care of garbage and trash, perhaps? The dutiful citizen cleans up after himself and makes sure to get all the household rubbish to the proper location at

32. Austin Delaney begins his review of Naipaul's *An Area of Darkness: An Experience of India* with the comment that "This book is a sustained, high I.Q. whine about India. A spoiled Brahmin from Trinidad, Mr. Naipaul became, during a year's tour, one of the literary world's most accomplished turd-watchers. No aspect of Indian public life is so carefully chronicled, so ingeniously introduced into chapter after chapter. The mere sight of a bare bottom sends him into a frenzy of distaste." Austin Delaney, "Mother India as Bitch," *Transition* 26 (1966): 50.

33. There are many reasons for not conflating what Chakrabarty describes as "modernity" with "civilized behavior." The kind of trash snooping at the center of Chapter 1 appears to be perfectly compatible with the practices and institutions characteristic of modernity as understood by Chakrabarty; and yet whether we agree with Justice Brennan that unwarranted trash snooping is "uncivilized," the term hardly seems unfamiliar in such contexts.

the proper time; the responsible dustbin men carry out their appointed tasks. The very name for both the household and the larger trash containers, the *poubelle*, we recall, honors the hearty 19th-century French bureaucrat who brought such cleanliness and order to Paris. But M. Poubelle was hardly the first or the last person to be charged with developing sustained methods of trying to rid Paris and the Seine of garbage, trash, and human and animal waste. Calvino doesn't mention the treatment of sewage (he does, we recall, compare the pleasure and importance of throwing things out to that of defecation, though he delivers the allusion quickly and does not linger over it—his essay is perhaps too "civilized" to do so). But as Dominique Laporte highlights with considerable glee in *History of Shit*,[34] among Poubelle's sanitation-minded predecessors was no less a personage than King François, who in November 1539 issued an edict that includes the following:

> François, King of France by the Grace of God, makes known to all present and all to come our displeasure at the considerable deterioration visited upon our good city of Paris and its surroundings, which has in a great many places so degenerated into ruin and destruction that one cannot journey through it either by carriage or on horseback without meeting with great peril and inconvenience. This city and its surroundings... [are] so filthy and glutted with mud, animal excrement, rubble and other offals that one and all have seen fit to leave heaped before their doors, against all reason as well as against the ordinances

---

34. Dominique Laporte, *History of Shit*, translated by Nadia Benabid and Rodolphe el-Khoury, with an introduction by Rodolphe el-Khoury (Cambridge, MA: MIT Press, 2002).

of our predecessors, that it provokes great horror and greater
displeasure in all valiant persons of substance.

. . . We forbid all emptying or tossing out into the streets
and squares . . . of refuse, offals, or putrefactions, as well as all
waters whatever their nature.

. . . We forbid all and any persons to leave or dispose of any
manner of fodder, animal wastes, soots and ashes, mud or any
other kind of unspeakable wastes on the streets.[35]

What does it take for "valiant persons of substance" to get "all and
any persons" to share their "horror" of and "displeasure" over the
unmistakable and ubiquitous sight and smell of "unspeakable
wastes"? King François appears to have had faith in royal edicts and
their enforcement (though probably, according to Laporte, enforcement was not very rigorous and the king himself violated the edict
with abandon).[36] The late 20th-century Paris in which Calvino
perfected his household and civic *poubellian* duties appears to have
approached closely the king's ideal if not his practice: among other
things, over the centuries a complex sewer system has been built
and rebuilt, and tours of the sewers have been available since the
early 1800s. Indeed, on Internet sites such as Tripadvisor, visitors
rather uniformly allow that such a tour isn't a bad "getaway" and
in fact the "smell isn't as bad" as one might think. There also is a
Sewers Museum in this city of Victor Hugo's *Les Misérables*.

Presumably, critics such as Gandhi, Chaudhuri, Naipaul, and
others would not propose a thoroughly Parisian solution for what
they see as the fouling of open spaces of India. But at least some of
the current efforts to create an "Open Defecation-Free India" are

35. Laporte, *History of Shit*, 3–5.
36. Laporte, *History of Shit*, 12.

built on assumptions not unlike those informing the design of the sewage system in Paris and the creation of incentives inviting people to use the system for the purposes for which it was designed.

According to Donald Reid's *Paris and Paris Sewermen: Realities and Representations*, 19th-century French sanitarians such as Alexandre-Jean-Baptiste Parent-Duchâtelet and other "public health experts and engineers condemned fear and disgust as irrational, uncivilized responses." Reaching for "a fundamentally romantic reconciliation of people and their refuse," such reformers insisted that "the danger to civilization came from unthinking repression of waste; only by processing this refuse could society conquer its anxieties and turn to profit the hidden worth of what it rejected."[37] If the remarkable sewers of Rome were one of the wonders of its civilization, so too could be those of Paris. And if the sewers were "civilizing agent[s],"[38] so too was the sewerman, "an embodiment of the health, order, and civilization which modern technology could produce."[39] Design or redesign the sewers properly so that they can adequately deal with human waste; make clear that they are places in which civilized and civilizing workers can labor in health and with dignity; invite the public down and encourage them to take justified pride in this particular achievement of French civilization.

If Parisian sanitarians linked the possibility of civilized attitudes about trash, garbage, and especially human waste to *not* feeling disgust,[40] according to journalist Rose George some current sanitarians in India hope to convince the large

---

37. Donald Reid, *Paris Sewers and Sewermen: Realities and Representations* (Cambridge: Harvard University Press, 1991), 3–4

38. Reid, *Paris Sewers*, 36.

39. Reid, *Paris Sewers*, 114.

40. In "Sense and Sensibilities: Disgust and the Meanings of Odors in Late Nineteenth-Century Paris," *Historical Reflections/Réflexions Historique* 28, no. 1 (2002): 211–249, David S. Barnes describes the strong link between feeling disgust and being "civilized,"

number of open defecators to come to their senses (quite literally) by *igniting* their disgust at the fecal breadth and depth of their neighborhoods; such disgust, the reformers hope, will induce people to develop solutions, the success of which will underwrite not only fierce pride but an unwillingness to revert to unhygienic and disgraceful habits.[41] Proponents of such Community-Led Total Sanitation projects (CLTS) came to recognize that simply providing people with latrines and warning them about the link between poor health and the inevitable spread of fecal matter due to open defecation is likely to be fruitless. After all, Rose George points out, just because doctors know that smoking is harmful doesn't mean they themselves give it up. She reports that close observation of what convinced people in Benin, for example, to turn from open defecation to latrines indicated that

> their principal reasons were to avoid embarrassment when visitors came; to make the house complete; not to have the chore of walking to get water; and to feel royal.[42]

which the reformers Reid refers to thought they must resist. During the "Great Stink" of 1880 and then again in 1895, many "disgusted, indignant, civilized" Parisians made clear their alarm that their city, a "paragon of modern, civilized life," was turning into a "cesspool" (Reid, *Paris Sewers*, 35, 25).

41. Rose George, "Open Defecation-Free India," in *The Big Necessity: The Unmentionable World of Human Waste and Why It Matters* (New York: Metropolitan Books, 2008), 173–197. See also her website, rosegeorge.com/site/about, for her continuing articles and blog entries on the sanitation situation in India and around the world. George alludes to the lack of civilized behavior in defecatory practices not in connection with India but with her native England: she has described as "Toilet Barbarians" the public officials who toilet by toilet are dismantling public bathrooms in Yorkshire and across England. George, "Why We Must Have Relief from the Toilet Barbarians," *Yorkshire Post*, February 12, 2012, http://www.yorkshirepost.co.uk/news/debate/columnists/rose_george_why_we_must_have_relief_from_the_toilet_barbarians_1_4266255.

42. George, *The Big Necessity*, 181.

Indeed, not having to walk to fetch water is particularly important for women and girls: in India, it's not only terrifically awkward and difficult to defecate in public in a sari; it can be dangerous, especially when it is done alone and in the dark. Moreover, George reports, many women who have been involved in CLTS projects have developed "enough confidence to start speaking in meetings, then to tie wife-beating husbands to lampposts, then to set up self-help groups."[43] More recently, according to news accounts echoing a case described by Rose George, a woman in India refused to stay at the home of her new husband until proper sanitation was provided; at the same time, women have been both scolded by a sanitation minister for wanting cell phones more than toilets and told by the country's former president, Pratibha Patil, that because sanitation is especially important for women's dignity, health, and safety, they ought to be at the forefront of efforts to end open defecation and protect water and land resources.[44]

The recent WHO/UNICEF report and frequent articles in the Indian press suggest that what Chakrabarty describes as the modernist sensibility has taken hold strongly: concerns about hygiene, safety, and economic vitality appear to be widespread; in the words of a member of the Ministry of Urban Development, "Progress is significant and in the right direction."[45] Reports don't much record the arrogant revulsion of relative outsiders but register insiders' sense of shame, fear, and deprivation of dignity.

43. George, *The Big Necessity*, 182.
44. K. Balchand, "President Asks Women to Lead Sanitation Revolution," *The Hindu*, March 22, 2012, http://www.thehindu.com/news/national/president-asks-women-to-lead-sanitation-revolution/article3026009.ece.
45. Jason Gale, "India Failing to Control Open Defecation Blunts Nation's Growth," *Bloomberg*, March 3, 2009, http://www.bloomberg.com/apps/news?sid=aErNiP_V4RLc&pid=newsarchive.

Bindeshwar Pathak, a determined longtime campaigner linking the situation of Dalit "scavengers" to issues of public toilets, has argued that assigning responsibility for cleaning up after others to one segment of society has allowed policymakers in particular to ignore the vast sanitation problems facing the nation[46]—echoing a mentality, surely not confined to India, described by one sanitation expert as "my crap is your problem."[47] The question of responsibility for taking out the trash and dealing with the waste turns out to involve one set of problems for the Dalits, another for all those affected by the lack of sanitary land and resources despite the Dalits' labor, and yet another for those anxious about India's standing among the "civilized" people of the world and its prospects for sustained economic vitality.

Taking out the trash and garbage is an everyday form of labor that Tallis doesn't do, perhaps doesn't even think it important to do; this is held to reflect badly on his personality and character.

Taking out the trash involves labor that Calvino considers a source of considerable satisfaction, not only from the pleasure he takes in performing it but also because of its thought-producing capacity. At the same time, he does not fail to acknowledge that the related labor of picking up the trash of others appears to be among few possibilities for immigrants, though it is work that seems to provide a taste, as it were, of lives they may wish some day to live themselves.

In the case of Dalits, the labor of picking up trash and waste is a badge of deeply entrenched social, political, economic, and

46. Gale, "India Failing."
47. George, *The Big Necessity*, 184.

116

spiritual positions they occupy (though there long have been efforts to rethink this). Dalits live in a society in which many complementary forces continue to relegate them to the job of cleaning up the waste and trash of others, making it difficult to join in Calvino's celebration of filling the *poubelle* or to share the dustbin men's hopes of moving on to another job.

Overall, these three examples suggest that garbage and trash are not something to be too closely associated with, literally or symbolically. Tallis is not immune to inferences made about his character drawn from his being unable to deal with his own daily detritus and that of his distracted and disorderly housemates. For quite different reasons and with quite different consequences, Dalits' spiritual contamination is held to be reflected in their occupational association with garbage and waste. It is only because of Calvino's alchemical ability to find philosophically rich themes in the contents of his *poubelle*, and his relatively privileged social and economic standing, that he can be so intimately connected with his waste and garbage without its suggesting even a whiff of contamination. Indeed his rapt attention to and delight in the resources he divines in his garbage almost have the effect of sanitizing and deodorizing it.

Trash and our relative relations to it play a prominent role in efforts to articulate and underscore significant differences among us. But why have we enlisted trash to do such work? It doesn't appear to be simply that we think trash is dirty, that we don't like dirt, and that we think people who deal with dirt must in some sense be dirty.

Hilda goes to great lengths to describe the muck and debris with which Tallis allows himself to be surrounded. What does that add to her otherwise already extensive assessment of his incompetence and inadequacy? Perhaps she believes that it is one thing for Tallis to fail to live up to the career expectations of a man of his ethnic and class background, but that it is quite another thing for him to live in the midst of dirt and grime. It is as if the rubbishy redolence permeating his being establishes him as beyond the pale, incapable of living up to the basic demands of civilized life.

In the case of the Dalits, trash and waste appear to provide a particularly handy means of responding to the ontological and epistemological challenges connected with establishing claims about deep differences between the Dalits and everyone else: for if there are indeed divergences among humans so great as to be irreversible and inerasable, how are we to know that they exist, given that there also are so many similarities among us? Are there any readily intelligible signs of such differences? Well, if the crucial distinction is between those who are pure and those who are not, and we can't determine simply by looking at people who is and is not pure, perhaps we can tell the difference by looking at the materials they handle day in and day out. Of course, "purity" and "impurity" don't have the same meaning in the case of one's spiritual state as they do in the case of one's bodily condition, but still, handling trash, waste, garbage, carcasses, and so forth offers the possibility of a reliably visible sign of a permanent but invisible blight. It might be helpful in this connection to recall that Aristotle, in the *Politics*, thought it would be ever so much easier to tell the difference between those who, he claimed, are free and those who are slaves by nature, if the outward difference between them were as clear as that between human bodies and statues of the gods.[48]

---

48. Aristotle, *Politics* 1254b34–36, in *The Complete Works of Aristotle: The Revised Oxford Translation*, Vol. 2, edited by Jonathan Barnes (Princeton, NJ: Princeton University Press, 1984).

Trash is a point of contact between Calvino and the dustbin men in a way that his correspondence, for example, as a point of contact between him and those who handle his mail, is not. Calvino comes close to treating what goes into the *poubelle* as human remains. He certainly does not explicitly argue that "life's leftovers" should be handled with the same reverence as the bodies of deceased humans. But Calvino implicitly describes trash and garbage as brimming with proof of human life—even though he sees them as a reminder of a state to which we are not looking forward. Trash may be, as he says, "alien" to us, but it is our alien creation. Despite the explicit correlation he makes between who we are/what we keep and who we are not/what we toss away, much of what he says also suggests that it is a mistake to think that throwing something out means it has ceased to be part of our lives; we shouldn't assume that what we throw out has entirely lost the animation with which we have imbued it. For it to be out of the orbit of our care is not the same as its being lifeless. In it are the remains of our days, and our days still linger in it. Perhaps, paradoxically, that is one of the sources of our disregarding or disdaining people who pick up our discards (as opposed to those who pick up our mail)—such attitudes promise to shore up our efforts to make sure our connection with our rejectamenta is broken. It is now in the hands of others, now *their* stuff. Our desire to distance ourselves from it points to our recognition that it nonetheless is or was ours. (If this sounds Freudian, well bully for Freud.)

No doubt these three examples are just a very few out of a vast history of formal and informal associations of trash with character over time and across cultures. Though the fact of such association is probably not surprising, some features of our exploration of that association seem to stand in rather stunning contrast to notions about trash we've explored in earlier chapters.

Recall, for instance, the examples in Chapter 1 of celebrity watchers and narcotics agents pawing through the trash of other people. One common reaction to such activity, at least in some parts of the world, is to speak of a kind of "sacredness" about one's trash: as if, yes, a person has thrown it out, but doesn't the trash carry enough of the history, the presence, of the person who did the tossing, to make it a rather serious violation to paw through it? And yet people whose job it is to pick up the trash are not treated as if they are dealing with sacred matter by any means. Hilda certainly doesn't think of Tallis as surrounding himself with anything sacred. The Dalits are assigned the task of dealing with what is considered radically impure. Calvino savors the handling of his own trash not because he thinks of it as sacred but because he believes that tossing stuff out is crucial to clarifying who he is.

Even if a person's trash is thought to be severed from its owner, and to that extent to have become ownerless, those whose job is to pick it up may come to be identified by their relation to it, as if it now belongs to them, belongs with them. It's not their trash, but to varying degrees, depending on the context, something important about them is thought to be revealed in their work of handling it. While Calvino unpeels who he is by throwing things out, the garbage men reveal who they are by picking it up; if Calvino undergoes purification by *poubelle*, the dustbin men become subject to possible pollution of their persons (at least temporarily). The Dalits' alleged impurity is perfect partner to the impurity of what they gather up.

Calvino's concerns about the treatment and future prospects of the dustbin men, and much of the literature about the conditions under which most Dalits continue to work and live, may tempt us to think of the dustbin men and Dalits as being treated as trash, as being—albeit in different ways in their different contexts—their societies' rejects, disposable and disposed-of people. There no doubt is something to that, especially to the extent that they are thrown to and left to fester at the margins of their societies. Moreover, it seems to be true, especially in the case of those conceived of as permanently polluted, that unlike secondhand goods—rejected objects that are given a second or third or fourth life in formal and informal segments of economies around the world[49]—once a human reject always a human reject,[50] the patina of pollution being exceedingly difficult to remove when the commitment to preserve it has broad and deep support in the society.

49. See, for example, Nicky Gregson and Louise Crewe, *Second-Hand Cultures* (New York: Berg, 2003).

50. It apparently is enormously difficult for so-called white trash in the United States to free themselves of the label and its implications (some so referred to, on the contrary, proudly and emphatically embrace the terminology). See, for example, Jeffrey A. Brown, "Class and Feminine Excess: The Strange Case of Anna Nicole Smith," *Feminist Review* 81 (2005): 74–94; Dorothy Allison, *Bastard Out of Carolina* (New York: Penguin Plume, 1993); and *Trash* (New York: Penguin Plume, 2002). People referred to as "white trash" don't necessarily have any particular connection to the handling of waste and trash: indeed, being employed in sanitation work would appear to be at odds with the powerful stereotypes of "white trash" as lazy, inebriated, sexually promiscuous, incestuous, incapable of or uninterested in holding a job, impoverished with no one to blame but themselves, dirty, and a disgrace to the "white race" (see, for example, Matt Wray and Annalee Newitz, eds., *White Trash: Race and Class in America* [New York: Routledge, 1997]). The association with trash is meant to underscore not their work but their alleged blight on the world, their status as human detritus, their "trashy," "low-class" ways.

Chapter 4

Evolutionary Trash

You've no doubt received the memo: human beings are born and eventually we die. Each of us has come into existence and then, sooner or later, each of us will go out of existence. Moreover, according to evolutionary theory, the same is likely to be true of our species, *Homo sapiens*. We are relative newcomers to the universe, and sooner or later—we seem to be going out of our way to making it sooner—our species probably will become extinct. In the meantime, we have the chance to think about many, many things, including how our species came to be (a not unworthy way to avoid thinking about where it may be going). The account offered by evolutionary theory is that we evolved, descended from, earlier forms of life. But why bring this up in a book exploring the intimate ties between humans and the rich realm of rejectamenta?

According to a common understanding of evolutionary theory, the process through which we and all other living things emerged is extravagantly wasteful. Though not all evolutionary theorists emphasize the place of waste in evolution, the idea enjoys widespread currency and has a colorful history. Charles Darwin himself described nature as "clumsy, wasteful, blundering." But such a notion was shocking and repugnant to many of his contemporaries and continues to this day to be heartily resisted in various religious, educational, and scientific quarters. Just what has been so disturbing about an account of human origins and of the natural world of which we are a part in which waste and wastefulness play a prominent role? Why and to whom is such a portrait of *Homo sapiens* so disconcerting?

Evolutionary theory[1] portrays the emergence over time of different populations of living things and the inheritable changes that take place within them. In offering an explanation of the source of those changes and their results, it supplies an account of diversity within a population and diversity among populations. It tells us how our species came about through such changes. We weren't the first form of life, but even if somehow we had been, as a species we couldn't have stayed around were it not for the wherewithal to meet the challenges and threats of the environments in which we live and success in reproducing before we die. For we are environmentally dependent and sensitive critters, and our surroundings change in ways that on the whole we cannot predict or control. Unless at least some members of a species are capable of surviving in environments in which other members cannot, it's curtains for that species. Species that cannot adapt to environmental change become extinct. The kinds of changes taking place within species,

---

1. There is not, of course, a single "evolutionary theory." Reflections on evolution certainly predate the work of Darwin, and there have been many developments since his *On the Origin of Species* was published in 1859. The "modern synthesis" that emerged in the first half of the 20th century pulled together, among other things, Darwinian ideas about natural selection and Mendelian accounts of genes and genetic mutation. As is clear in what follows, many details, for example about the structure and function of DNA, continue to be worked out.

and from one species to another, are in part (how large a part continues to be explored) a result of environmental pressures to adapt or die. But how are such changes possible?

Well, it turns out that the defining genetic information that is inherited from one generation to the next can undergo mutation. Such mutation doesn't necessarily assist the individual organism or the species in adapting to environmental pressures; it might be harmful, or it might not matter one way or the other. In any event, the mutation doesn't come about because it is helpful or harmful or neutral; it just comes about. Mutations don't happen for a purpose. They just happen. If the species is lucky, the mutation will enable it to survive or at least not stand in the way of its survival. Even then, mutations that are beneficial in one environment may cease to be so in another.

In short, individuals and the species of which they are a part cannot be guaranteed to survive willy-nilly. Species that cannot adapt cannot survive: to have survived in threatening environmental conditions is to have adapted to them. The very process that enables a species to survive also can create conditions under which a new species can emerge, a population of organisms enough like the one from which they emerged to be seen as their descendants but enough unlike them to not be able to reproduce with them.

In a letter to his friend Joseph Hooker, Charles Darwin exclaimed, "What a book a Devil's chaplain might write on the clumsy, wasteful, blundering low & horridly cruel works of nature!"[2] One hundred fifty years later, allusions abound to the "prodigiously

2. "Darwin, C. R., to Hooker, J. D.," Darwin Correspondence Database, http://www.darwinproject.ac.uk/entry-1924.

wasteful" process of evolution,[3] to the "messy and wasteful" nature of adaptation,[4] to nature's not being a "planned economy, carefully designed to eliminate extravagance and waste"[5] but on the contrary "breathtakingly wasteful and inefficient."[6] What is alleged to be so wasteful about nature, especially as seen through the dioramic frame of evolutionary theory?

1. To begin with, mutation appears to be wasteful in at least two ways. Most mutations are harmful: they make it more likely, even if they don't necessarily ensure, that the organisms and thus perhaps the species in which they occur will be tossed into the evolutionary wastebasket. In this sense, nature seems to be an excellent waste-generator.

Moreover, of those mutations that are not harmful and do not threaten the survival of the organisms in which they arise, some are better than others at equipping the organisms to adapt to specific environmental conditions. Because those conditions can change in ways that affect survival, species that are well adapted to only one set of conditions are likely not to survive as long as those with the potential to adapt to a wide variety of conditions. As one biologist has put it, the "emergence of complex ecological relationships"—a satisfactory fit between changing environmental conditions and organisms that find themselves called on to adapt to them—depends on "the availability of usable resources and the existence of a species pool from which ecological players can be

3. Daniel Dennett, *Darwin's Dangerous Idea: Evolution and the Meanings of Life* (New York: Simon and Schuster, 1995), 184.
4. Stephen Jay Gould, *The Structure of Evolutionary Theory* (Cambridge, MA: Harvard University Press, 2002), 122.
5. Richard Dawkins, *The Greatest Show on Earth: The Evidence for Evolution* (New York: Free Press, 2009), 375.
6. Philip Kitcher, *Living with Darwin: Evolution, Design, and the Future of Faith* (New York: Oxford University Press, 2007), 124.

drafted."[7] So a certain amount of genetic variation within a species is necessary for it to adapt under a range of conditions, but not all such variation will prove to be useful, not all the "ecological players" will be "drafted." The production of genotypic stock or inventory may simply be wasteful, in a sense similar to the production of inventory by automobile producers: a great deal of time, labor, and expense goes into the production of vehicle inventory, but much of that goes to waste if what is produced and ready at hand is not desirable to customers. Indeed the idea behind "zero inventory" is that companies can on the whole respond more nimbly and efficiently to changes in the market by adapting to real-time, just-in-time demand.[8] Biological organisms have never been in the position of Henry Ford, who could make sure that demand would follow supply: the Model T famously came in three colors, black, black, and black. To the extent to which unused potential constitutes a kind of waste, mutations that survive but don't seem to benefit the organism, even though they do no harm, are wasteful.[9]

2. Having an inventory of potentially useful but unused genetic material is one thing; but there also appears to be a massive amount of genetic material—in humans more than 90% of our DNA—that seems to lack even potential use: so-called junk DNA. Even though it appears (or has until recently) to have no function

7. Robert Dorit, "Biological Complexity," in *Scientists Confront Intelligent Design and Creationism*, ed. Andrew J. Petto and Laurie R. Godfrey (New York: Norton, 2007), 246.
8. For a careful exploration of the view that "inventory reflects underlying waste and that eliminating waste causes inventory to drop and productivity to rise," see Willard I. Zangwill, "The Limits of Japanese Production Theory," *INTERFACES* 22, no. 5 (September–October 1992): 14–25. See also the Japan Management Association, "Just-In-Time-Toyota," in *The Industrial Design Reader*, ed. Carma Gorman (New York: Allworth Press, 2003), 211–213.
9. This doesn't mean, as we shall see later, that evolutionary theorists necessarily assume that genetic inventory so far unused couldn't possibly be of use in the future; maybe what is going on is prudent hoarding!

or value, it has not disappeared; indeed, it busily and insistently replicates itself. It's one thing to keep stuff around that might be useful—but this *looks* like senseless clutter, lacking past, present, or future usefulness.[10]

3. Vestiges—such as the vermiform appendix in humans—are a kind of waste in the sense that they no longer are of use, but unlike allegedly "junk" DNA, they at least have the good grace to have done "a useful job in our long-dead ancestors."[11] They are remnants, leftovers, evolution's museum pieces. Our finding them quaint or fascinating is not the same thing as their performing a useful function for the organisms in which they loiter about.[12] And their hanging on can be dangerous: people can die from a burst appendix, for example.

4. There are many examples of organisms that have come into and managed to stay in existence whose construction or functioning nevertheless seems to involve a waste of resources, a supply greatly in excess of what seems necessary for the task at hand. Darwin's written works are full of comments on such waste: for example, what he described as the "incalculable waste of . . . pollen, eggs and immature beings" (from the 1844 Essay);[13] "the astonishing waste of pollen by our fir-trees."[14] A favorite example of some contemporary evolutionary theorists is the laryngeal nerve of the

---

10. Here, too, as we shall see later, evolutionary biologists have come to reassess the view of this material as "junk."
11. Dawkins, *Greatest Show*, 340.
12. Once again, this is not to say that there hasn't been speculation about a possible but so far unidentified use to the organism, as we shall see later.
13. Charles Darwin, *The Foundations of the Origin of Species. Two Essays Written in 1842 and 1844*, ed. Francis Darwin (Cambridge: Cambridge University Press, 1909), http://darwin-online.org.uk/content/frameset?itemID=F1556&viewtype=text&pageseq=1.
14. Charles Darwin, *On the Origin of Species, a Facsimile of the First Edition*, Introduction by Ernst Mayr (Cambridge, MA: Harvard University Press, 1964), 472.

giraffe, which instead of going directly from brain to larynx, heads past the larynx and back up, taking an extra 10–15 feet.[15]

So the evolution of organisms and the populations of which they are a part depend on events and processes that appear to be wasteful in several senses of "waste" and its close semantic cousins such as "trash" and "junk":

a. Trash as that which is rejected, thrown out: for example, the condition of an organism in which as a result of harmful mutations the organism has been rejected, tossed out, thrown away, exterminated. There has been a fruitless expense of energy.

b. Waste as potentially useful but unused excess: genetic inventory that provides a source of latent but unrealized capacity to adapt to environmental conditions.

c. Waste as unused excess with no past or potential use: allegedly "junk" DNA.[16]

d. Junk as stuff that had a use once but has no present use, yet is still around, hasn't been tossed out (and could prove to be dangerous): vestiges.

e. Waste as inefficient use of resources, in particular, as purposeless excess: over-abundant pollination, extra-long laryngeal nerve. It's useless, it's going to waste, or much less of it could be used to carry out the work it performs.

Given the appearance of such waste and trash and junk, it may seem—especially in our anthropomorphizing moods—as

15. E.g., Dawkins, *Greatest Show*, 363–364.
16. We shall see below why describing this DNA as junk rather than trash has turned out to be considered remarkably apt.

if nature's household operates on principles not unlike those Thorstein Veblen held to be characteristic of the Gilded Age leisure class and its emulators: as if it is boldly and conspicuously wasteful, going out of its way to exhibit how it can afford to overspend its resources, how it is not beholden to ideals of usefulness and efficiency. Such extravagance, abundance, excess, profligacy! Moreover, while Veblen acknowledged how useful in fact such wastefulness was for the attainment and maintenance of social status—conspicuous wastefulness in that sense itself didn't go to waste but helped establish and maintain one's place in the social hierarchy—there doesn't appear to be a similar kind of usefulness-at-the-next-level in the case of nature. To whom or to what is nature showing off or trying to prove something? Its wastefulness has no apparent further function—except perhaps as a reminder of the difference between nature and that part of it called *Homo sapiens* (not unlike that between the leisure class and those who can't live like them). In light of the apparent waste and trash and junk enumerated above, it looks as if nature can afford to be spendthrift, indeed to flaunt its extravagantly wasteful ways. But the resources and time available to humans do not appear to be unlimited, and our survival depends on our husbanding such resources and taking care to use them frugally. From this perspective, it seems fortunate that we can put our minds and our efforts toward the prevention of waste, if we so wish: our history is full of waste-preventing, efficiency-producing schemes, such as the division of labor (consult worthies such as Plato and Adam Smith); "scientific management" of the workplace (give thanks or blame to the likes of Frederick Winslow Taylor and Lillian and Frank Gilbreth); "fuel-efficient" cars; the composting of food scraps; handy hints for the frugal housekeeper ("An old toothbrush is great for scrubbing around faucets in the bath or kitchen . . . . Recycle those old powder puffs. Wash them in soapy water, rinse well and dry thoroughly. They are excellent for polishing silverware, copper and brass.")[17] But—to continue in the anthropomorphizing mood—nature appears not to have such worries, to have no shame and no regrets, not even think twice about cavalierly creating stuff only to then throw it out, madly producing matter for which it appears to have imagined no use at all, and producing much more than it needs to stay in business.

Let's assume for the moment that this is the case, that by ordinary human standards of what constitutes waste, nature is a champion at creating it. But so what? Why should that be a matter of interest or of concern? After all, humans are wasteful, often prodigiously so; they are part of nature, so why does the wastefulness of nature seem worthy of attention?

If the reference to Veblen reminds us that in some contexts humans are impressed by the capacity to waste, it is also true that in other contexts we applaud our fellow humans for their ability to avoid being wasteful. Assuming that when we predicate wastefulness of nature, we mean more or less the same thing as when we predicate wastefulness of human beings, the description of nature as wasteful can cut at least two ways, reflecting our ambivalence.

On the one hand, the ability to waste with impunity, to not have to worry about careful and efficient use of resources, might be seen as indicative of nature's majestic strength and unfathomable power, especially in comparison with pathetic little humanity's hardscrabble, penny-pinching existence. A version of such awe appears in one of Darwin's early diaries:

17. *Why Didn't I Think of That? Bright Ideas for Housekeeping, Garden, Kitchen and More* (Memphis: Wimmer, 1993), 64, 74.

Many of [the world's] creatures, so low in the scale of nature, are most exquisite in their forms & rich colours. It creates a feeling of wonder that so much beauty should be apparently created for such little purpose.[18]

Indeed, comments on the awe-inspiring fecundity of the natural world were not uncommon at the time: it is "as if a design had existed of displaying to the astonished eyes of mortals the unbounded resources of creative power."[19]

On the other hand, such fecundity is inseparable from extravagant and gratuitous waste, suggesting quite a different picture of nature, one according to which it, unlike that little pocket of scarcity-fearing humanity within it, is ill equipped to design carefully and intelligently, and to carry out such plans. Think, for example, of the potter turned industrialist, Josiah Wedgwood: owner of a very successful factory (and, by the way, the grandfather of Charles Darwin and of Darwin's cousin and wife, Emma), Wedgwood was an advocate of "scientific management" *avant la lettre*, devising and rigorously enforcing rules and procedures aimed at minimizing the waste of labor and materials.[20] Nature may seem like a real amateur in comparison. Certainly some of Darwin's contemporaries implied as much:

18. Charles Darwin, *Charles Darwin's Diary of the Voyage of H.M.S. "Beagle,"* ed. Nora Barlow (Cambridge: Cambridge University Press, 1934), 23. Quoted in Frank Burch Brown, "The Evolution of Darwin's Theism," *Journal of the History of Biology* 19, no. 1 (Spring 1986): 11.
19. P. M. Roget, *Animal and Vegetable Physiology with Reference to Natural Theology*, 2 vols. (London, 1834), Vol. 1, 48. Quoted in Richard R. Yeo, "The Principle of Plenitude and Natural Theology in Nineteenth-Century Britain," *British Journal for the History of Science* 19, no. 3 (November 1986): 268.
20. See Neil McKendrick, "Josiah Wedgwood and Factory Discipline," *Historical Journal* 4, no. 1 (1961): 30–55.

To work in vain in the sense of producing means of life which are not used, embryos which are never vivified, germs which are not developed, is so far from being contrary to the usual proceedings of nature, that it is an operation which is constantly going on, in every part of nature.[21]

As already apparent, the question of whether nature is profligate and wasteful was not an idle question in the cultural context in which Darwin worked, wrote, and published. And it is hardly an idle question now, as is clear from ongoing skirmishes about the relative virtues of evolutionary theory and what is called "intelligent design" as explanations of the natural world and its denizens, including the heavy-brained featherless biped known as *Homo sapiens*. There is considerable and perhaps surprising variation in the positions staked out over whether there is waste in nature and, if there is, what that means for the hypothesis[22] of intelligent design. Seatbelts please.

1. In products of intelligent design there is no waste.
    a. Nature is the product of intelligent design and therefore there is no waste in nature.
    b. There is waste in nature and therefore it is not the product of intelligent design.
2. There is waste in nature, but that doesn't count against nature being the product of intelligent design.
3. There is no waste in nature, but that doesn't count toward nature being the product of intelligent design.
4. In nature there is neither waste nor the absence of waste.

21. William Whewell, *Of the Plurality of Worlds: An Essay. Also a Dialogue on the Same Subject*, 2nd ed.(London, 1854), 334. Quoted in Yeo, "Principle of Plenitude," 278.
22. As we shall see below, the very meaning of "hypothesis" plays no small role in the contretemps under discussion here.

Now to each of these in some detail.

1a. We begin with contradictory conclusions drawn by those who agree that waste would not be found in products of intelligent design. The first argument runs something like this:

In products of intelligent design there is no waste.
The natural world is the product of intelligent design.
Therefore there is no waste in nature.

Darwin not only found himself unable to ignore ways in which nature is "wasteful," "clumsy," "blundering," even "cruel"; he quipped that such features would be of great interest and importance to an imagined "Devil's chaplain" because he recognized that they appeared to present a serious challenge to beliefs about the natural world and its creation shared by many influential scientists and divines active in Darwin's time. According to the "natural theology" espoused by the likes of William Paley and at least to some extent and for some time embraced by Darwin himself, observation of the natural world yielded conclusions about its origin arrived at by a route different from but fully compatible with divine revelation. No special means of disclosure was required to appreciate the magnificent fit of living things to their environments. Anyone with normally working senses and ordinary capacities for making logical inferences could recognize the intricate and ingenious design to be found in nature and draw the conclusion that such design surely is the work of a highly intelligent designer. For after all, we don't think that a watch or a ship or a house just happens to come into existence. Without some kind of design, even of the most haphazard kind, such items just couldn't have come together in that way.

Think of watches that are particularly good at keeping time, ships that lend themselves well to being navigated through rough and changing seas, houses that provide shelter from the elements even as they take advantage of their surroundings: we rightly take these to be strong evidence of good and careful design. And so when we come across organisms having shapes and structures that seem exquisitely fitted to the environments in which they are found, doesn't it make sense to take them, too, to be powerful evidence of design—but in their case, design not by humans, but by a force or forces far more powerful, far more intelligent, far more ingenious? How else can we explain the fact that flowers are structured so they can be cross-pollinated by bees, that the wing of an eagle equips it so beautifully for flying, the leg and single toe of the horse for running, the structure of the human eye for responding to differences in light—as Darwin himself put it, "all those exquisite adaptations of one part of the organisation to another part, and to the conditions of life, and of one distinct organic being to another being"?[23]

In any world that such an intelligence designed and had the power to bring about, there would be no fuss, no mess.[24] Such an intelligence doesn't have to waste time on false starts or what in

23. Darwin, *Origin*, 60–61.
24. One might be tempted here to think of a "genius" like Mozart as the closest human example of the kind of intelligence Paley had in mind: even in Mozart's youth, or so some of the stories about him go, his compositions flowed effortlessly, flawlessly, without sputter or in need of correction. But insofar as the miracle of such genius is that it is a capacity that doesn't seem to require much thought at all—something that seems to have occurred to Plato in his portrayal of the rhapsode Ion as merely a vessel of forces beyond his control—it may not serve the purposes of proponents of intelligent design. The intelligent design for which human design provides the weak model would

David Hume's work are described as "rude essays," very rough drafts.[25] Surely, unlike the bumbling human scholar, such an intelligence wouldn't need to keep old versions of the essay on hand just in case they turn out to contain useful gems or fruitful mistakes. Of course, if such superhuman intelligence were not also benevolent, it might design and create a world of useless things and beings, a world of trash (here the masterminds of planned obsolescence might come to mind), or one in which some things and beings were junk or trash and others were not. But a supremely intelligent and powerful designer/creator that was also benevolent would neither intentionally nor unintentionally create waste or junk. To refer to things and to people as junk is to announce their disposability and to undermine the claim to intelligence and benevolence in their purported designer/ creator. That no doubt is why Tammy Faye Bakker, she of TV evangelical fame and notoriety, may have surprised and shocked some of her followers when she appeared to refuse to demonize gay and lesbian people: "We're all just people made out of the same old dirt, and God didn't make any junk."[26]

"Who made this junk?" denigrates both the product and the producer. Hence, thinkers of a Paleyan stripe contend that if something or some process in nature looks like junk or trash or waste to us, we needn't assume that's because of the lack of skillful and

seem to involve more mental labor than the kind of effortless creation attributed to "genius." See Plato, *Two Comic Dialogues: Ion and Hippias Major*, ed. Paul Woodruff (Indianapolis: Hackett, 1983).

25. David Hume, *Dialogues Concerning Natural Religion*, 2nd ed., ed. Richard H. Popkin (Indianapolis: Hackett, 1988), 37.

26. Anita Gates, "Tammy Faye Bakker, 65, Emotive TV Evangelist, Dies," *New York Times*, July 23, 2007, A21.

loving design by which it was produced; rather, it's a reflection of the inevitable difference in mental and moral capacity between us and the superhuman intelligent being or forces by which we came into being.

In short, Darwin's work emerged in a context in which an argument along the following lines was widely embraced:

- There is a remarkable, often strikingly beautiful fit of living things to their environment.
- This remarkable fit is best explained by a kind of intelligent design suggested by but far superior to that of human design.
- The presence of waste in a design process or designed product tells against the intelligence and power of the designer.
- Since this world is the product of intelligent design, there is no waste. If there appears to be waste, that's only because humans can't fully fathom what is going on in nature.

1b. But as hinted at in comments made by Darwin, there's another response among those who begin with the premise that waste would never be found in anything that is the product of intelligent design:

In products of intelligent design there is no waste.
The natural world is full of waste.
Therefore it cannot be the product of intelligent design.

A number of Paley's intellectual descendants flourishing in the late 20th and early 21st centuries argue that there are some processes in nature that are so complex, requiring so many parts operating in such exquisite harmony, that they cannot be adequately accounted for by mutation and natural selection. The biochemist Michael Behe, for example, cites flagella and cilia, the amazing little motors found in some bacteria. The mechanisms of natural selection, he insists, cannot possibly explain how these little marvels came about. But the explanatory failure of natural selection does not leave us in the lurch. Another explanation "flows naturally from the data":

> The straightforward conclusion is that many biochemical systems were designed. They were designed *not* by the laws of nature, not by chance and necessity. Rather, they were *planned*. The designer knew what the systems would look like when they were completed; the designer took steps to bring the systems about. Life on earth at its most fundamental level, in its most critical components, is the product of intelligent activity.[27]

Underscoring the promise of a Paleyan natural theology that no special gift or capacity for revelation is required to reach the conclusion that intelligent design is responsible for life on earth, Behe adds:

> Inferring that biochemical systems were designed by an intelligent agent is a humdrum process that requires no new principles of logic or science. It comes simply from the hard work that biochemistry has done over the past forty years, combined with consideration of the way in which we reach conclusions of design every day.[28]

27. Michael Behe, "Molecular Machines: Experimental Support for the Design Inference," in *Intelligent Design Creationism and Its Critics: Philosophical, Theological and Scientific Perspectives*, ed. Robert T. Pennock (Cambridge, MA: MIT Press, 2001), 254. Emphasis in the original. Behe's argument also appears in his *Darwin's Black Box: The Biochemical Challenge to Evolution* (New York: Free Press, 1996).
28. Behe, "Molecular Machines," 254.

Just as Darwin and some of his colleagues regarded the wastefulness found in nature to pose a problem for the hypothesis of intelligent design in the 19th century, many contemporary evolutionary theorists take such waste to be among the difficulties facing current versions of intelligent design: since an intelligent designer surely would not create waste, if there is waste there can't be intelligent design; but there is waste, so intelligent design cannot be an adequate explanation of the natural world.

For example, Philip Kitcher, who has been following and responding to Behe's defenses of intelligent design for well over a decade, has argued that anyone who puts forward intelligent design as an explanation of nature's workings better be prepared to offer details about how the explanation works. The account ought to provide "a set of coherent principles that identify the ways in which intelligence is directed and what its powers and limitations are."[29] After all, one might add, if Behe insists that it requires no esoteric knowledge of logic or science to see that intelligent design is at work, surely we ought to have some idea about the nature of this intelligence and how it operates. Among difficulties Kitcher finds in Behe's brief for intelligent design (these are in addition to his criticisms of Behe's arguments against natural selection) is the apparent incompatibility between the hypothesis of intelligent design and the broad and deep scattering of waste across the allegedly intelligently designed natural landscape:

> Apparently Intelligence isn't directed toward eliminating the junk from genomes or removing vestigial structures like the whale's pelvis.... It's possible, of course, that although directed

29. Kitcher, *Living with Darwin*, 105.

toward these ends, Intelligence is simply unable to bring them about. So any satisfactory principles must differentiate between the bacterial flagellum, blood-clotting cascade, and similar places where Intelligence [according to Behe] shows its prowess, and the accumulated junk, vestigial structures, and genetic blunders, where it remains in abeyance.[30]

Like Paley and Darwin, Kitcher (along with Gould, Dawkins, and others) takes the presence of waste in nature to count against the idea that the natural world is the product of intelligent design. Unlike Paley, but like Darwin (at least in some of his less guarded moments), Kitcher thinks that what we take to be waste is in fact waste, and that instead of writing it off as simply an appearance, and preserving the hypothesis of intelligent design, we must accept it and regard it as among the factors counting against that hypothesis.

2. *There is waste in nature, but that doesn't count against nature being the product of intelligent design.*

Paley's response to the problem that waste in nature provides an argument against intelligent design was to deny that there is waste, and to explain the appearance of it by reference to the limits of the human mind. Michael Behe takes a somewhat different tack. In response to the kind of concern we just saw Kitcher raise, Behe doesn't deny that there are imperfections, including waste, in the natural world. But he insists that we should no more count that against the existence of intelligent design than we count planned obsolescence against the possibility of the designer having many goals, aims that might override efficiency or perfection.[31] For him the crucial question is whether we must postulate intelligent design, not whether we can know all the aims and standards of an intelligent designer. In effect, then, his position seems to be that while there is enough similarity between the products of human design and superhuman intelligent design for us to infer with certainty that there is intelligent design, there is enough difference for us not to expect to know everything about what the super-designer is up to.

So, unlike Paley, Behe apparently is willing both to accept that there is waste and deny that its existence counts against the hypothesis of intelligent design. This turns out, however, neither to appease his critics nor soothe his potential allies. The inevitable ignorance of what the designer is up to alleged by Behe is for Kitcher a strong argument against the explanatory adequacy of intelligent design: Behe has got to offer something better than "intelligent design explains nature, but I can't really tell you how it works; how could a mere human fathom the soul of an intelligent designer?" And for some students of religion it means that the intelligent designer Behe postulates cannot be said to resemble the "all-knowing, all-powerful, and perfectly good . . . God of traditional theism": for whether or not Behe has shored up the notion of an intelligent designer, he hasn't ruled out the possibility that that designer is neither omnipotent nor benevolent.[32]

Moreover, if our model for understanding design in the natural world is supposed to be design as executed by humans, we have to consider the possibility (alluded to only very briefly by Behe) that we have very good reason to think that sometimes waste is in fact

31. David B. Myers, "New Design Arguments: Old Millian Objections," *Religious Studies* 36, no. 2 (June 2000): 150.
32. Myers, "New Design Arguments," 142.

the proud product of intelligent design. For though human design as we know it typically involves unintentional waste (my plans for this book, for example, didn't include the many false starts I have now discarded), sometimes the waste is intended, is central to the design: think of throwaway razors, or that nifty little smartphone buzzing in your pocket. Indeed, a high level of intelligence and ingeniousness in human designers is revealed in our capacity not to prevent waste but to create it. It's not necessarily that the object is designed to break or disintegrate or collapse or burst into flames (though that might sometimes be the case); it might rather be that it is loaded with features that are intended to be used for only a relatively short period of time. A smartphone is built in such a way that owners will have increasing difficulty using it for the multiple purposes they are assumed to have in mind, which of course can include not only maintaining communication with others or recording music, but impressing observers with one's good taste and up-to-date fashion sense. Why wouldn't a superhuman intelligent designer relish designing things intended to be disposed of—especially if one important difference between human and superhuman intelligent design is that the latter, unlike the former, can get along just fine, thank you, without the need to be frugal or conserve resources? Not only devils can be divas of disposability.

3. *There is no waste in nature, but that doesn't count toward nature being the product of intelligent design.*

One doesn't have to embrace the tenets of natural theology to doubt that what appears to be waste really is waste. There are at least two reasons that defenders of evolutionary theory not enamored of intelligent design might seize the opportunity to demonstrate that there is no or next to no waste in nature.

First, there is a practical matter: the appearance of waste in nature becomes an invitation to engage in research that can show that such appearances are belied by what actually is going on. Researchers aren't necessarily threatened by or worried about the appearance of waste; they're simply motivated to try to uncover functions obscured by its appearance.

For example, the idea that some DNA is useless junk has struck some investigators as being so unlikely that, appreciating the distinction in other contexts between junk and trash, they have wondered whether such DNA, like junk in the attic, after all can or does perform some functions. Unlike trash, junk has not been thrown out—at least not yet. Indeed, in recognition of this difference, Stephen Jay Gould withdrew the concern he and Jürgen Brosius had expressed, in a 1992 article, about what they saw as "the current disrespectful (in a vernacular sense) terminology of junk DNA and pseudogenes." They thought such language had "been masking the central evolutionary concept that features of no current utility may hold crucial evolutionary importance as recruitable sources of future change."[33] In his 2002 book *The Structure of Evolutionary Theory,* Gould reported having come to appreciate that "junk" is in fact a perfectly appropriate term for something that is "currently useless, but harmless (as opposed to garbage), and replete with potential future value."[34]

And for some time now it has been becoming clear, as one team of researchers put it, that there is "a surprisingly large amount of potential treasures among the stretches of ["junk"] DNA sequence

33. Jürgen Brosius and Stephen Jay Gould, "On 'Genomenclature': A Comprehensive (and Respectful) Taxonomy for Pseudogenes and Other 'Junk DNA,'" *Proceedings of the National Academy of Sciences of the United States of America* 89, no. 22 (November 15, 1992): 10709.

34. Gould, *Structure,* 1270.

that evolution has saved for us"[35]—for example, providing some kind of support for the straightforwardly useful DNA. "Risking personification of biological processes, we can say that evolution is too wise to waste this valuable information . . . repetitive DNA should be called not junk DNA [pace Gould's reminder about the meaning of "junk"] but a genomic scrap-yard because it is a reservoir of ready-to-use-segments for nature's evolutionary experiments."[36]

Of course not all such "experiments" will be of positive use to the organism and indeed may function to hasten its demise: so-called junk DNA has been linked with certain diseases, such as a form of muscular dystrophy.[37] But some of it also has been claimed to be crucial to the "high speed of evolution of human lineage brain size"[38]—perhaps the path of *Homo* to *sapiens* was accelerated thanks to some apparently useless "junk" in our DNA.

It's as if calling some DNA "junk" amounted to throwing down a gauntlet to which curious and clever investigators would respond by showing that it isn't junk—or that it is junk, but that doesn't mean there is no point in exploring the uses to which it has been or might be put: it may be junk but that ain't the same as being in the trash.

35. Mark Johnston and Gary D. Stormo, "Heirlooms in the Attic," *Science, New Series* 302, no. 5647 (November 7, 2003): 997.

36. Wojciech Makalowski, "Not Junk after All," *Science, New Series* 300, no. 5623 (May 23, 2003): 1247.

37. Gina Kolata, "Reanimated 'Junk' DNA Is Found to Cause Disease," *New York Times*, August 19, 2010, http://www.nytimes.com/2010/08/20/science/20gene.html?modu le=Search&mabReward=relbias%3Ar%2C%7B%221%22%3A%22RI%3A11%22%7D; and "Bits of Mystery DNA, Far from 'Junk,' Play Crucial Role," *New York Times*, September 5, 2012, http://www.nytimes.com/2012/09/06/science/far-from-junk-dna-dark-matter-proves-crucial-to-health.html?pagewanted=all&module=Search&mabR eward=relbias%3Ar%2C%7B%221%22%3A%22RI%3A11%22%7D.

38. Roy J. Britten, "Transposable Element Insertions Have Strongly Affected Human Evolution," *Proceedings of the National Academy of Sciences of the United States of America* 107, no. 46 (November 16, 2010): 19945.

As for the idea that vestiges constitute waste, it seems to be widely accepted by biologists that since "it is quite unlikely that structures completely without function would be preserved, certain functions must be assumed to persist."[39] Perhaps the vestige is so closely wound up in human development or otherwise plays such a crucial role that its disappearance would be harmful. Maybe it now serves a new function of which we remain unaware. "Hence, a vestigium should not generally be considered without function, or only with respect to its ancestral, adult roles."[40] So what appears to be waste, in the form of DNA that doesn't seem to have any function, or vestiges that hang around despite having been deprived of any justification for their presence, is welcomed by researchers as an invitation to dig more deeply, to locate and describe heretofore undiscovered uses.

But is their enthusiasm simply a practical professional heuristic? Or might there be a *second* source of the eagerness of some investigators to topple the idea that there is waste in nature—namely, a concern that an article of professional faith is at stake, a worry that the presence of waste in nature would in fact undermine a central tenet of evolutionary theory? Is the presence of waste in nature as much of an embarrassment to evolutionary theorists or other biologists as it has been to proponents of intelligent design?

Stephen Jay Gould has said that the important reminder of the distinction between junk and garbage that led him to back off his criticism of the use of "junk" in the description of repetitive DNA came from Sydney Brenner, a Nobel laureate in genetics.

39. Gerd B. Müller, "Vestigial Organs and Structures," *Encyclopedia of Evolution*, ed. Mark Pagel (Oxford: Oxford University Press, 2005), http://www.oxfordreference.com.libproxy.smith.edu:2048/view/10.1093/acref/9780195122008.001.0001/acref-9780195122008-e-415?rskey=MjrzBT&result=1.
40. Müller, "Vestigial Organs."

Brenner saw Gould's scolding as characteristic of a widespread but unfounded belief among scientists that "all organisms are perfect and that everything within them is there for a function . . . that patently useless features of existing organisms are there as investments for the future. . . . [Such scientists] are all convinced by the argument that if this DNA were totally useless, natural selection would already have removed it. Consequently, it must have a function that still remains to be discovered."[41] But Brenner reminds his colleagues that natural selection is not so narrowly selective. He concedes that "were the extra DNA to become disadvantageous, it would become subject to selection, just as junk that takes up too much space, or is beginning to smell, is instantly converted to garbage."[42] However, he thinks it is a mistake to assume that anything within an organism must have a current use because otherwise it would have been selected against, that is, eliminated: to assume this is to forget that it is only *deleterious* mutations that don't make it through the sieve of natural selection. Those that do make it through might be useful, but they might not. That everything that is harmful is sooner or later eliminated does not mean that everything that survives elimination must be useful. It might be, but it might be useless, albeit harmless.

There is something quite striking about Brenner's characterization of the assumption he thinks is held by many of his colleagues in genetics: he is in effect charging that they cannot countenance the idea that there is waste in nature because they think that natural selection rules out such a possibility. If that is the case, such

41. Gould, *Structure*, 1269, quoting Sydney Brenner, "Refuge of Spandrels," *Current Biology* 8, no. 19 (1998): R669.
42. Brenner, "Refuge," 669.

proponents of natural selection are as allergic as proponents of intelligent design to the idea that nature is wasteful: they hold not only that the absence of waste in nature does not count toward intelligent design and that natural selection can explain the absence of waste, but also that natural selection requires that there be no waste.

Somewhat analogous attempts to banish the impression that nature is wasteful, but not in order to clear away obstacles to intelligent design, have appeared in comments by observers of complex ecosystems; they claim that whatever waste does show up in nature nevertheless will soon be taken care of by organisms ready and eager to make opportune use of such waste. For example, environmental ethicist Holmes Rolston III has urged us to consider that what appears to be waste in nature really isn't—that nature is economical in the sense that some use is always or almost always found for what comes into being. Rolston acknowledges that the case for waste seems easy to make:

> The proliferation and die-off [of pupfish] is extravagant, indifferent reproductive power. Heavy-seeded trees, such as oaks or hickories, may produce 200 million acorns or nuts to replace themselves once or twice, and light-seeded trees, like cottonwoods produce billions. A pair of robins may produce thirty eggs to replace themselves once. Mother Nature seems spendthrift.[43]

But Mother Nature, he counters, is no such thing. "One organism's waste is another organism's treasure," he says, just what we might expect in light of the fact that

43. Holmes Rolston III, "Disvalues in Nature," *Monist* 75, no. 2 (April 1992): 268–269.

all living things are marginally pressed for survival. . . . Wherever there is available free energy and biomass, a life form typically evolves to exploit those resources. . . . Truth is, there is not much "waste" in natural systems, though there is exuberance and fecundity. What there is, if immediately a disvalue, is systemically transformed into something of value.[44]

Rolston's point seems to be that organisms that have in their genetic repertoire (however that came about) the capacity to make use of the waste found in nature are likely to be able to make better use of their surroundings than those that don't.

Biologist Robert Dorit, like Rolston, describes complex ecosystems as being virtually free of waste. But in addition he seems especially eager to point out that it doesn't take the work of an intelligent designer to explain this absence of waste.

The arrival of every new participant in an ecosystem . . . creates novel ecological opportunities for parasites, symbionts, and predators. Ecosystem complexity increases (up to a point), entrained by this positive-feedback loop. In a complex process of trial and error, new participants try to gain a foothold in an increasingly crowded environment. Some species cannot successfully insert into the maturing ecosystem, others are displaced by more effective competitors. A similar triage may be occurring at the ecosystem level: Unstable networks of ecological interactions give way to more robust networks of interaction. . . . The result, in the absence of a designer, is a complex ecosystem in which little appears to go to waste.[45]

44. Rolston III, "Disvalues," 269–270.
45. Dorit, "Biological Complexity," 246.

Dorit seems to be concerned that defenders of intelligent design may take the absence of waste in complex ecosystems to count toward their hypothesis—they may think that if the presence of waste anywhere in nature points to the absence of design, then the absence of waste points to the presence of design. Of course, logically speaking, the latter does not follow from the former: the proposition that if there is waste then there is no intelligent design does not imply the proposition that if there is no waste then there is intelligent design. But Dorit seems to think it is important to block that inference.

It's worth pointing out that the arguments of Rolston and Dorit in fact are at odds with the idea that there is no waste in nature— or at least with the idea that there is no trash. In his brief for the absence of waste in a "self-assembling" system, one that exists "in the absence of a designer," Dorit cites examples such as life forms coming to take over in environments newly "denuded by catastrophic events (fire, hurricane)," species "displaced" by competitors, and "unstable networks" giving way to "more robust networks of interaction."[46] There is absence of waste in some sense, yes: an environmental neighborhood is not lost, its resources not gone to waste, even though its most recent inhabitants were destroyed; and the reserve systems from which "ecological players can be drafted" are actually put to use, their potential is not wasted.

But surely there is waste in another sense, certainly a lot of trash, in the form of what's left after the fire or hurricane, or in the demise of the just exterminated species. The economy of nature Dorit is describing is not one that prevents trash; it is one that "repurposes" it. Rolston does a little riff on a familiar old saw in saying that "One organism's waste is another organism's treasure." But we can't say both that one person's trash is another person's treasure, and also

46. Dorit, "Biological Complexity," 246.

insist that there is no trash. If there is no trash to begin with, no one can turn it into treasure. Perhaps a more perspicuous way to make the point being urged by Rolston and Dorit is that there may be trash but it won't go to waste (a reminder that just as in some circumstances it is important to distinguish between junk and trash, so also it can be important to distinguish between trash and waste).

What Rolston and Dorit describe seems quite compatible with thinking of ecosystems as neighborhoods in which trash is generated but not left dormant. Like the tonier precincts of a big city favored by a mayor who makes sure the trash there is collected frequently and on schedule, ecosystems produce lots of trash but also (albeit without mayors) get rid of it: for example, some dead or decaying organic matter turns out to be lunch for the hungry saprophyte. On this view, the tidiness of fit of organisms to changing environments is not the result of a well-thought-out ingenious design that prevents waste, but of nature's opportunistic, trash-to-treasure bent, its let's-clean-up-the-mess-I-just-made ethic: let's not let the yummy trash go to waste. Or less anthropomorphically: organisms that can make use of the detritus around them may have a better chance of survival than those that cannot.

4. *In nature there is neither waste nor the absence of waste.*

"Waste," "trash," "junk," and the family of terms of which they are a part have a strong normative dimension. It is true that sometimes their use simply reflects the location of something— something is "in the trash" or "in the wastebasket"—or refers to the physical state of something, as in describing an apple in the fridge as being in a condition of deliquescence. But most uses of the terms reflect a judgment about the value of a thing or person or process in light of certain ends or purposes. It's when things no longer adequately serve the purposes for which we employed them that we throw them into the trash (at least when we do so intentionally). Their being in the trash announces their loss of usefulness. We have not thought of a way to "repurpose" them, though of course other people might do so: as we are often reminded, one person's trash may become another person's treasure. We describe the use of something for a purpose we regard as unworthy or undesirable or unattainable as a waste of time or energy or resource. Time can only be said to be "wasted" if there are thought to be appropriate and inappropriate uses of it. John Locke described uncultivated land as "wasted" because, he claimed, God gave land to humans to produce sustenance: "land that is left wholly to nature, that hath no improvement of pasturage, tillage, or planting, is called, as indeed it is, *waste*."[47]

So when we judge something in nature to be waste we seem to be assuming that it fails to function in the way and toward the ends that we take to be appropriate for it or that it serves. It is "wasteful" of nature to create something that exists only long enough to be thrown into the trash or has a potential for use that goes unrealized only if we assume that there must be a use for that thing and that that use should be realized. It is "wasteful" of nature to store stuff that no longer is useful only if we assume that nature could and should do spring housecleaning. It is "wasteful" of nature to have used all that time and energy creating a species and then toss it away, only if we assume that nature would never and should never go to such ultimately fruitless expense. The reputation of vestiges and "junk DNA" as wasteful can only be reversed if their usefulness can be demonstrated. The judgment that the giraffe's

47. John Locke, *Second Treatise of Government*, ed. C. B. Macpherson (Indianapolis: Hackett, 1980 [1690]), §42.

laryngeal nerve is a "waste of resources" rests on the assumption that a much shorter one could carry out the same function more economically and efficiently.

But we must consider the possibility that trying to decide whether something in nature is or is not waste is like trying to decide whether Saturday is or is not orange. Saturday is neither orange nor not orange. Just as days of the week don't have colors (except in a strongly metaphorical sense) in light of which we could sensibly formulate and assess the judgment that Saturday is or is not orange, so perhaps there is no goal or purpose to ground the judgment that something in nature is or is not waste—there is no norm of efficiency, or of extravagance, in light of which the giraffe's laryngeal nerve, for example, is or is not a waste of resources.

Such a possibility may at first glance seem bizarre. After all, we seem to have no difficulty making perfectly good sense of the descriptions of nature as wasteful made by Darwin, Dawkins, Gould, or Kitcher; we seem to have no trouble at all understanding the claim to the contrary that there really is no waste in nature, whether made by a natural theologian such as Paley or current students of ecology such as Rolston and Dorit. (Whether we agree or disagree with the views so expressed is another matter.)

But we do seem to be extrapolating from norms that have developed in the context of our judgment about the human use of resources such as time and labor and money. Does *nature* have norms, purposes, or goals in light of which it can be judged to be wasteful or not wasteful? What are we attributing to nature if we say or imply that it does have such norms or purposes or goals? Is nature the kind of entity that can be and can have a vested interest in being efficient, or delight in being profligate? Does it measure its own workings and find itself now with too little, now too much, and now just the right amount?

There are some old and familiar problems here about how to make sense of nature without thereby characterizing it in ways that may obscure its workings more than help reveal and explain them. For example, should we follow Aristotle in attributing purposes though not personality to nature?[48] Are "teleological notions . . . essential or merely heuristic for understanding biological phenomena"?[49] Such problems surely are not going to be solved here, only noted. Darwin faced a version of them as he laid out his notion of natural selection. He hoped to be able to use the phrase "natural selection" and yet block the inference that he was referring to a process involving conscious agency. Responding to critics' concern that "selection" implies a kind of personification of nature, in the third and all succeeding editions of the *Origin* Darwin replied:

> It is difficult to avoid personifying the word Nature; but I mean by Nature, only the aggregate action and product of many natural laws, and by laws the sequence of events as ascertained by us. With a little familiarity such superficial objections will be forgotten.[50]

Darwin may seem to be courting circularity here by using "natural" to clarify what he means by "Nature." But it seems clear that he is seeking ways to avoid committing himself to a view of nature or the natural that involves a notion of something like human agency. One of the reasons "selection" might have seemed an appropriate

48. See, for example, Anthony Preus, "Aristotle's 'Nature Uses . . . ,'" *Apeiron* 3, no. 2 (July 1969): 20–33.

49. Colin Allen and Marc Bekoff, "Biological Function, Adaptation, and Natural Design," *Philosophy of Science* 62, no. 4 (December 1995): 610.

50. Quoted in Philip R. Sloan, "'The Sense of Sublimity': Darwin on Nature and Divinity," *Osiris*, 2nd series 16 (2001): 266.

choice to Darwin for describing a process in nature is that he and many of his contemporaries were very well acquainted with humans' selective breeding of plants and animals. But he wished to choke off the possibility that nature "selects" in the same sense— that nature, like the human breeder, engages in picking and choosing, rejecting and tossing. For an organism to be "selected" is not for it to be picked out, chosen, awarded the prize, but to have survived changes occurring as the result of natural laws operating on the organism in which the trait appears, under the environmental conditions in which it is found. When a species ceases to have organisms that can adapt to threatening changes in their environment, the organisms and the species disappear. Off they go, into the evolutionary landfill. It is true that those that remain do so not simply at random, and it may seem as if they were "selected" on account of their capacity to survive. But "selection" is misleading, if it suggests that there is a selecting agent doing the picking and choosing, that some organisms are picked out, and others rejected, like tomatoes at the market. For in fact all that is going on is that in the face of environmental threat some survive and some do not.

Using "selection" with the usual connotations of conscious choice flatters survivors, insofar as it gives a sense that there is a reason for their surviving, that a choice was made, that what happened was neither irrational nor non-rational, that it was based on something. Survival does depend on there being an orderly process, on there being favorable conditions in the organism and in the environment. But it also is not unlike the luck of the draw: given the constitution of the organism, it happened to be in the right place at the right time.

The idea that nature is not the kind of being or entity that has norms, and that therefore strictly speaking can be neither wasteful nor non-wasteful by adhering or failing to adhere to such norms, may seem deflationary, to put the kibosh on the kind of explorations at the heart of this chapter. But whether being in the business of describing nature as wasteful or not wasteful involves a category mistake—a misunderstanding along the lines of thinking of Saturday as orange or not orange—such descriptions have been crucial to some of the grounds of the fervid exchanges between proponents of intelligent design and evolutionary theorists. We could try to call off the game on account of the darkness of a conceptual misdemeanor, insist on a ceasefire, pull the rug out from under their apparent disagreements (please do help yourself to a metaphor). Or we could, as we have here, use the occasion to highlight significant details about the terms of the engagement.

The natural theology of William Paley and less explicitly the intelligent design hypothesis of Michael Behe involve the assumption that there really is no significant difference between religious exploration and scientific investigation, that it is not as if one is comparing apples and oranges, or pushpin and poetry. According to their views, the careful observations and inferences that yield conclusions about nature also turn out to yield conclusions about the source of the undeniable design exhibited in nature. Such moves involve a wager: that natural theology, and intelligent design, will gain credibility by being seen as compatible with scientific investigation. But of course there is also a risk: if intelligent design is seen as a scientific hypothesis, it will be subject to testing by scientific methods. Part of the cost for theology of going "natural" is that it at least has to acknowledge the possibility of counter-arguments based on observations of nature. You can't ask for membership in the club and hope to enjoy only its privileges and not its responsibilities.

Darwin had been a close reader of Paley, and intelligent design was a live hypothesis for him, one for which there appeared to be powerful evidence in nature. But he could not ignore what seemed to him and others to be undeniable evidence of widespread wastefulness in nature. The broad perspective from which nature appears to be designed is also a perspective from which it appears to be wasteful. Though the question of whether nature is wasteful was hardly the only question that posed doubts about intelligent design for Darwin and others, it was a powerful consideration. And as we've seen, there continues to be quite a lot at stake in the question of whether nature is wasteful.

Unlike Darwin, most contemporary evolutionary theorists don't take intelligent design to be a live hypothesis, or to be a real hypothesis at all—something offered in the expectation that it can and should continue to be explored and tested according to methods characteristic of science. Philip Kitcher, for example, is hardly alone in characterizing intelligent design as "discarded science, dead science":[51] there is no reason for it to be included in biology curricula, he argues, except as part of attempts to understand the history of scientific thought. But he recognizes that intelligent design has considerable influence as a strongly and widely held belief, one that is not going to go away simply because in most scientific quarters it has been declared dead on arrival. It is in this context that Kitcher gives particular weight to the wastefulness of nature, having it play a central role in backing proponents of intelligent design into a corner of their own making from which they can't escape without considerable damage. He is in effect saying, Let's assume for the sake of argument that belief in intelligent design is not simply a matter of faith,[52] but a belief that is open to

51. Kitcher, *Living with Darwin*, 12.
52. Here understanding by "faith" is something not immune to doubt but something not properly a matter for ordinary scientific adjudication.

being supported by or undermined by scientific investigation. If you want to describe the workings of nature as due to intelligent design, then you better be prepared to account for "the mess, the inefficiency, the waste"[53] so undeniably a part of what we observe in nature. It's not fair to ask us to keep our eyes open for signs of design but then demand that we close them or discount them when we see signs of waste.

The fact that the question of wastefulness in nature continues to appear in exchanges between proponents of intelligent design and evolutionary theorists suggests that in some respects the debates haven't changed very much over the past century and a half. Certainly science has changed, though as is clear in the case of Michael Behe and some other supporters of intelligent design, advances in scientific understanding have been invoked in hopes of strengthening the evidence for intelligent design (as in "what else could account for those amazing little bacterial motors?").

In any event, it looks as if the question of whether nature is or is not wasteful won't disappear as long as defenders and opponents of intelligent design wish to continue to argue with each other. Not a bad gig for the concept of wastefulness in nature: "Go ahead and call my use in this context a 'category mistake' all you want—those disputants need me in order to keep their battles alive!"

If *Homo sapiens* is looking for a way to plump up its résumé, evolutionary theory doesn't seem to have much to offer—especially in comparison with something like Paley's version of intelligent design, which can make the road to our arrival seem more like careful preparation for the birth of a beloved and longed-for royal baby

53. Kitcher, *Living with Darwin*, 125.

than the rough, rocky, and aleatory route along which evolution bumped us into existence. As readers of David Hume's *Dialogues Concerning Natural Religion* notice, according to intelligent design, human beings get to feel twice blessed: we are the products of an intelligent designer, and in case we feel our parade is rained on by the knowledge that every other living thing is, too, we can point out that it's the human capacity for design that comes closest to the skill and the power of the Grand Gucci. In the portrait provided by evolutionary theory, our reputation seems multiply muddied: a complete picture book of our genealogy includes many critters we might want to photoshop out; the processes by which we finally emerged appear to be riddled with waste and trash and junk; and if there is any human capacity that might serve as a model for understanding such processes it is our notorious albeit sometimes celebrated capacity to waste resources, create trash, keep junk around. If explanations offered by intelligent design highlight and extrapolate from *Homo* as gloriously *sapiens*, many of those offered by evolutionary theory seem to give top billing to *Homo* in its most *trasho* moments.

Though we humans haven't really seemed to mind making trash and waste, indeed are gifted and prolific creators of it, many of us don't much cotton to the possibility that it is as a result of nature's trashing and wasting that we came about, and that our future most likely involves our becoming just another chunk of detritus in evolution's graveyard. It may seem small consolation to be told that the worms will be delighted. But then it hardly seems cause for celebration to be assured that that's just what the designer had in mind.[54]

---

54. In high hopes it won't sully his reputation: Thanks to Jeff Ramsey for helpful advice early on when I began wandering through the thicket of literature explored in this chapter.

Chapter 5

Desire, Dissatisfaction, and Disposability

Trash. Mounds and mounds and still more mounds of trash. Whole plastic islands of it. We humans—some of us much more than others—have become prodigious producers of it. The irony of our being surrounded (again, some of us much more so than others) by the very matter we have tried so earnestly to get rid of might be a bit droll were it not for the enormous problems that we dedicated and determined disposers cause ourselves and our planetary home. Still, such troubles—well and widely examined elsewhere by many others—do not exhaust the significance of trash in human life.[1]

---

1. See, for example, Heather Rogers, *Gone Tomorrow: The Hidden Life of Garbage* (New York: New Press, 2006); Annie Leonard, with Ariane Conrad, *The Story of Stuff: How Our Obsession with Stuff Is Trashing the Planet, Our Communities, and Our Health—and a Vision for Change* (New York: Free Press, 2010). For a vivid and inviting exploration of the many ways in which humans are related to trash—a study that inspired my own work but covers topics different from those examined here—see Gay Hawkins, *The Ethics of Waste: How We Relate to Rubbish* (Lanham, MD: Rowman and Littlefield, 2006).

Try as we might to distance ourselves from trash and waste, our relation to them is really quite intimate. As we have seen, they can be used to provide juicy, or boring, details of our individual and communal histories. Being able to afford to be wasteful has been relied on to attest to our social status. How well or poorly we carry out responsibilities as handlers or haulers of trash appears to provide promising information about not only our social or economic status but our moral state and psychological health. The very thought that we, precious humanity, emerged from a wasteful evolutionary process can seem threatening to the grounds of our dignity and to fly in the face of more attractive accounts of our coming into existence. In these various ways, something significant about us is thought to infuse our being on account of our relation to trash and waste.

Humanity announces its presence in the designation of something as trash: matter becomes *trash* as a result of a particular kind of treatment in the practices of human beings—our having used them (or in any event having had them), discarded them, declared their uselessness or valuelessness or undesirability. That is why to rescue something from the trash is not only to remove it from a particular location but to undo its status as trash, to transform it, as the saying goes, into treasure.[2] Nothing about the object has changed, only the judgment or valuation accorded it by a human being. It might or might not be in a state of decay or disintegration, might or might not be damaged or beyond repair.

Trash thus sometimes testifies to the history of our desiring to have something, acquiring it, not being satisfied by it or ultimately

---

2. Such a claim carries the implication that artworks made from trash are no longer trash. Artists who create installations made from trash presumably don't want their works to be confused with what is to be tossed in the dumpster.

growing dissatisfied with it, and finally discarding it. While that particular path to disposal will be our main focus here, it would be misleading to suggest that the production of trash always reflects such an itinerary. Desire for something is only one of many possible routes by which we come to have things, and dissatisfaction is only one of many possible paths along which we come to dispose of them. Desire is neither a necessary nor sufficient condition of acquisition. The stuff we accumulate includes things we don't especially long for but nevertheless judge to be necessary or simply useful for everyday existence (most women I know don't really long for tampons, for example). Many a household in contemporary Japan overflows with items that are not wanted but have been received as gifts.[3] And there no doubt are many things we desire but do not or cannot acquire.

Moreover, dissatisfaction is neither a necessary nor sufficient condition of disposal. Among our discards might be items with which we are not at all unhappy, maybe even wish we didn't have to dispose of. And among the things we do not discard may be items with which we are dissatisfied: I really wanted that shirt, was fortunate enough to be able to acquire it, but now have come to dislike its color. But I've kept it around, thinking it might be useful to wear some day while re-painting the bathroom, or to cut up for rags. It is not trash, but it is a kind of junk, inasmuch as "junk" often is used to refer to items kept on reserve for possible future service (recall the fortuitousness of the concept of "junk DNA"). Perhaps I plan to donate it to a secondhand clothing distributor. In fact, I may have come to think that having it but not using it is wasteful: I haven't turned it into waste in a sense in which "waste" can be very close in meaning to "trash" but in the sense of failing to find a use for it.

3. See Inge Daniels, "The 'Social Death' of Unused Gifts: Surplus and Value in Contemporary Japan," *Journal of Material Culture* 14, no. 3 (2009): 385–408.

I haven't thrown it into the trash but I have let it go to waste (for example, by not making it available for another person's use). So the road to the dump does not necessarily include stops along the way at desire and dissatisfaction. Our focus here is on a route that does include them, a path that begins at desire, bumps into dissatisfaction, and ends at the landfill. Many of the venerable travel guides that include commentary on the trip from desire to dissatisfaction ignore the final leg to trash-making. But it is there that further details in the portrait of the intimate relation between humans and our trash will appear.

Our exploration begins with some reminders about the familiarity of dissatisfaction. It is a condition that has been a topic of considerable quip and commentary, predominantly by those not particularly concerned about a connection between dissatisfaction and trash-making.

Much attests to our awareness of dissatisfaction as an everpresent risk of desire. Desires can be fulfilled or unfulfilled, met or not met, and typically, though not always, their being met brings pleasure, their not being met brings pain or displeasure. Because simply desiring something or someone or some state of affairs provides no guarantee that the desire will be fulfilled, there is always the risk, often a big risk, that one's desire will go unsatisfied, unfulfilled. Such looming possibility appears to be well known and well remarked on. A familiar example is Tennyson's famous insistence on the advisability of taking desire-related risk: "It is better to have loved and lost than never to have loved at all;"[4] or the Rolling

4. Alfred, Lord Tennyson, *In Memoriam*, Norton Critical Edition, ed. Erik Gray (New York: Norton, 2003), 44.

Stones' laments that "You Can't Always Get What You Want" and
"(I can't get no) Satisfaction." Though the Stones don't comment
on whether such longing was worth it despite the lack of satisfaction, the songs underscore the fact of the risk.

This is not to say that the risks of desire are evenly distributed
among the lot of desiring humans. As Amartya Sen has pointed
out, referring to a context quite different from those in which
Tennyson wrote and the Stones sang,

> The defeated and the down-trodden come to lack the cour-
> age to desire things that others more favourably treated by
> society desire with easy confidence. The absence of desire for
> things beyond one's means may not reflect any deficiency of
> valuing, but only an absence of hope, and a fear of inevitable
> disappointment.[5]

The risks of desire include much more than the possibility
that they might not be fulfilled, might go unsatisfied. Obtaining
the object of desire has its own notorious risks. In Bernard Shaw's
famous formulation, "There are two tragedies in life. One is to lose
your heart's desire. The other is to gain it."[6] Students of consumption have identified "buyer's remorse"[7] and other "varieties of

5. Amartya Sen, "The Standard of Living: Lecture I, Concepts and Critiques," in *The Standard of Living*, ed. Geoffrey Hawthorn (Cambridge: Cambridge University Press, 1987), 10–11.

6. George Bernard Shaw, Act 4 of *Man and Superman: A Comedy and a Philosophy*, Introduction by Stanley Weintraub (New York: Penguin, 2000 [1903]), 208. A similar *aperçu* appears in Act 3 of Oscar Wilde's *Lady Windermere's Fan*: "In this world there are only two tragedies. One is not getting what one wants, and the other is getting it. The last is much the worst, the last is a real tragedy!" In *The Importance of Being Earnest and Other Plays*, ed. Peter Raby (New York: Oxford, 1995 [1893]), 44.

7. See, for example, Arthur Asa Berger, *Shop 'Til You Drop: Consumer Behavior and American Culture* (Lanham, MD: Rowman and Littlefield, 2005), 199ff.

consumer disappointment"[8] as characteristic of what the economist Tibor Scitovksy called the Joyless Economy.[9] Getting what
one wants does not necessarily bring satisfaction. But even if it
does, there is no guarantee that such satisfaction will last, that one
will not grow dissatisfied.

For instance, the object (in the broad sense that also includes
persons) presently satisfying my desire might cease to have the
properties in virtue of which I find it so desirable. Such a possibility is acknowledged explicitly and vividly in the kind of marriage
vows in which people articulate a commitment to stay with and
stand by each other "through sickness and health, 'til death do us
part." Making such vows requires one to acknowledge, at some
level or another, that at least some of the characteristics of the person I desire right now may cease to exist in the future, and that this
is likely to have consequences which I cannot precisely predict but
ought to be prepared for.

It also is possible that though the object of my desire continues
to have the properties in virtue of which I found it desirable, I no
longer find those properties desirable. If in the earlier example I got
what I wanted but it's no longer got what I want, here I got what
I wanted but I no longer want what it's got; it hasn't changed, but
I have. I got what I wanted, and that which I wanted hasn't changed,
but my wants have changed. There's that Chevy Suburban Charlie
long had coveted and finally bought but now is the source of his
considerable chagrin. The Suburban hasn't changed, but Charlie's
desires have. It's not that his needs have shifted, that he still loves
that big machine but has to get rid of it on pain of not being able

8. Albert Hirschman, *Shifting Involvements: Private Interest and Public Action* (Princeton,
NJ: Princeton University Press, 1982), 25ff.
9. Tibor Scitovsky, *The Joyless Economy: The Psychology of Human Satisfaction*, rev. ed.
(New York: Oxford University Press, 1992).

to keep food on the table and pay the mortgage. No, he's come to be convinced that its very existence is a threat to the environment and that his having acquired and insured it is a waste of money. He doesn't want it anymore. He doesn't say, "I wish I could keep it," but rather, "Whatever got into me?" He got what he wanted and now he simply feels stuck with it, this bulky evidence not of his current desires but his past ones. Among the risks he has taken in satisfying his desire is that a desire now past and thoroughly denounced will be shadowing him in the form of that hulk in the garage.

In short, if not getting what one desires leads to unhappiness, so, eventually, might success in doing so, since I may not feel satisfied with what I obtain, and even if I do, that satisfaction is not guaranteed to last.

So then, is dissatisfaction—either as failure to get what I want, lack of satisfaction even when getting it, or the disappearance of any satisfaction that had accompanied having it—the lot of humankind? And if so, why? Is there anything we can or should do about it?

These questions occupy vital space in philosophical traditions west and east: students of Plato and of Buddhism are offered rich opportunities to explore the nature of dissatisfaction and to consider how individuals and the communities in which they live can temper it or otherwise manage it. Moreover, dissatisfaction has come to play a crucial role in economies heavily dependent on consumption.

The fact that the presence of trash leads us back to the dissatisfaction of human beings doesn't mean that those who have explored dissatisfaction have been interested in its relation to the generation of trash. But as we'll see, their treatments of dissatisfaction nevertheless can invitingly inform our understanding of the intimate relation between humans and their rejectamenta.

PLATO ON DISSATISFACTION

The driving concern in Plato's *Republic*[10] is whether those who lead just lives are better off, happier, more likely to flourish as human beings than those who do not lead just lives. Socrates agrees to examine this question at the urgent request of his young companions Glaucon and Adeimantus. By the time the threesome complete their inquiry and reach the conclusion that justice is indeed much more advantageous than injustice, it is clear that the prospects of a person enjoying the blessings of a just life are likely to be ruined should insatiable desire, and the dissatisfaction that inevitably accompanies it, prevail within that person. In short, an important upshot of the *Republic* is that anyone interested in creating justice needs to understand the nature and source of dissatisfaction and its capacity to undermine the conditions under which justice can exist.

The exploration of whether a firm foundation can be found for the view that a person is better off being just than being unjust takes off in earnest in Book II. Socrates, Glaucon, and Adeimantus agree that locating where justice resides in the *polis* or city-state can help us understand where justice resides in a person's soul, since the former can offer a view of the latter "writ large." So they begin to speculate about the conditions under which a *polis* comes into existence. Socrates suggests that such small city-like entities arise because "none of us is self-sufficient, but we all need many things" (369b)—at the very least food, shelter, and clothing. Glaucon and Adeimantus grant Socrates' assumption that given natural differences in people's abilities, the best way to provide

---

10. Plato, *Republic*, trans. G. M. A. Grube; rev. C. D. C. Reeve (Indianapolis: Hackett, 1992). Further references to the text are given in parentheses.

for such necessities will be a division of labor: "more plentiful and better-quality goods are more easily produced if each person does one thing for which he is naturally suited, does it at the right time, and is released from having to do any of the others" (370c). Socrates offers a description of the array of goods that these usefully employed members of the city will thereby be able to enjoy:

> They'll produce bread, wine, clothes, and shoes, won't they? They'll build houses, work naked and barefoot in the summer, and wear adequate clothing and shoes in the winter. For food, they'll knead and cook the flour and meal they've made from wheat and barley. They'll put their honest cakes and loaves on reeds or clean leaves, and, reclining on beds strewn with yew and myrtle, they'll feast with their children, drink their wine, and, crowned with wreaths, hymn the gods. They'll enjoy sex with one another but bear no more children than their resources allow, lest they fall into either poverty or war. (372a–b)

With a little prodding from Glaucon, Socrates allows that he has forgotten that "they'll obviously need salt, olives, boiled roots, and vegetables of the sort they cook in the country. We'll give them desserts, too, of course, consisting of figs, chickpeas, and beans, and they'll roast myrtle and acorns before the fire, drinking moderately" (372c–d).

Glaucon, however, retorts that even with such an amendment, Socrates might as well be "founding a city for pigs" (372d). Pigs might be satisfied with such a limited life, but humans aren't, and, Glaucon continues, there is no reason why they should be. Oh, replies Socrates, then the city we imagine coming into existence is not what one would call a "healthy" one but rather a "luxurious" one, in which people will demand and be provided with more than what they simply need: more objects ("couches, tables, and other furniture . . . perfumed oils, incense" [373a]), and more kinds of people ("hunters, for example, and artists or imitators . . . poets and their assistants, actors, choral dancers, contractors, and makers of all kinds of devices, including, among other things, those needed for the adornment of women" [373b]). Denizens of this luxurious city will want to eat meat, and the expanded need for land thereby required will lead to war between this city and its neighbors, "if they too have surrendered themselves to the *endless acquisition* [emphasis added] of money and have overstepped the limit of their necessities." The latter, roughly speaking, includes items such as food, clothing, and shelter (373e), the desire for which one cannot desist from on pain of doing harm to oneself, as opposed to goods that are not beneficial, or even harmful, to one's health, the desire for which one can desist from if one is brought up under the right conditions (558d–559d).

Glaucon's position seems to be that a life in which people are merely satisfied, in the sense that they will get what they need, won't be satisfying enough. Characteristically human desires go beyond that which people merely need, even beyond their living in comfort and peace. Glaucon does not disagree with Socrates' characterization of humans in the luxurious city as wanting a much broader range of goods and services than those available in the healthy city, indeed as not only wanting to acquire more than they need but engaged in "endless acquisition." And Socrates does not object to the shift of focus: it will not be the healthy city but rather the luxurious one in which the investigation of the nature of justice will be carried out—not despite but because it's the "fat city" or "luxurious city," not the "healthy" one, in which dissatisfaction will arise and become a significant liability. We learn more about the nature of this "fat city" dissatisfaction throughout the rest of the *Republic*.

In this dialogue,[11] Plato attributes to the character Socrates a view of a person's soul as having three aspects—reason, spirit, and appetite. Each element has its characteristic desires: reason loves learning, "is always straining to know where the truth lies"; spirit "is wholly dedicated to the pursuit of control, victory, and high repute"; appetite loves food, drink, sex, and money (581a–b). Appetitive desires in particular are said to be by their very nature insatiable. It's not just that there is no end to them, that no sooner has one ceased than another comes along behind it, in the endless attempts to acquire yet more. Getting the object of one's appetitive desires—succeeding in "feed[ing], fatten[ing], and fornicat[ing]"—fails to bring satisfaction, since the appetitive element of the soul is like a "vessel full of holes" (586b). This incapacity for satisfaction is an inherent condition of appetitive desires.

One or another of the three elements will be dominant in each person, and differences among people will mirror such intrapsychic dominance. Those in whom reason is regnant belong to the class of philosophers; they should be prevailed on to rule the community. Those in whom high spirit rules belong to the class of guardians; they serve the community best by guarding against external and internal enemies. Those in whom appetite takes over belong to the class of laborers; the task for which they are best suited is the production of basic provisions and services.

But what does all this have to do with justice and whether being just profits humans more than being unjust? Well, justice turns out to be constituted in individuals by a kind of harmonious order in the soul, an order dependent on each "part" or aspect of the soul

---

11. For a discussion of the somewhat different accounts of the structure and nature of desire in other Platonic dialogues, see Charles H. Kahn, "Plato's Theory of Desire," *Review of Metaphysics* 41, no. 1 (September 1987): 77–103.

having and being limited to the exercise of its appropriate function; similarly, justice in a community or *polis* depends upon harmonious order among those in each of the three broad classes of people, a balance that can exist only if each class understands and agrees to its place and stays in it. Those in whom appetitive desires predominate (according to Plato, that is the majority of humankind [586b]) threaten such order. There cannot be order in a soul ruled by desires incapable of satisfaction, nor in a polity when there is no check on people who will go to any end to try to sate such desires. Concord is possible, however, if the consequences of such inevitable dissatisfaction can be contained by construction of a polity in which people not under the sway of their own appetitive desires rule those in whom self-control is out of the question.[12]

So, according to the *Republic,* appetitive desires are insatiable. They either are not fulfilled at all or their fulfillment fails to bring satisfaction. Yet despite that, one doesn't cease to respond to their ceaseless importuning. One always wants more. Such dissatisfaction is likely to be ruinous to the prospects of justice, of harmonious order in individuals and communities, unless those in whom it prevails are kept in check.

But there are desires that can be satisfied and remain satisfied: reason's desires, those prevailing in philosopher-rulers. What is it about such desires that protects them from dissatisfaction?

For the very small band of people in whom reason reigns over other elements of the soul, there is not only the possibility of avoiding or mitigating much of the risk of appetitive desire but

---

12. Philosopher-rulers, those in whom reason predominates, cannot do their appointed work without the help of the guardians, in whom spirit predominates. But spirited desires are themselves no less at risk of getting out of control than those of the appetite: "love of honor" may make one "envious," "love of victory" make one "violent" (586c–d).

also the promise of fabulous rewards to be reaped, of satisfactions unknown to, indeed unimaginable to appetitive desire—pleasures that are "stable and pure" (586a). According to Diotima, described in Plato's *Symposium*[13] by Socrates as his instructor in love, those driven by their appetitive desires and bedazzled by the brightness of baubles, or the lovely flesh of another human being, mistake the passing beauty and charm of things or of people for Beauty itself, Eternal Beauty, that in virtue of which beautiful things are beautiful but which, unlike such things, neither comes into nor goes out of existence, never fades, never ceases to satisfy. Desire for such Beauty, not for the derivative and transient beauty of beautiful things, is not to be found in the appetitive element of the soul but only in the element that reasons. The objects of appetitive desire, and the desire itself, are transitory, waxing and waning, coming into and going out of existence. But the objects of reason's desire, the Forms, are eternal and unchanging, and reason itself, once released from the body in which it is entombed, is immortal. There is no end to the rapture of an immortal soul contemplating the Forms.[14] There is no risk that one will not be satisfied, or will become dissatisfied on account of the object's losing what made it desirable, or on account of one's ceasing to find the object desirable even though it has not changed.

Moreover, one need not worry about being able to care for or maintain commitment to the object of one's desire in order to keep it alive or functioning well. Forms are care-free. They have no

---

13. Plato, *Symposium*, trans., with Introduction and Notes, by Alexander Nehamas and Paul Woodruff (Indianapolis: Hackett, 1989).

14. There is some unclarity about the details of Plato's position: in the *Symposium* he insists that one loves or desires only things that are not present. So the picture of satisfaction he proposes has to do either with eternally sustained desire in the continuous presence of eternally existing objects of desire (*Republic*) or the absence of desire but under conditions in which one has been and continues to be satisfied (*Symposium*).

shelf-date. Corruptible by neither moth nor rust, they are never in need of repair or tune-up and polishing or preserving or restoring. They cannot disintegrate, crumble, go to waste—they are not subject to forces that have such effects. They cannot be trashed—there is no way to get rid of them. And (leaping ahead many centuries) they are Anselmic: like St. Anselm's God, "a being than which no greater can be conceived," these are entities than which no grander can be imagined. One needn't worry about greedy consumers of such splendid entities, about some souls taking so much that nothing is left for anyone else. Nor is there reason to envy others for having what you lack. One immortal soul's enjoyment of the Forms in no way is an obstacle to any other immortal soul's enjoyment. Greed and envy, indeed war, are conditions that can attend appetitive desires but not those of reason.

For all his attention to appetitive desire and the risks and perils to which its insatiability exposes embodied beings, Plato did not have as a major concern the production of trash and rubbish, or the disposition of garbage and sewage.[15] Worries about such things are not in the list of potentially threatening implications of human life organized on the model of the "fat city" rather than the "healthy city." There certainly are indications that Plato thought that assignment of tasks not based on a division of labor respecting and reflecting what people are "naturally" suited for would involve a waste of time and energy; that any attempt to sate desires that by their very nature do not provide satisfaction is an irrational waste of effort; and that material things by definition go to

---

15. A rich canvassing of scattered comments in the Platonic corpus about waste and trash can be found in Astrid Lindenlauf's fascinating "Waste Management in Ancient Greece from the Homeric to the Classical Period: Concepts and Practices of Waste, Dirt, Recycling and Disposal" (Ph.D. dissertation, University College London, 2000), http://discovery.ucl.ac.uk/1317693/.

waste in the sense that they decay and disintegrate and disappear (in that regard the material world is a wasteland). Plato did not have a specific view about trash and waste and what to do with them, nor was he explicitly concerned about the waste of natural resources.[16] But when we look at some familiar Platonic doctrines with rejectamenta on our minds, we are invited not only to dwell on Plato's treatment of dissatisfaction but to highlight some features of the Forms, and of the reasoning souls that are in a position to contemplate them, that otherwise might not stand out: in the realm of the Forms, the only realm in which the highest form of soul-flourishing can occur, a realm in which the risks of appetitive desire endemic to embodied life have been resoundingly rebuffed, trash and waste are impossible. In this context, where there is no dissatisfaction there also is no trash, for the very conditions Plato describes in which dissatisfaction cannot occur are those in which nothing is disposable and nothing wastes away.

BUDDHISM AND DISSATISFACTION

Though there are a variety of Buddhist schools and traditions, one thread running strongly through all of them warns of the perils of craving, of the suffering bound to accompany the attachment at its core. Though presumably humans cannot live without some kind and degree of desire, if only for food and water, it is easy for our desires to lead us astray, especially insofar as we are ignorant of or choose to ignore the fact that desire opens

---

16. Plato clearly anticipated battles over land in the "luxurious city," whose dwellers will demand ever more foodstuffs, especially meat, and land on which to grow them. This will lead to war among neighbors and thus prompts the need for soldiers. See *Republic*, 373d ff.

us up to a craving for and attachment to what is impermanent. Such attachment is bound to make us suffer, since what we are attached to does not endure. But it is not as if there is nothing we can do about such dissatisfaction. The Four Noble Truths of Buddhism posit a way out:

- Human life is characterized by suffering.
- Among the principal causes of such suffering is the desire for and attachment to things that are by their very nature impermanent.
- It is possible to mitigate such suffering.
- Humans can overcome their ignorance of the impermanence of things and of the accompanying irrationality of desire for and attachment to them. There are right ways of living that can help minimize the risks of the terrible admixture of ignorance and desire.

The risk of fervent desires not being satisfied can be reduced to the degree that one learns to detach from them, to not be concerned to satisfy them, knowing that attempts to do so will only lead to suffering. In the state of detachment one can instead simply note one's desires and the illusory promise of pleasure they carry. The risks connected with the satisfaction of desire will be mitigated by one's recognition that in the end, getting what you want brings suffering just as certainly as wanting it and not getting it; dissatisfaction is bound to set in.

The idea is not that we should try to banish desire—the urgent wish to banish desire is itself something to which we could become quite attached. Instead, we can simply acknowledge the presence of our desires. The hopes and expectations they inspire are illusory. What isn't illusory is the understanding that suffering is bound to follow on both successful and unsuccessful attempts to try to satisfy our cravings.

Buddhist accounts of the nature, sources, and consequences of dissatisfaction have some intriguing implications for the relation between dissatisfaction and the creation of waste or trash. Buddhism focuses on the impermanent nature of living and non-living things: they are transient, evanescent, impermanent, short-lived. They fade away, vanish. They decay—indeed, according to the *Book of the Great Decease*, as he died the Buddha once more and for the last time urged his companions to keep in mind that "decay is the inherent state of all contingent things."[17] All such things are waste, not in the sense that they are thrown away or disposed of (a use of "waste" that is close to "trash"), or in the sense that they have not been put to proper use (as if they were allowed to "go to waste"), but in the sense that they disintegrate, decompose, cease to be. It is our failure to attend to this feature of the things around us that makes our desire for them bring painful dissatisfaction in its wake. Here the waste associated with desire and its inevitable dissatisfaction has to do with the fact not that desire leads to the production of waste but that in the grip of desire we ignore the wasting-away nature of what we grasp for, thereby risking, indeed ensuring, our suffering. That is, the immediate link to waste here is not that we might create waste on account of our desire and accompanying dissatisfaction but that we won't recognize the decay inherent in the very nature of what we desire and thus will invite our dissatisfaction in the very process of trying to avoid that condition.

---

17. *Dialogues of the Buddha*, 4th ed., translated from the Pali of the Digha-Nikaya by T. W. Rhys Davids (Oxford: Pali Text Society, 2002), Part II, 173.

Because dissatisfaction with something is a major contributor to getting rid of it, in offering a means of reducing the risk of dissatisfaction Buddhism implicitly offers a means of reducing the risk of trash production. Those who do not grasp for things will not grow dissatisfied with them and thus will not act on such dissatisfaction by rejecting them, throwing them out. Detachment prevents the suffering inevitably attendant on attachment. It thereby takes the teeth out of the risk that desire will lead to the production of trash.

But wait. Short of attaining the extinction of craving in the state of Nirvana, one is likely to find oneself attached to this or that thing, this or that person. Suppose one manages to detach, to "let go" of the craving and the object craved. What then is the status of the person or thing let go? How is detachment different from rejection, throwing away? Do I manage to detach by convincing myself that someone or something is not worthy of attachment? And if so, doesn't that mean I've judged them to be unworthy of my desire, to be undesirable? How is that different from thinking of them as disposable, trashable? Isn't the desire "to have and to hold" persons and things a powerful measure of our regard for them and of our willingness to care for them? And if so, isn't a failure to attach, or success in detaching, a way of treating someone or something as dispensable? Does avoiding dissatisfaction in order to decrease the risk of trash production actually risk trash production by rendering all living and non-living things rejectable? After all, the Buddha left behind his wife and infant son—in the name of renunciation.

A Buddhist response probably would go something like this: first, we misunderstand the nature of desire and attachment if we think that desiring someone or something heightens their value or status, if we believe that in craving their company we evince a higher regard for them and are more likely to look out for their welfare than we would in the absence of such avid desire.

On the contrary, we are setting them up to be the occasion for our inevitable dissatisfaction with them and thus for our disposing of them. People as well as things can be turned into trash.

Second, detachment or non-clinging is not the same thing as aversion or disgust, and unlike them is not in tension with compassion and care. It is not desire for and attachment to someone or something that makes them worthy of compassion and care—in fact, insofar as attachment is likely to eventuate in dissatisfaction it may undermine concern for what once was and no longer is desired. A compassionate being is concerned to lessen the suffering in the world; but in the grip of passionate desire one ignores the suffering so inevitably bound up with that desire.

So, the Buddhist might argue, there is a significant difference between dissatisfaction with something and detachment from it. If one acquires something on account of the satisfaction it promises, it's highly likely that one will put it aside or dispose of it once dissatisfaction sets in. Detachment is based not on aversion toward or a desire to get rid of something, but on awareness that of the many kinds of relation one might have to persons or things, intense desire for and clinging to them is based on ignorance of their impermanent nature and of the transience of desire.

A Buddhist perspective, then, suggests that trash can be understood as one of the consequences of and thus testimony to the powerful but defeasible existence of the dissatisfaction attending desire.

DISSATISFACTION AND THE CELEBRATION OF CONSUMPTION

If some of Plato's major works describe dissatisfaction as the lot of most of humanity (albeit a fate that is mitigable under the right rule), and Buddhism portrays dissatisfaction as part of the human condition (albeit a condition that can be significantly moderated with the right training and habits), consumer-centered economies treat dissatisfaction as a calling.

The US economy is not the only but certainly a prime example of an economy based on high consumption of disposable goods— goods created to be used for a short time and then got rid of. It hasn't always been that way and may be shifting gears somewhat. But let's look for a few minutes first at how such an economy decreases—yes, oddly enough, *decreases*—the displeasure of dissatisfaction (without its ceasing to be dissatisfaction), indeed elevates it to a kind of welcome duty of citizenship.

A consumer-centered economy certainly seems to increase the likelihood of dissatisfaction. Indeed, as we've seen, consumption-oriented economies have been characterized by some as "joyless," as almost inevitably leading to disappointment or regret. But consider: the pain of one's dissatisfaction with the goods one once desired and then acquired is alleviated by the fact that such dissatisfaction takes on a different and more positive valence in the consumer-centered economy. It doesn't matter if I cease to be satisfied, or rather it matters in a positive way: though merchants and companies surely hope that I will be satisfied by my acquisitions, and will let others know how satisfied I am, I'm expected not to be satisfied for very long. As Zygmunt Bauman has pointed out,

> Ideally, nothing should be embraced by a consumer firmly, nothing should command a commitment till death do us part, no needs should be seen as fully satisfied, no desires considered ultimate. There ought to be a proviso "until further notice" attached to any oath of loyalty and any commitment. It is but the volatility, the in-built temporality of all engagements, that

truly counts; it counts more than the commitment itself which is anyway not allowed to outlast the time necessary for consuming the object of desire (or, rather, the time sufficient for the desirability of that object to wane).[18]

The economy only appears to leave me in the lurch: yes, I'm expected to cease to be satisfied by the goods in my possession, but that is in order to leave room for me to consider and to want new things, which in their turn will cease to satisfy, too. My satisfaction is temporary, but so is my dissatisfaction. As a good consumer I not only expect but in fact may even begin to look forward to the moment of dissatisfaction. Dissatisfaction isn't just a risk; it is in fact a pretty sure outcome, a part of the regular rhythm of my life as a desiring subject.

My dissatisfaction thus can be seen as evidence of a particular kind of labor I perform for the economy. We perhaps most readily associate labor with those who produce the abundance of goods that satisfy and then cease to satisfy us, and also with those who repair them (though of course disposable goods are not meant to be repaired) or haul them away from our living quarters. The point is not simply that shoppers account for something like two-thirds to three-quarters of economic activity in a perfervid consumer society such as that of the United States.[19] In an economy of disposability, consumers are counted on to perform a special form of emotional labor: the steady work not of the producer but

18. Zygmunt Bauman, *Globalization: The Human Consequences* (New York: Columbia University Press, 1998), 81.
19. In the second quarter of 2012, for example, "personal consumption expenditures" accounted for 71% of the total Gross Domestic Product—24% of that going for durable (7.7%) and non-durable (16.3%) goods, 47% for services. Christopher Swann, "GDP and the Economy: Second Estimates for the Second Quarter of 2012," *Survey of Current Business* 92, no. 9 (September 2012): 1–10.

that of the assiduous shopper who creates the disvalue of the thing through her eventual dismissal and disposal of it, be it on account of disdain, disgust, disenchantment, disappointment, or some other form of dissatisfaction. Consumers had to be taught to labor in this particular way: for example, along about 1955 the scholar and arts administrator Eric Larrabee commented that the car of the 1950s

> taught its owners to consume, and its makers to produce, for an economy in which the strictures of historical scarcity no longer apply. It has made waste through overconsumption one of the indispensable gears of that economy, and has made it socially acceptable as well.[20]

It is perhaps hard for us to imagine that "the twentieth century [was] the first period of recorded history in which huge masses of the population have come to accept change as natural and desirable."[21] Such emotional and evaluative labor—coming to regard something as not worth keeping, as disposable, and as such much more desirable than stuff that is meant to last—was and remains crucial to an economy that depends heavily on high levels of consumption and produces the accompanying inevitable disposal of once desirable goods. If those goods as newly produced reflect the labor of those who produced them, those same goods piled up for the waste hauler reflect the labor of dutiful disdainers.

20. Eric Larrabee, 'The Great Love Affair,' *Industrial Design* 2, no. 5 (1955): 98. Quoted in Nigel Whiteley, "Toward a Throw-Away Culture: Consumerism, 'Style Obsolescence,' and Cultural Theory in the 1950s and 1960s," *Oxford Art Journal* 10, no. 2 (1987): 8.
21. J. Gordon Lippincott, *Design for Business* (Chicago: P. Theobald, 1947), 8. Quoted in Whiteley, "Throw-Away Culture," 10.

The rhythm of my dissatisfaction is not only performing an important economic function. One of the purported reasons for the frequency with which my desires for stuff cycle through satisfaction and dissatisfaction is that things are always getting better. There are no Anselmic goods among the things that might be mine: I don't expect whatever I have to be that than which nothing greater can be conceived and produced, so whatever my current dissatisfaction, I can only look forward to something that will bring even more satisfaction than that which once but no longer satisfies me.

I needn't worry much about caring for what I have. It's not really meant to be cared for, fussed over, lovingly preserved, or dexterously mended. There's no call for my labor in that regard. A world of disposables is a carefree world. It's designed to be carefree:

> Consumer goods are meant to be used up and to disappear: the idea of temporariness and transitoriness is intrinsic to their very denomination as objects of consumption; consumer goods have *memento mori* written all over them, even if with an invisible ink.[22]

And thus, I need not worry about being weighed down by the gravity or deadly heft of my past desires, or the results of my having acted on them. There's no reason for me or anyone else to be confused or puzzled by the apparent incoherence of the history of my desires, of the ups and downs of my satisfaction and dissatisfaction. The person who craved last year's iPhone isn't the same person who now finds it pretty contemptible, for

22. Zygmunt Bauman, *Work, Consumerism, and the New Poor* (New York: Open University Press, 2005), 29.

whatever identity I crafted with and through my worldly goods is discarded as soon as they are. Charlie need not be embarrassed by that dated version of himself having lusted after a Chevy Suburban. After all, each new thing I acquire is a better thing, and I a better, more up-to-date version of myself for all that. The perils of failing to be thrifty, or becoming greedy, or envying those who have what I do not, are considerably reduced by the ready turnover of abundant, relatively cheap, and not unfashionable goods, and by my obviously being held in warm regard by companies stumbling over themselves to let me know how creditworthy I am.

And if I'm asked, "As a dutifully dissatisfied consumer, aren't you creating a lot of waste?" I'm primed to reply: "Probably. In an economy of disposability, most of what I acquire will end up in the dump.[23] But listen up, everybody, no need to panic! Though I may not care for or about my discards, my local or state government is charged with doing so, with being the foster parents of my rejectamenta. And it's not as if nobody's working on whatever problems there are, right? We've got recycling; and there are lots of creative responses to the landfill problem and how to isolate and contain the really bad stuff in computers and cell phones and old TVs, such as the highly successful Waste Management Centre of Excellence in Edmonton, Alberta. Cities such as Oslo have become so adept at turning garbage and trash into energy that they have to import the stuff from elsewhere.[24] And Adam Smith hasn't been the only person to point out the good uses to which poor people can put the

---

23. See Andrew O'Hagan, "The Things We Throw Away," *London Review of Books* 29, no. 10 (May 24, 2007): 3–8.
24. John Tagliabue, "A City That Turns Garbage into Energy Copes with a Shortage," *New York Times*, April 30, 2013, A9.

hand-me-downs of the wealthy.[25] In any event, no one has the right to tell me that I have to keep and care for old stuff, that I can't toss it, as long as I don't break any laws in doing so."

Dissatisfaction is the high calling of consumers vital to an economy centered on the acquisition of disposable things. Whether the dross we thereby create can be kept from despoiling the planet remains a source of great worry—despite the cheery response ready at hand for the happily dissatisfied consumer.

We've been looking at treatments of dissatisfaction and the relation of dissatisfaction to both desire and disposal. Plato was concerned about dissatisfaction not because it can lead to trash production but because it is such a disruptive force in human life—in individuals and the communities of which they are a part. The focus of Buddhist attention to dissatisfaction has been not so much the path it blazes to trash production (though certainly some Buddhists have been exploring such a connection recently)[26] but its centrality to the suffering characteristic of all humanity, and its origins in craving—in longing for that which in our ignorance we do not understand to be incapable of satisfying us. Finally, it appears that economies dependent on steady and intense consumer activity

25. Smith argued that because the "proud and unfeeling landlord" can't possibly make use of "all the baubles and trinkets which are employed in the economy of greatness," he will pass them on to those who work for him, "all of whom thus derive from his luxury and caprice that share of the necessities of life which they would in vain have expected from his humanity or his justice." Adam Smith, *The Theory of Moral Sentiments* (Amherst, NY: Prometheus Books, 2000), 264.

26. See, for example, Stephanie Kaza, "Penetrating the Tangle," in *Hooked! Buddhist Writings on Greed, Desire, and the Urge to Consume*, ed. Stephanie Kaza (Boston: Shambala, 2005), 139–151; Peter Daniels, "Buddhism and the Transformation to Sustainable Economies," *Society and Economy* 29, no. 2 (August 2007): 155–180.

have a stake in stoking dissatisfaction, elevating it as the high calling of life in the checkout lane.

What do these accounts have to tell us, explicitly or implicitly, about the relation between dissatisfaction and trash? If Plato were around and asked what he thinks about all our trash, he might well proffer something along these lines: "Well, I actually didn't have much to say about the creation of trash and waste, but I'm not at all surprised by how much of that stuff humans now produce. I warned you about the dangers of not keeping insatiable appetite and thus dissatisfaction in check, and spoke to you of the delights that would be yours (well, at least some of you) by way of the Forms and the unending satisfaction they alone can offer. In trash we observe the victory of dissatisfaction, the inevitable result of the privileging of the fleeting pleasures of the physical world over the unending satisfaction accompanying contemplation of the eternal and unchanging Forms. I told you about the beast but you fed it anyway."

From a Buddhist perspective, in trash we can read the suffering of human existence. Though we can read such suffering in most everything else as well, trash offers a particularly vivid, indeed fragrant, reminder of our predilection to bring on dissatisfaction, an inevitable consequence of not thinking twice about the entrapment of desire or the impermanent nature of that which we crave. But as we gaze on trash, and understand it in this way, perhaps we can use it as a prod to consider seriously the path that Buddhism offers out of such entrapment. At the same time, tours of landfills, trips to trash-saturated beaches, and visits to garbage heaps around the world now serving as home to generations of families living at the margins of wealth-infested cities might suggest to us the irony that the least impermanent of all the impermanent things around us is our trash. It has monumental powers of endurance: much of what we throw away is likely to last longer than we do.

And from an enthusiast of consumer-centered economies we may well hear: well, I suppose the production of such massive amounts of trash is likely to happen when you turn dissatisfaction from a state of displeasure into a welcome vocation and a cash cow. Trash tells us what a thriving economy looks like, bringing to our attention how much and how often its celebrators and sustainers throw stuff away. But not to worry. All this trash won't go to waste: there already are plenty of people making money on it, more and more municipalities finding ways to generate energy from it.

There's an old and familiar adage, often attributed to Benjamin Franklin, "Waste not, want not." Among the common meanings of the phrase is the idea that those who are careful not to let what they have go to waste (for example, their food) or who are careful not to spend their time, money, and other resources on things and activities that they don't really need or probably won't use (for example, home exercise equipment) will not find themselves in want of what they need or most fervently desire. So understood, "want" in this pithy aphorism means "lack": those who do not waste their resources will help keep themselves from lacking the means to obtain what matters most to them. That is, the "want not" part of the phrase is not an injunction not to desire. It is part of a piece of advice enshrined in a hypothetical: if you aim to not find yourself without what you really need or desire, then don't waste your resources. The whole phrase might be invoked to warn people that if they spend their money on "luxuries" they are likely to find themselves without "necessities," but it need not be used only in that way. For example, it might be employed in a context in which someone is being encouraged to think carefully about what they really need so that they can save their pennies for a comforting splurge. In one of its more intriguing invocations, the phrase appears in a study of proposed uses of waste itself, in this case animal and human waste. In "Waste Not, Want Not: Excrement and Economy in Nineteenth-Century France," Dana Simmons recounts earnest efforts to "feed the poor without the aid of urban factories."[27] All that is needed in order to make sure the urban poor get adequate nutrition, the argument goes, is the extraction of their excrement, not their factory labor, in the production of the food supply.

Despite the fact that in the familiar "Waste not, want not," "want" typically means "lack" and not "desire," the phrase invites us to look at the three treatments of dissatisfaction and its relation to trash as offering urgent variations on the homely piece of wisdom.

"Want Not, Waste Not." Both the Platonist and the Buddhist perspectives imply, though as we've seen do not explicitly offer, advice of the following sort: if you aim to reduce the production of waste, well then, don't want so much, don't coddle and cosset and cultivate your desires. Given the nature of desire (in Plato's case, appetitive desire in particular) and the dissatisfaction inevitably following in its wake, indulging desire is bound to take you on a very disappointing crash course—one result of which we see in the trashing of the planet.

"Want! Waste!" The last thing champions of hyper-consumerist economies want you to do is stop wanting. Keep wanting! It only gets better! Yes, all that wanting is indeed a precursor to dissatisfaction and then to disposal. But that's fine: the economy needs

27. Dana Simmons, "Waste Not, Want Not: Excrement and Economy in Nineteenth-Century France," *Representations* 96, no. 1 (Fall 2006): 75.

your dissatisfaction, and if that means waste, more waste, and yet again waste, not to worry. We'll make sure that people want your trash, too. So please want! Please waste!

One measure of the intimacy of our relation to trash, then, can be described in this way: trash occupies pride of place on the family crest of *Homo besottica*, a being in thrall to the perfidious promises of desire, who on some accounts cannot or will not pay attention to the inevitability of dissatisfaction, and from some quarters is urged to accept dissatisfaction, indeed, to greet it with glee.

Chapter 6

On Knowing Waste
When You See It

Thorstein Veblen acknowledged that in describing leisure class life as embracing "conspicuous waste," he was employing a term that "in the speech of everyday life . . . carries an undertone of deprecation" and that he thus appeared to be charging the masters of conspicuous waste with engaging in "an illegitimate expenditure of human products or of human life."[1] Veblen insisted that he was simply using "waste" in a narrow, non-denunciatory sense, in accordance with which activities that do not serve the "human life process impersonally"[2] are wasteful. Whether or not Veblen was being disingenuous, he rightly reminded us that judging an act or a person to be wasteful is at least prima facie a form of disapproval.

This is perhaps particularly clear in the case of describing someone as wasting food. The necessity of food for human

1. Thorstein Veblen, *The Theory of the Leisure Class: An Economic Study of Institutions* (New York: Modern Library, 1931 [1899]), 97.
2. Veblen, *Leisure*, 99.

survival grounds prudential and ethical interest in its not going to waste. Given our undeniable need for the nutrition food provides, it seems both irrational and irresponsible to fail to make good use of it before it perishes. Indeed, the waste of food appears right up there among the top spectacles performed in the theater of human folly and bad behavior.

Or so it might seem—until we recall that in the history of humankind, food has not been only about nutrition and survival, just as clothing has not been simply about protection and warmth. Madness and moral mayhem hardly exhaust the repertoire of tales told by food waste.

After a sobering update on some of the latest chapters in the ongoing saga of humanity's apparently wanton waste of food, we shall explore some moments in the rich and complex history of reflection on the significance of food and the wasting of it: John Milton's proposal, in his rendering of the Book of Genesis, that food spoilage emerged only when humanity fell from a state of innocence; the prevention of food waste as the foundation for property rights, in John Locke's *Second Treatise of Government*; and the significance of food waste in rituals of feasting.

FOOD WASTE: CURRENT ASSESSMENTS

The United Nations Food and Agricultural Organization (FAO) estimates that one-third of the amount of food intended for human consumption ends up being wasted or lost.[3] The effects of such waste are not experienced uniformly. A portrait

---

3. Food and Agriculture Organization of the United Nations, "Food Loss and Food Waste," http://www.fao.org/food-loss-and-food-waste/en/.

of food distribution across the globe today strongly suggests something like feasts for some and famine or food insecurity for others. Food waste and food loss are important factors in the creation and maintenance of such asymmetry. In *Waste: Uncovering the Global Food Scandal*, Tristram Stuart has pulled together persuasive evidence that efforts going into the production of food wasted in wealthy countries such as the United States and Britain could be redirected to feed almost all those in the world not receiving adequate nourishment, and that a reduction in food surplus in well-supplied countries, in conjunction with a reduction of post-harvest losses in relatively poor countries, would substantially save the supply of food around the globe.[4] Moreover, given the multiple resources needed to produce food, its waste and loss also threaten the sustainability of land and water and have implications for climate change.

Consumers are by no means the only or the greatest wasters of food. No doubt in places such as the United States and England, palpable evidence of great quantities of food gone to waste is visible in household refrigerators, the plates of restaurant patrons, and the municipal landfills to which garbage is hauled. But tracking down records of how much food is wasted by farmers, food corporations, restaurants, caterers, and supermarkets is not easy (Stuart, xxi, 11). Unlike the growing number of conscientious citizens keeping blogs about how much food waste and other trash they dispose of, these major creators of food waste are reluctant to compile data about their waste and, on the whole, their governments have not been eager to require them to do so. (Gleaners and

---

4. Tristram Stuart, *Waste: Uncovering the Global Food Scandal* (New York: Norton, 2009), xvi. Further references appear in parentheses.

dumpster divers around the world may have excellent information about such matters, however.)

Food is a heavily marketed commodity, and supermarkets in particular create and reflect market standards for the desirability and acceptability of food. Just because farmers or fishers produce something edible and nutritious doesn't mean it will be attractive to those who supply food markets. If market owners insist that people won't buy forked carrots, slightly bruised apples, or knobby cucumbers, then tough luck for farmers, who by some estimates can lose up to a third of a year's harvest (Stuart, 102). (Recently at the local food co-op, a vegetable farmer watched a few of us shoppers engage in gleeful neighborly competition to pick out the weirdest carrots from the batch the farmer had just delivered. Commenting on how difficult it is to sell such produce, he thanked us. The carrots not only were cause for merriment and delight but were delicious—indeed, on the whole, much tastier than their perfectly-shaped-for-efficient packing-and-shipping "normal" sisters and brothers.) Farmers also may over-produce in order to ensure that they match what they have contracted to supply. It's true that such excess food might be plowed back into the land, but to infer that therefore no waste is involved is to ignore the enormous cost of land, water, labor, and capital involved in producing the food to begin with.

Once the food that survives aesthetic and efficiency standards gets on market shelves, there is no guarantee that it won't end up in the dumpsters behind the store. Among the many factors conspiring to produce such waste are the mostly meaningless "sell by," "use by," "best until" tags; a presumed customer desire to see shelves full of the freshest and prettiest items; and fear that selling slightly "old" stuff or even making sure it goes to survival centers would inspire customers to wait for the bargains or go to the centers.

Attitudes toward food waste can differ rather starkly across cultures. For example, unlike the majority Han Chinese, for whom hospitality includes making sure to offer more food than can possibly be eaten by guests or patrons, Muslim Uighers in China take pride in preventing waste in the preparation and distribution of food (Stuart, 199–210). A culture's attitudes can vary over time: countries such as the United States and Great Britain certainly have shown in wartime that anti-food-waste campaigns can be successful. But they and many other countries have evolved a food supply system that in effect requires waste, and they tolerate, indeed seem to encourage, its acceptance, or they are at least quite ready and willing to obscure its scope.

There is, however, growing acknowledgment of the extent of food waste, along with earnest promises to diminish it at all points along the production and consumption lines. For example, the European Commission has published a multi-language 10-step program for household waste reduction.[5] The European Parliament, building on statistics provided by the FAO, has issued a report that among other things targets all sectors of the food supply chain in efforts to reduce waste and devise more efficient and just schemes of distribution.[6] (Initiatives emerging from the European Union perhaps have a better chance of getting some respect now that their earlier highly ridiculed regulations governing the degree of bend in bananas and curvature in cucumbers appear to have been dropped.)

5. European Commission, "Food and Feed Safety," 2012, http://ec.europa.eu/food/food/sustainability/index_en.htm.
6. European Parliament, "Report on How to Avoid Food Wastage," 2011, http://www.europarl.europa.eu/sides/getDoc.do?type=REPORT&reference=A7-2011-0430&language=EN.

UNEATEN APPLES AND THE FALL
FROM INNOCENCE

Forth reaching to the fruit, she plucked, she ate.

John Milton, *Paradise Lost*, IX, 781

The idea that wasting food is irrational and irresponsible may appear to be self-evident: human labor is needed to find or make food, and much of that labor is considerably more time-consuming and back-breaking than picking an apple from a tree (though picking many apples from many trees is not only demanding work but is likely to involve exposure to toxins). Moreover, a tree that offers abundant fruit one season may have withered and died by the next. The supply of nutritious foodstuff is precarious and hard-won, and this would seem to provide strong grounds for judging its waste to be foolish and harmful.

No wonder, then, that we humans have imagined paradises in which food is readily and inexhaustibly available. A prime example is at the center of *Paradise Lost*, John Milton's expansive treatment of the story of Adam and Eve in the Garden of Eden.[7] (Quotations from the text are plentiful, to allow readers unfamiliar with Milton's masterpiece to get a sense of its beauty and reach, and to lay before those who already know the work evidence supporting the perhaps surprising claim I'm making here about Eve's motivation.)

On Milton's rendering of Genesis, the Paradise in which God placed Adam and Eve was a land of plenty. Food was abundant

---

7. John Milton, *Paradise Lost*, in *John Milton: The Major Works*, ed. Stephen Orgel and Jonathan Goldberg (New York: Oxford, 1991 [1674]). Further references to *Paradise Lost* are given in parentheses.

and delicious. Neither scarcity nor anxious fear of it threatened. The Garden offered "choice/Unlimited of manifold delights" (IV, 434–435). While the Garden needed some tending, the trees some lopping and pruning, the labor involved was not particularly arduous, just taxing enough to whet the appetite (IV, 328–335). The God who placed Adam and Eve "here/In all this happiness" (IV, 416–417) put but one burden, one restraint on them: so free and welcome were they in the Garden of Eden, and so endowed with creaturely magnificence, that "The only sign of our obedience left/ Among so many signs of power and rule/Conferred upon us, and dominion given/Over all other creatures" (IV, 428–432) was not to taste from the tree of knowledge.

Adam and Eve had but a vague idea of what would happen were they to disobey this one firm though "easy charge" (IV, 421), this "easy prohibition" (IV, 433): death—"what e'er death is,/Some dreadful thing no doubt" (IV, 425–426). The scarcity and hard labor that would be their lot after the fall appears even farther from their conceptual repertoire than death (though at the same time it would be odd for them—and Milton's readers—to marvel at the bounty God put at their disposal did they not in some sense have a concept of unbountiful conditions). And in their prelapsarian state, when scarcity was at best a vague conception and still far from a looming possibility, there would seem to be no concern about food going to waste—certainly not insofar as the waste of food becomes problematic and worrisome only or especially when supply is limited and labor is taxing. Book IV of *Paradise Lost* is full of assurances that in Paradise such worries are banished, indeed hardly imaginable.

Still, if such abundance ruled out scarcity, didn't it at the same time create waste? Wasn't there more than enough food for Adam and Eve? If so, was not such excess wasteful? It turns out that this possibility eventually dawned upon Eve and was decisive in her coming to take the fatal bite from the tree of knowledge.

Just as the possibility of scarcity is alluded to distantly in the exclamations of joy at the marvel of abundance, so the possibility of food going to waste through spoilage sits on the far conceptual horizon in descriptions of plentiful fruits and other growing things in the Garden. The Garden appears to be waste-free, but not on account of some fine economy of nature according to which one species' leavings—the uneaten apple core, for example, or the decaying windfall—readily became another species' takings. There is no effort to assure readers that food unneeded and uneaten by Adam and Eve was devoured by animals or turned into compost. Rather, it is as if God's fruits have a kind of built-in preservative:

> For many are the trees of God that grow
> In Paradise, and various, yet unknown
> To us, in *such abundance lies our choice,*
> *As leaves a greater store of fruit untouched,*
> *Still hanging incorruptible,* till men
> Grow up to their provision, and more hands
> Help to disburden nature of her birth.
>
> (IX, 618–624 [emphasis added])

There is glorious excess, and yet nothing spoils.[8] The fruit does not "corrupt," does not decay, before it can be used by the Garden's inhabitants (like them, it does not suffer death). In that

---

8. There is a suggestion, at IV, 729–731, that the "delicious place" into which God has placed Adam and Eve is so abundant that some fruit falls to the ground before they need it. And yet as they are being led out of Paradise Eve wonders what it will be like to no longer enjoy "immortal fruits" (XI, 285).

sense it does not go to waste. But in the same breath in which she comments on such "incorruptibility," Eve also notes that the fruit goes untouched, and will remain untouched at least until, in accordance with both God's instructions and plans that she and Adam have discussed, they produce descendants who will join them in their labors and their meals. The idea that fruit untouched and uneaten could constitute waste in the sense of its not being put to proper use first occurred to Eve in a dream in which she observes an angel-like figure addressing the "tree of interdicted knowledge" (V, 52):

> And O fair plant, said he, with fruit surcharged,
> Deigns none to ease thy load and taste thy sweet,
> Nor God, nor man; is knowledge so despised?
> Or envy, or what reserve forbids to taste?
> Forbid who will, none shall from me withhold
> Longer thy offered good, *why else set here?*
>
> (V, 58–59, 62–63 [emphasis added])

Proceeding thence to pluck and eat the fruit, this creature, "shaped and winged like one of those from heaven" (V, 55), is emboldened to proclaim that goods such as knowledge and fruit actually grow in abundance the more they are shared, and thus increase rather than diminish the glory of the being who created them (V, 72–74).

Eve is chilled by this parade of images, and tells Adam "O how glad I waked/To find this but a dream!" (V, 92–93). And yet the dream portends her own future: later, very much awake in the Garden, she allows herself to be beguiled by Satan, present now not as a figure in a dream but in the form of a serpent, that "fittest imp of fraud" (IX, 89), that "wily adder" (IX, 625). As if having become Satan's understudy,[9] Eve reasons that God's prohibition against eating the fruit from the tree of knowledge is incoherent and that fear of the sure death its transgression is said to threaten is unwarranted. In keeping us from knowledge of good and evil (IX, 709, 723, 752), God thereby "Forbids us good, forbids us to be wise."[10] Surely "Such prohibitions bind not" (IX, 759–760). If something is good, and available to us, there is no reason for us not to have it, indeed every reason for us to have it. And we can't have it unless we know it: "For good unknown, sure is not had, or had/And yet unknown, is as not had at all" (IX, 756–757). Moreover, there now is proof that having what has been forbidden is not bad, does not bring death—that is, proof that "knowledge of good" is *not* "bought dear by knowing ill" (IV, 221): for the serpent has eaten, and yet clearly has lived to tell the tale.

> How dies the serpent? he hath eaten and lives,
> And knows, and speaks, and reasons, and discerns. (IX, 764–765)

Like the serpent, Eve then reaches forth to the forbidden fruit. She plucks, she eats (IX, 781). Addressing the tree of knowledge, she declares that it makes no sense to let "thy fair fruit . . . hang, as to no end created" (IX, 798–799). Surely the tree with its fruit was created to be used, and surely its use is to be eaten. It would

---

9. Eve is not aware that Satan was confident that the knowledge she seeks will indeed be her and Adam's undoing: "Sleep on/Blest pair; and O yet happiest if ye seek no happier state, and know to know no more" (IV, 774–775).

10. A thorough exploration of the soundness of either God's or Eve's reasoning is not among the present purposes of this essay. But such an exploration, as Monique Roelofs has pointed out in conversation, would involve asking whether Eve (and Adam) are presumed to have enough knowledge already of good and evil to know that disobedience is evil.

be wasteful not to treat it accordingly. Eve will "ease" its "fertile burden" (IX, 801). God's prohibition against tasting of the tree of knowledge is incoherent and premised on an unfounded threat; in forbidding the eating of such abundant fruit, God also enjoins wastefulness. What a silly that God is—creating such beautiful and beneficial stuff and then letting it go to waste, indeed requiring that it go to waste, by forbidding its use! It won't go to waste in the sense of decaying—it is "incorruptible"—but it will go to waste in the sense of not being put to use. God, Eve might be said to imply, has a limited notion of what constitutes waste.

But there is an economy of waste that Eve has not foreseen. In the name of not letting the fruits of the Garden go to waste in remaining unused, Eve inaugurates a new and decidedly unparadisaical era in her and Adam's life, indeed in the lives of all their human descendants: Eve and Adam's transgression brings about a veritable wasteland in which formerly "incorruptible" fruit now suffers decay and formerly deathless humans now will turn back to dust (X, 208, 770, 1085). The moment Eve told Adam of her "fatal trespass" (IX, 889), the splendid roses in the garland he had been preparing for her "faded" and were "shed" (IX, 893). The "verdure" of Paradise disappears, is "spoiled" (XI, 832); the cattle die "of rot and murrain [infectious disease]" (XII, 179). The devilish "dogs of hell" are set free "to waste and havoc" the world and also to "lick up the draff and filth/Which man's polluting sin with taint hath shed/On what was pure, till crammed and gorged, nigh burst/With sucked and glutted offal" (X, 616–617, 630–634).

When Eve acted to make sure that a part of God's bounty did not go to waste in one sense—to go unused—she guaranteed that it all would go to waste in another—to become subject to "corruption," spoilage, rot, demise through decay or death.

Change in the nature of nature—from being incorruptible to being all too corruptible—is accompanied by, indeed caused by, the emergence of humans' claims to know waste when they see it: from Eve's confident perspective, surely unused fruit has a purpose that goes unfulfilled unless it is eaten—and unavailable knowledge has a purpose that goes unmet unless humans can avail themselves of it.

But such judgment, it turns out—judgment about what does and does not constitute waste, what does and does not constitute proper use—God regards as being beyond the ken and outside the jurisdiction of humanity. Humans enjoy manifold gifts in God's Paradise, but good judgment about waste is not among them. Humans are not in a position to know why things were created, what purpose they might serve, and their not recognizing and accepting this limitation is at the heart of their disastrous downfall: Eve's thinking she knows the proper use of that forbidden if enticingly available apple is integral to her act of disobedience and the descent from God's grace it precipitated.

This particular gap in human knowledge and judgment is noted at several places in *Paradise Lost*. The archangel Raphael offers Adam instruction about the significance of the differences between humans and their maker. Humans should recognize the limits of what they can know; unlike God, they are not omniscient, and they can get terribly lost and make disastrous mistakes when they try to venture outside the generous limits God has set.

> . . . knowledge is as food, and needs no less
> Her temperance over appetite, to know
> In measure what the mind may well contain,
> Oppresses else with surfeit, and soon turns
> Wisdom to folly, as nourishment to wind. (VII, 126–130)

Among the excellences of God in comparison with which humanity, however blessed, fares poorly, is God's knowledge of how "to value right/The good before him"; anyone else "perverts best things/To worst abuse, or to their meanest use" (IV, 201–204). Humans are apt to misjudge the purposes for which God created things, the ends they are designed to serve. At one point Adam tells Raphael that he finds it quite puzzling that God, author of "wise and frugal" nature, has created with "superfluous hand" (VIII, 26–27) stars vastly disproportionate in number to what is necessary to pour light on this small, single, and distant earth.[11] Raphael patiently responds to Adam, almost as if to a child, that God does not "divulge/His secrets to be scanned by them who ought/Rather admire"; in fact, God simply laughs at the pointless disputes humans get into over matters way beyond their ken (VIII, 73–78). If Adam wants to understand the point of all that great distance between the stars and earth, he might well consider the possibility that it is in order "That man know he dwells not in his own," and that otherwise all that space is "Ordained for uses to his Lord best known" (VIII, 104, 107). Adam listens carefully to Raphael's counsel that while Adam is favored with the "joy" of "this Paradise/And thy fair Eve," "heaven is for thee too high/To know what passes there," and Adam thus should be, only can be, "lowly wise" (VIII, 171–173). Adam comes to accept and endorse the view that humans best use their minds to reflect on "That which before us lies in daily life," not what for humans must remain "obscure and subtle" (VIII, 192–193), such

---

11. In Book IV Eve asks Adam why the stars shine all night, "when sleep hath shut all eyes" (IV, 658). Adam has a ready answer: so that no part of the earth would be left in "total darkness" and suffer thereby the extinguishing of life (IV, 665–666). But in the passages in Book VIII referred to above, he reveals to Raphael that he doesn't understand why it takes so many stars to achieve this end.

as how things are to be valued and used and thus what constitutes their being wasted.

And yet in Book IX, Adam does not hesitate to counsel Eve concerning what constitutes a waste of human effort: Eve suggests that they "divide [their] labours" (IX, 214) tending the "wanton growth" (IX, 211) in the Garden, for otherwise they are likely to waste time smiling and talking while working side by side. Allowing that surely "nothing lovelier can be found/In woman, than to study household good,/And good works in her husband to promote" (IX, 232–234), Adam nonetheless urges that God has not made the health of the Garden turn on such efficiency: "For not to irksome toil, but to delight/He made us, and delight to reason joined./These paths and bowers doubt not but our joint hands/ Will keep from wilderness with ease" (IX, 242–243). However, Adam does not insist that his view about waste of time and labor must prevail over Eve's, and does not try to stop her from heading off alone on a path that leaves her open to the final and fatal suasion of the serpent.

John Milton invites us to think of Paradise—the mythical home for the Old Testament's first man and woman—as a place in which food is not only not scarce but magnificently bounteous. In all that excess there is no waste, in the sense that fruit does not spoil, however long it is on the tree. But once Eve posited that there was another kind of waste in the Garden—the unrealized potential of what might be gained from eating of the tree of knowledge—the world became a wasteland and the threat of scarcity entered into human life. Eve's disobedient decision to consume the fruit of the forbidden tree took root in the fertile ground of her confidently assuming the authority to judge what is waste and what is not.

FOOD WASTE AND PROPERTY RIGHTS

In Milton's rendition of Genesis, food waste has a striking role in the history of the relation between humanity and God. In John Locke's *Second Treatise of Government*, food waste is crucial to the foundation of the rights of humans to the resources God gave them.[12]

The natural world in which Locke locates humanity is God-given but also marked by signs of our expulsion from Paradise. God gave us this world with all its rich floral and faunal resources, and blessed us with the capacity to reason, which allows us "to make use of [the world] to the best advantage of life, and convenience."[13] But this world is, after all, post-lapsarian: we have to labor much harder and longer than did the still-innocent Adam and Eve, and earth's apples are no longer "incorruptible." Since this world was given to us "in common" (§25), we all have a right to its resources. But there are both conditions for and limits on the exercise of this right. Your labor entitles you to a portion of what is given in common. Go forth and pluck, gather, hunt, and fish. But not to your heart's content. For there are limits to what a person can make his or hers: God gave us all this plenty for us to "enjoy," that is, to "make use of to any advantage of life before it spoils" (§31). "Nothing was made by God for man to spoil or destroy" (§31).

12. In her lively *Making Waste: Leftovers and the Eighteenth-Century Imagination* (Princeton, NJ: Princeton University Press, 2010), Sophie Gee describes a preoccupation with waste among writers in the century following that in which Milton and Locke flourished.

13. John Locke, *Second Treatise of Government*, ed. C. B. Macpherson (Indianapolis: Hackett, 1980 [1690]), §26. References to the text appear hereafter in parentheses.

It is not just the edible items humans come across in nature that can be of use to them in obtaining sustenance. There is also the land. And indeed by the time Locke was writing the *Second Treatise*, toward the end of the 17th century, the *"chief matter of property"* of English denizens was "now not the fruits of the earth, and the beasts that subsist on it, but *the earth itself*" (§32, emphasis in the original). Man and woman are no less entitled, indeed no less bound, to make use of the land than they are to gather what nature offers independently of their digging into the soil. *"As much land* as a man tills, plants, improves, cultivates, and can use the product of, so much is his *property"* (§32, emphasis in the original). But there are limits here, too, on appropriating common land: as long as one leaves "as much" and "as good" land as existed before the appropriation, it's as if one has taken "nothing at all" (§33).[14]

Cultivating land properly improves its value. Appropriators actually "increase the common stock of mankind": a single acre of cultivated land could easily produce many times the "provisions" of "an acre of land of an equal richness lying waste in common" (§37). If there is waste in allowing food to rot, meat to putrefy, so too there is waste when land that might be cultivated goes unfurrowed and unplanted. Indeed "we shall find the benefit of it amount to little more than nothing" (§42). Think about bread: it is only because of the tremendous labor that has gone into the cultivation of land, the invention of tools, the distribution of the final product, that it is available to us as bread—"nature and the earth furnished only the almost worthless materials" (§43). They may be "materials of plenty" (§41), but their potential is not realized apart from

---

14. Locke famously, or infamously, appends this proviso: once money exists, he posits, it can rightfully be used to appropriate more land than one can use, as long as those who don't own the land can benefit from what is produced on it (§46).

human labor. Our capacity to toil is thus implicitly a greater gift to us from God than what God provides independently of our labor.

In Locke's post-Edenic world, God has provided bounteously for humanity (though much of that bounty depends on cultivating what otherwise is wasteland), but the waste of food is an ever-present possibility that humans must be on watch for scrupulously. The occurrence of waste in nature—food waste in particular—is clear evidence that a person has mismanaged, misused God's plenty. You are welcome to pluck apples from a tree, to kill a deer you come across in the woods, in order to sustain your life. But if you allow the apples to spoil, or let the animal flesh putrefy, you have abused your right to the riches God has provided. You also are not only welcome but commanded by God "to subdue the earth, i.e., improve it for the benefit of life" (§32), not leave it in a state of waste, that is, uncultivated.

There are then according to Locke at least two senses in which food waste is to be understood: (1) as the loss, the draining away, of the use value of existing foodstuffs (e.g., rotten apples, stinking carcasses); (2) as the untapped, unrealized potential of land to be cultivated in order to create foodstuffs, something Locke espied across the Atlantic:

> for I ask, whether in the wild woods and uncultivated waste of *America*, left to nature, without any improvement, tillage or husbandry, a thousand acres yield the needy and wretched inhabitants as many conveniences of life, as ten acres of equally fertile land do in *Devonshire*, where they are well cultivated? (§37; emphasis in the original)

Locke here adopts the very view about waste—in particular about our capacity and authority to judge what is waste and what is not—that was Eve's undoing: Eve disobediently assumed that she knew the proper use of the apple. Locke takes it as a given that God counts on our ability to know the proper use of the resources around us. God wants us to see land that might be cultivated as lying in waste should it not be tilled. Of what value can such land be if it is not used to create food? For Locke, "land that is left wholly to nature, that hath no improvement of pasturage, tillage, or planting, is called, as indeed it is, *waste*" (§42).

This understanding of food waste is central to a Lockean inspired view according to which settlers from elsewhere had the right, in fact the duty, to take possession of uncultivated lands in America.[15] According to Locke, the only or in any event the far superior use of land is to cultivate it. He implicitly rules out the possibility that any other use of the land, any other value it could have, could be relevant—for example, the Miltonic ideas that God's glory might be revealed in bounteous excess, and that humanity's limitations are exposed in their inability to judge what is or is not wasteful in God's designs; or the notion that hunting and gathering are adequate and respectful ways of sustaining life. God gave the world "to the use of the industrious and rational" (§34), but the "wretched inhabitants" across the sea appear unable to

---

15. For example, "Locke's argument from divine command to cultivate those '*great Tracts*' of unappropriated land became the classic theoretical expression of the agriculturalist argument for European *dominium* over American land." David Armitage, "John Locke, Carolina, and the 'Two Treatises of Government,'" *Political Theory* 32, no. 5 (October 2004): 618. A view similar to Locke's had appeared in Thomas More's *Utopia* and in the works of Grotius and Pufendorf: see Karl Olivecrona, "Locke's Theory of Appropriation," *Philosophical Quarterly* 24, no. 96 (July 1974): 220–234; Thomas Flanagan, "The Agricultural Argument and Original Appropriation: Indian Lands and Political Philosophy," *Canadian Journal of Political Science/Revue canadienne de science politique* 22, no. 3 (September 1989): 589–602; and Barbara Arneil, "Trade, Plantations, and Property: John Locke and the Economic Defense of Colonialism," *Journal of the History of Ideas* 55, no. 4 (October 1994): 591–609.

treat the land as a breadbasket-in-waiting, to understand that God commands us "to subdue the earth, i.e., improve it for the benefit of life" (§32).

In the case of both Milton and Locke we can see that because food has significance beyond its role in sustaining human life, and "waste" is a normative term, there are bound to be differences over whether a particular use of food is wasteful, along with struggles over whose view ought to prevail. In Milton, the idea is broached that humans fail to honor the splendor, power, and authority of God when they insist that they know what is useful for humans and what is not; in Locke, there is the claim that it's precisely when humans fail to mine the world for what is useful to humanity that they go against God's will, and that others have the right, in fact, the obligation, to go forth and cultivate. In *Paradise Lost* we are said to not be good judges of what constitutes waste; in *The Second Treatise* we are instructed that the capacity for reason that God gave humans enables us, indeed requires us, to judge what is wasteful and what is not.

FEASTS

Damaris Cudworth, or Lady Masham, a dear friend of John Locke's, is reported to have said that he strongly disliked waste in any form.[16] One wonders what he made, then, of the fact that humanity, in all its motley glory and across time and culture, has given the wasting of food a central role in celebrating life, in glaring back defiantly into the face of scarcity, and in establishing or maintaining social relations.

16. Maurice Cranston, "Locke and Liberty," *Wilson Quarterly* 10, no. 5 (Winter 1986): 93.

Feasts have a prominent place in human history. Communal and commensal, they come in great variety: they can be religious, irreligious, or non-religious in intent; they may be designed by and for royalty or peasantry; sometimes they function to confirm existing social hierarchies, other times to temporarily dislodge them (or do the former by doing the latter); they might sanctify order or celebrate disorder. But among the basic elements of feasts, whatever their mood and aim, are food and drink. And, if at all possible, the victuals are to be as plentiful and delicious as possible, even at what may be extraordinary expense to the individual or community creating them.[17] The specialness of the food marks the specialness of the occasion: feasts typically are offered to show honor, respect, or gratitude for some person or deity, or to underscore the importance of an event such as a birth, a death, a wedding, a victory; they may lubricate the economy in the creation and discharge of debt. The provision and intake of more than enough food and drink typically is called for.

Feasts thus are likely to involve waste in a number of ways: the very idea of a feast tends to suggest that there will be not only enough but an inordinate amount for all the participants. In ancient feasts it was not unusual for there to be containers at hand into which revelers might vomit and thereby make room for yet another dish, another draught. Frugality is supposed to be out of the question.

While the excess might be given to animals or humans not among the feasters (for example, a 14th-century English court

---

17. See, for example, Michael Dietler, "Theorizing the Feast: Rituals of Consumption, Commensal Politics, and Power in African Contexts," in *Feasts: Archaeological and Ethnographic Perspectives on Food, Politics and Power*, ed. Michael Dietler and Brian Hayden (Washington, DC: Smithsonian Institution, 2001), 82, 96.

might include an "almoner" among whose tasks was to direct leftovers from the feast to the poor),[18] it might also be left to rot. (The post-Thanksgiving behavior of many North Americans has centuries-old antecedents.) Providing enough to waste is part of the point of the feast. That is among the reasons that a Luo family in west Kenya, for example, might exhaust its supply of food, knowing that some of it will quickly become garbage, rather than keep themselves from going through a period of near starvation,[19] or why an about-to-be married couple in the United States put themselves in hock for a splendid and heavily garbage-producing feast for family and friends.

What are we to make of what appears to be wanton, intentional waste of food at feasts? Three perspectives on the matter stand out:

(One) Evidence of Human Folly and Failure. At one level the waste typically associated with feasts would seem to provide abundant evidence of irrational or reprehensible behavior: why would we go out of our way to waste food, given the labor and resources that go into the production, preparation, and presentation of the offerings at the feast and that are required for the daunting cleanup job afterward? In light of the signal importance of food to our survival and the looming threat of its becoming scarce, there are much better uses of food than allowing it to go to waste, indeed, planning on its going to waste. It's not for nothing that Veblen noted the tight connection between describing behavior as wasteful and impugning the wasters of engaging in bad behavior. From this perspective, the question

18. Roy Strong, Feast: A History of Grand Eating (London: Pimlico, 2003), 91.
19. Dietler, "Theorizing the Feast," 96.

then isn't really whether there's something wrong with wasting food but whether anything other than human folly or moral failure can be its source. (*Two*) *Invitation to Consider Possible Uses of Food Waste.* But maybe we are all too quick to see the waste of food at feasts as lacking any possible usefulness or purpose, as being revelatory simply of wasters' inability or unwillingness to reflect on the detriment of their behavior to themselves or to others. Though the excess food in such feasts is going to waste in the sense of spoiling instead of being consumed, more likely than not it is not going to waste in another sense, for the provision of the food and the unused excess appear to be crucial to the social or political work the feast performs. Among the most studied deployments of food and other provisions for such purposes is the *potlatch*, a ritual ceremony engaged in by some of the indigenous peoples of the Pacific northwest of the United States and Canada.[20] The origin and meaning of such events continue to be under considerable debate.[21] But one crucial element of the potlatch is the showering of guests with extravagant and clearly excessive amounts of food. That this vital resource would go to waste (in the sense of not being fully consumed) was part of the meaning and function of offering it: such a gift both established the authority and power

20. Veblen was quite interested in the potlatch as a prime example of the "conspicuous consumption of goods [as] a means of reputability"; even if the "presents and feasts had probably another origin than that of naïve ostentation, . . . they acquired their utility for this purpose very early" (*Leisure*, 75).
21. See, for example, Joseph Masco, "Competitive Displays: Negotiating Genealogical Rights to the Potlatch at the American Museum of Natural History," *American Anthropologist*, New Series 98, no. 4 (December 1996): 837–852.

of the giver over the recipients and put the latter under obligation to and in competition with those who had provided such largesse.

Does the social, political, and economic usefulness of the apparent waste of food in rituals such as the potlatch remove the grounds on which such waste is subject to disapproval as given above in Perspective One? After all, seen in the light of Perspective Two, the waste of food appears to be contrary neither to self-interest nor to certain forms of social or political obligation recognized in one's community. It has a calculable function in complex patterns of human interaction.

Certainly many missionaries and lawmakers in Canada and the United States did not think that understanding the function of food and other forms of waste integral to the potlatch should halt attempts to outlaw or otherwise get rid of such rituals. One superintendent of Indian affairs in Northwest Canada in the late 19th century had no difficulty recognizing that the waste of food and property ritualized in the potlatch was crucial to the maintenance of long-established practices among the indigenous peoples whose minds and habits he hoped to change. Indeed, he and other critics apparently "came to realize . . . that what was called potlatching was the heart of the cultural system of the Northwest Coast and was related to numerous parts of the complete social system of the natives."[22] But recognition of the cultural importance of the potlatch did nothing to moderate the consternation of critics who judged the habits of the native

22. Forrest E. LaViolette, *The Struggle for Survival: Indian Cultures and the Protestant Ethic in British Columbia* (Toronto: University of Toronto Press, 1961), 36–37.

inhabitants to be "uncivilized." They took it to be just further evidence of "how radically unlike" Europeans the indigenous peoples were.[23]

This kind of reaction has in turn been seen as imperialistic and moralistic, as a wholesale ethnocentric misunderstanding not just of the waste of food and property but of a way of life in which such waste has a perfectly understandable place. Moreover, according to this take on the potlatch's critics, it's not as if "civilized" Europeans and their colonizing countrymen in North America don't have similar feasts and rituals serving similar social functions: indigenous people themselves pointed out that Christmas and the 4th of July, for example, are ritual occasions on which "'money is spent in squandrous profusion with no benefits to the poor of your race.'"[24]

From this second perspective, then, the object of disapproval shifts from the wasters of food (as in Perspective One) onto those judged to be too ethnocentric and too complicit in projects of cultural, religious, and economic domination to see that the waste of food and property in the potlatch is just one among many uses of food in what some anthropologists and other social scientists have called "status quests."[25] Perhaps if it were serving no useful function at all, had no discernible purpose, it would invite disapproval. But in fact it's no more and no less rational and responsible than many similar habits and practices of the Europeans who are appalled by it. The halos of rationality, calculability, and solemn duty have not disappeared after all.

23. LaViolette, *Struggle*, 32.
24. LaViolette, *Struggle*, 70.
25. See, for example, *Food and the Status Quest: An Interdisciplinary Perspective*, ed. Polly Wiessner and Wulf Schiefenhoevel (Providence, RI: Berghahn Books, 1996).

(*Three*) *Excessive Spending of Resources as Evidence of Freedom.*
Adopters of a third perspective disagree with the premise
of the first and smell a rat in the second.

While they perhaps agree that the ordinary use of "waste"
carries a judgment of disapproval—as Veblen said, it "carries an
undertone of deprecation"—they take this common connotation
of the word to be based on a misunderstanding of life on the planet
and to depend on a widespread but terribly misleading idea that
the world we occupy is much more like the post-fall hardscrabble
environment John Locke described than the prelapsarian paradise Milton versified. A major figure in this connection is Georges
Bataille, who rejected the idea that humans are by the very nature
of things always faced with the threat of resource depletion, including our own energy:

> It is not necessity but its contrary, "luxury," that presents living
> matter and mankind with their fundamental problems.[26]

Our world depends on the energy of the sun, which, Bataille
insists, is inexhaustible and is available for our use[27] without
our having to give something in return—it "squander[s] without reciprocation" (*Accursed*, 38). Our problem is not what to do
about scarcity but what to do about the excess energy available

26. Georges Bataille, *The Accursed Share: An Essay on General Economy*, Vol. I, trans. Robert
Hurley (New York: Zone Books, 1988), 12. Emphasis in the original. Further references
appear in parentheses.
27. Just how available that energy actually is or will remain is not under consideration here.
But for doubts about Bataille's understanding of the extent of usable energy, see Allan
Stoekl, "Excess and Depletion: Bataille's Surprisingly Ethical Model of Expenditure,"
in *Reading Bataille Now*, ed. Shannon Winnubst (Bloomington: Indiana University
Press, 2007), 252–284.

to us and to all living organisms—energy that far exceeds what we need to consume in order to maintain our present state, grow, and reproduce; energy that one way or another, for better or for worse, in the exuberance of love or in the heated ravages of war, we will expend because we are bound to expend. True, Bataille readily concedes, it's not as if we have handled this problem well: for example, writing in the 1930s, he points out that there appears to be "a deficiency of resources," exhibited, for instance, in the "extreme poverty in India" (*Accursed*, 39). But this appearance of scarcity on the human scene—the hunger and threat of starvation that propels people in the direction of putting all their energy into survival—Bataille sees as reflecting not an implacably given condition of life but rather the result of the expenditure of excess energy in the creation and maintenance of systems of inequality. For example, he takes it that the situation in India cannot be "dissociated from the excesses of American resources" (*Accursed* 39).

According to Bataille, the presumption of scarcity as an integral part of "the [natural] laws that govern us" (*Accursed*, 12) (not the same as recognizing specific local conditions such as famine and dire poverty in which there is relative scarcity) mainly serves to give prominence to what he takes to be mendacious views about the appropriate economic and social arrangements for dealing with such alleged scarcity, according to which

- Those with very little, or nothing at all, are to sell the only thing they do have, their labor power, to those who are in a position to hire them.
- Everybody thereby has something to give and something to expect in return: you get my labor, I get your money, I give

what is now my money to someone else, who in turn provides me with what I need to survive.

- One must husband one's resources; to spend any time or energy on objects or activities without expectation of return messes up the fine-tuning of the arrangements that allow one to ward off poverty or starvation. When one "squanders without reciprocation," there is no way to make up for the loss.
- It is recognition of this that prompts some wasters of crucial resources to be angry with themselves, and their families and neighbors to be alarmed and disgusted by their behavior.[28]

Bataille vehemently rejects such a picture. The fool is not the one who in the face of scarcity spends his last funds on a waste-producing feast but the one who accepts the idea that sober recognition of scarcity obliges him not to endure loss without return.[29] The latter has forfeited the only real freedom humans have. For to the extent that we are reduced to thinking all our energy must go into preventing otherwise inevitable scarcity we become servile. "Acts undertaken with some rational end are only servile responses to a necessity. . . . It is . . . inhuman to abandon life to a chain of useful acts."[30] The spectacle of a man "glorifying necessary work and letting himself be emasculated by the fear of tomorrow" is pathetic.[31] "It is sad to say that *conscious humanity has remained a minor*; humanity recognizes the

28. In this connection, see Samuel Martínez, "The Struggle for Expenditure on a Caribbean Sugar Plantation," *Current Anthropology*, 51 (2010): 609–628.
29. Thus it presumably would be of interest to Bataille that typically the giver of the potlatch expects reciprocation: recipients incur the debt of giving a potlatch themselves.
30. Georges Bataille, "The Sorcerer's Apprentice," in *Visions of Excess: Selected Writings, 1927–1939*, ed. Allan Stoekl (Minneapolis: University of Minnesota Press, 2004), 231.
31. Georges Bataille, "The Practice of Joy before Death," in *Visions*, 237.

right to acquire, to conserve, and to consume rationally, but it excludes in principle *nonproductive expenditure*."[32] "A genuine luxury requires the complete contempt for riches, the somber indifference of the individual who refuses work and makes his life on the one hand an infinitely ruined splendor, and on the other, a silent insult to the laborious lie of the rich" (*Accursed*, 76–77). The slacker, not the servile utilitarian, represents humanity at its best, its freest.

We are now in a position to appreciate why Bataille would be suspicious of accounts of wasteful behavior, á la Perspective Two, that portray such behavior as being not so wasteful or useless after all but in fact quite instrumental in the pursuit of recognizable and at the very least not entirely unworthy ends. Bataille doesn't think wasteful expenditure needs salvaging by the earnest efforts of the high priests and priestesses of rationality and utility or those on guard duty against ethnocentrism. On the contrary, he thinks such attempts obscure what he regards as the sovereign acts of beings destined, indeed impelled, by "the general movement of exudation (of waste) of living matter" (*Accursed*, 23) to spend in excess, to live life without constantly checking in on the utility of one's behavior. From this perspective, one is not doing anyone a favor, not saving anyone from the shame or embarrassment or guilt of being foolish and irresponsible, by describing what appears to be wasteful behavior as really being purposeful or productive, as serving useful ends. To deny or mute the wastefulness of the act is to rob the person performing it of what gives her or him dignity as a human being.

32. Georges Bataille, "The Notion of Expenditure," in *Visions*, 117.

From Bataille's point of view, then, in thinking about the waste of food our interpretive repertoire need not be limited to just two possibilities, as if such behavior can only be understood either as something to be rued, as in Perspective One, or as a rational strategy for meeting a desired and not unworthy end, as in Perspective Two. Bataille thinks that such a limited palette doesn't have room for the possibility that there is and always will be excess energy to expend and that humanity's greatest freedom and most intense pleasure is experienced in excessive and exuberant expenditure without expectation of return or calculation of benefit. Though Bataille is not, as he takes others to be, in the business of trying to convince us that what appears to be wasteful really after all is not, it nonetheless seems to be an implication of his work that excess is waste only when judged against a picture of humanity as dwelling in a land not of inexhaustible plenty but of terrifying scarcity.

What's at stake in being able to establish yourself as someone who knows waste when you see it?

In Milton's *Paradise Lost*, the distinction between reliable and unreliable judges of waste is part of what distinguishes God from humanity. From God's perspective, there are some matters about which humans can't help but issue very imperfect judgments. Since humans don't know the purpose of things, neither Eve nor any other human is in a position to know what is and is not a waste of them. Moreover, Eve's thinking that she or any other of God's creatures had the wherewithal to exercise such judgment was a large part of her disobedience of God. Her thinking she knows what does and doesn't constitute waste was her undoing and thus ours.

According to Locke, the distinction between reliable and unreliable judges of waste is not a mark of the difference between God and humans, but rather of that between humans who have the capacity to exercise such judgment wisely and those who don't. The "wretched inhabitants" of the Americas are not good judges of what constitutes the proper use and thus the waste of the resources God gave humanity, and this is a measure of a crucial difference between them and those humans who do have good judgment about such matters. And it is only the views of the latter about what constitutes waste that can provide the proper foundations for the right to property.

Missionaries and lawmakers alarmed and appalled by the potlatch took what they saw as indigenous people's failure to understand the great harm of wasting food to be a measure of their distance from more civilized folk like themselves. Unable to recognize what really constitutes waste, the indigenous inhabitants of North America, officials argued, were in no condition to handle their own affairs.

Georges Bataille might ask whether there isn't a suspect assumption behind any attempt to distinguish between reliable and unreliable judges of waste—namely, that it is important to know what are the proper and best uses of things. For according to Bataille, being preoccupied with making sure our acts are useful and not wasteful is the sign of how far we have strayed from living in conditions of true freedom, how distant we are from being the exuberant and excessive creatures we are meant to be. If there is a distinction to be made, it is between those who worry about waste because they wrongly assume that our natural condition is one of scarcity, and those whose "excess" expenditure reminds us, intentionally or unintentionally, that in fact it's only in spending and giving without thought of benefit in return that we are living in freedom and not being servile, not being thoughtless devotees of utility. Ironically, the failure to understand that distinction has led us to use our abundant energy to create local conditions of scarcity in which waste indeed becomes worrisome.

In some grand sagas of human history and destiny, then, waste has been called upon to play a prominent role: the difference between reliable and unreliable judges of waste marks the difference between those who understand and those who don't understand what God expects of humans; it reveals the distance between those who really understand and those who fail to understand the meaning of human freedom and dignity. All in all, not a bad gig for waste.[33]

---

33. A highly abbreviated version of this chapter, indeed an *amuse-bouche*, appears as "Feast or Famine: On the Meaning of the Food We Waste," *Philosopher's Magazine* 61 (2013): 75–80.

Epilogue

The promised portrait of our intimate fellowship with trash has turned out to be more like a sestych, a six-panel installation. In each panel, significant distinctions among us turn out to track differences in our connections to the vast realm of refuse. Together, the vignettes highlight our dependence on rejectamenta to make sense of our lives and of our jostlings with each other. The following thumbnail sketches slightly recast what has been on display and include a detail or two from each of the panels as jogs to memory. Or, to shift metaphors, trash and waste here take a curtain call, having had starring roles in projects quite near and dear to the hearts of human beings.

The Knower and the Known. Rifling through rubbish is a common practice among those eager to gain kinds of knowledge about the lives of others not readily available through alternate means. Indeed some students of garbology think that especially significant information glitters in the dross of what we toss out. Because such gleanings may involve matters that discarders prefer not to be known, combing through the trash often portends the triumph of seeker over hider. (Just ask the narcotics agents who went after Billy Greenwood's garbage bags.)

The Fat Cats and the Stragglers. Displaying one's capacity to be wasteful has been a way of getting a leg up on others: I can afford to be wasteful, but you can't, at least not to the same degree. Take that, social inferior, economic laggard! (Consultant: Thorstein Veblen.)

The Scathed and the Unscathed. Handling trash—one's own or that of others—is not simply a household chore or mode of employment. There appears to be something that is the "right distance" from trash (this "something" is likely to vary across cultures or communities), and failing to strike such distance is held to mark the difference between those presumed to suffer from a character flaw or spiritual shortcoming and those not made subject to such presumption. (Tallis's filthy garbage-strewn house marked him in his family's eyes as psychologically wobbly and a sure loser.)

The Designed and the Disorderly. Just what are we, this species known as *Homo sapiens*, and how did we come about? What difference does it make if the story is: (a) the natural world of which we are a part is the work of a fabulously intelligent designer, one with plans and skills and powers far exceeding those of even the best human designers (and one who by the way must be especially proud of producing *Homo sapiens*); or (b) *Homo sapiens* evolved by means of a process that is extravagantly wasteful, surely a far cry from what any designer worth her or his salt would have wrought. Pray, what is our species: the crown jewel in an exquisitely designed world or just another event in nature's aleatory parade? A splendid and beautifully turned out creature or an accidental and decidedly unkempt tourist? (William Paley v. Charles Darwin *redux*, 21st century.)

The Enlightened and the Unenlightened. Some of our sages have told us that one of the differences between the enlightened and the benighted is that it is only the former who understand desire to be a major source of dissatisfaction in human life. These storied ancestors might have predicted that pumped up longing for the cornucopia of goods occupying center stage in consumerist societies ends in dissatisfaction, indeed invites it. Those who have seen the light about human nature, or so it is said, are attuned to the ever-present possibility of dissatisfaction and the trash-making to which it readily leads. Those still laboring in the darkness either don't pay attention to the power of dissatisfaction and the massive evidence of its presence in the rubbish littering the face of the earth, or they don't care about such matters; perhaps they even profit handsomely from cultivating dissatisfaction. (Plato and the Buddha take a tour of the local landfill.)

Reliable and Unreliable Judges. According to some accounts of great moments in human history, we would be well advised to consider the difference between those who have and those who lack good judgment about waste. If Eve only had understood that her judgment in matters of waste was no match for God's, humanity wouldn't have to endure the hardscrabble fate to which her disobedient fruit-plucking condemned us. And if those "wretched inhabitants" of the Americas only had acknowledged that invaders from elsewhere had a much more highly developed sense of what constitutes waste than they themselves did, maybe they could have held on to those contested lands. On the other hand, perhaps it's only the free and the brave among us who dare to expend excessively and with abandon. (John Milton, John Locke, and Georges Bataille make cameo appearances in *Return to Paradise*, soon to be a major motion picture.)

Cast in the above manner, the chapters in this book offer episodes in the long history of efforts we seem in no hurry to forgo: to gain power or advantage over others by being in possession of knowledge about them (*The Knower and the Known*); to establish superior social and economic rank (*The Fat Cats and the Stragglers*); to raise doubts about people's character and thereby marginalize them or exclude them from full citizenship (*The Scathed and the Unscathed*); to come up with authoritative accounts of human origins (*The Designed and the Disorderly*); to warn us of the perils associated with an insistent and hard-to-resist element in our makeup (*The Enlightened and the Unenlightened*); and to distinguish the brighter from the dimmer bulbs burning in the hall of human judgment (*Reliable and Unreliable Judges*).

The fact that trash and its many siblings have been recruited to drive home such distinctions lays bare the yeomanly value we are always at the ready to extract from the disvalued and decommissioned: no matter how hard we try to make sure that garbage and waste won't end up in our backyards, we heartily greet them as good neighbors and dependable partners in our rhetorical campaigns and relentless jockeying. We may want all that stuff out of sight, but hardly ever out of mind.

BIBLIOGRAPHY

Allen, Colin, and Marc Bekoff. "Biological Function, Adaptation, and Natural Design." *Philosophy of Science* 62, no. 4 (December 1995): 609–622.

Alley, Kelly D. *On the Banks of the Ganga: When Wastewater Meets a Sacred River.* Ann Arbor: University of Michigan Press, 2002.

Allison, Dorothy. *Bastard Out of Carolina.* New York: Penguin Plume, 1993.

Allison, Dorothy. *Trash.* New York: Penguin Plume, 2002.

Amis, Martin. "Age Will Win." http://www.theguardian.com/film/2001/dec/21/artsfeatures.fiction.

Amis, Martin. "Remembering Iris Murdoch." http://www.martinamisweb.com/commentary_files/ma_irismurdoch.doc.

Aristotle. *Politics.* In *The Complete Works of Aristotle: The Revised Oxford Translation,* Volume 2. Edited by Jonathan Barnes. Princeton, NJ: Princeton University Press, 1984.

Armitage, David. "John Locke, Carolina, and the 'Two Treatises of Government.'" *Political Theory* 32, no. 5 (October 2004): 602–627.

Arneil, Barbara. "Trade, Plantations, and Property: John Locke and the Economic Defense of Colonialism." *Journal of the History of Ideas* 55, no. 4 (October 1994): 591–609.

Balchand, K. "President Asks Women to Lead Sanitation Revolution." *The Hindu,* March 22, 2012. http://www.thehindu.com/news/national/president-asks-women-to-lead-sanitation-revolution/article3026009.ece.

Barnes, David S. "Sense and Sensibilities: Disgust and the Meanings of Odors in Late Nineteenth-Century Paris." *Historical Reflections/Réflexions Historique* 28, no. 1 (2002): 211–249.

Bataille, Georges. *The Accursed Share: An Essay on General Economy*. Volume I. Translated by Robert Hurley. New York: Zone Books, 1988.

Bataille, Georges. *Visions of Excess: Selected Writings, 1927–1939*. Edited by Allan Stoekl. Minneapolis: University of Minnesota Press, 2004.

Bauman, Zygmunt. *Globalization: The Human Consequences*. New York: Columbia University Press, 1998.

Bauman, Zygmunt. *Work, Consumerism, and the New Poor*. New York: Open University Press, 2005.

Bean, Susan S. "Toward a Semiotics of 'Purity' and 'Pollution' in India." *American Ethnologist* 8, no. 3 (August, 1981): 575–595.

Behe, Michael. "Molecular Machines: Experimental Support for the Design Inference." In *Intelligent Design Creationism and Its Critics: Philosophical, Theological and Scientific Perspectives*. Edited by Robert T. Pennock, 241–256. Cambridge, MA: MIT Press, 2001.

Behe, Michael. *Darwin's Black Box: The Biochemical Challenge to Evolution*. New York: Free Press, 1996.

Berger, Arthur Asa. *Shop 'til You Drop: Consumer Behavior and American Culture*. Lanham, MD: Rowman and Littlefield, 2005.

Beth, Sara. "Hindi Dalit Autobiography: An Exploration of Identity." *Modern Asian Studies* 41, no. 3 (May 2007): 545–574.

Bloom, Jonathan. *American Wasteland: How America Throws Away Nearly Half Its Food (And What We Can Do about It)*. Cambridge, MA: Da Capo, 2010.

Brantlinger, Patrick, and Richard Higgins. "Waste and Value: Thorstein Veblen and H. G. Wells." *Criticism* 48, no. 4 (Fall 2006): 453–475.

Brenner, Sydney. "Refuge of Spandrels." *Current Biology* 8, no. 19 (1998): R669.

Britten, Roy J. "Transposable Element Insertions Have Strongly Affected Human Evolution." *Proceedings of the National Academy of Sciences of the United States of America* 107, no. 46 (November 16, 2010): 19945–19948.

Brosius, Jürgen, and Stephen Jay Gould. "On 'Genomenclature': A Comprehensive (and Respectful) Taxonomy for Pseudogenes and Other 'Junk DNA.'" *Proceedings of the National Academy of Sciences of the United States of America* 89, no. 22 (November 15, 1992): 10706–10710.

Brown, Doug, editor. *Thorstein Veblen in the Twenty-First Century: A Commemoration of The Theory of the Leisure Class (1899–1999)*. Cheltenham, UK: Edward Elgar, 1998.

Brown, Frank Burch. "The Evolution of Darwin's Theism." *Journal of the History of Biology* 19, no. 1 (Spring 1986): 1–45.

Brown, Jeffery A. "Class and Feminine Excess: The Strange Case of Anna Nicole Smith." *Feminist Review* 81 (2005): 74–94.

California v. Greenwood. 486 U.S. 35 (1988).

California v. Rooney. 483 U.S. 307 (1987).

Calvino, Italo. "La Poubelle Agréée." In *The Road to San Giovanni*, 93–126. New York: Vintage, 1994.

Campbell, Colin. "Conspicuous Confusion? A Critique of Veblen's Theory of Conspicuous Consumption." *Sociological Theory* 13, no. 1 (March 1995): 37–47.

Chakrabarty, Dipesh. "Of Garbage, Modernity and the Citizen's Gaze." *Economic and Political Weekly* 27, no. 10/11 (March 7–14, 1992): 541–547. Reprinted in his *Habitations of Modernity: Essays in the Wake of Subaltern Studies*, 65–79. Chicago: University of Chicago Press, 2002.

Chameides, David. "365 Days of Trash: One Man's Attempt to Throw Nothing 'Away' for a Year ... and Beyond." http://365daysoftrash.blogspot.com/2007/12/365-days-of-trash.html.

Constitution of India. india.gov.in/my-government/constitution-india/constitution-india-full-text.

Cranston, Maurice. "Locke and Liberty." *Wilson Quarterly* 10, no. 5 (Winter 1986): 82–93.

Daniels, Inge. "The 'Social Death' of Unused Gifts: Surplus and Value in Contemporary Japan." *Journal of Material Culture* 14, no. 3 (2009): 385–408.

Daniels, Peter. "Buddhism and the Transformation to Sustainable Economies." *Society and Economy* 29, no. 2 (August 2007): 155–180.

Darwin, Charles. "Darwin, C. R., to Hooker, J. D." Darwin Correspondence Database. http://www.darwinproject.ac.uk/entry-1924.

Darwin, Charles. *On the Origin of Species, a Facsimile of the First Edition*. Introduction by Ernst Mayr. Cambridge, MA: Harvard University Press, 1964.

Darwin, Charles. *Charles Darwin's Diary of the Voyage of H.M.S. "Beagle."* Edited by Nora Barlow. Cambridge: Cambridge University Press, 1934.

Darwin, Charles. *The Foundations of the Origin of Species. Two Essays Written in 1842 and 1844*. Edited by Francis Darwin. Cambridge: Cambridge University Press, 1909. http://darwin-online.org.uk/content/frameset?itemID=F1556&viewtype=text&pageseq=1.

Dawkins, Richard. *The Greatest Show on Earth. The Evidence for Evolution*. New York: Free Press, 2009.

Delaney, Austin. "Mother India as Bitch." Review of *An Area of Darkness* by V. S. Naipaul. *Transition* 26 (1966): 50–51.

Dennett, Daniel. *Darwin's Dangerous Idea. Evolution and the Meanings of Life*. New York: Simon and Schuster, 1995.

Dhar, Aarti. "'India Will Achieve Sanitation Goals only by 2054.'" *The Hindu*, March 27, 2012. http://www.thehindu.com/news/national/india-will-achieve-sanitation-goals-only-by-2054/article3250852.ece.

Dialogues of the Buddha, 4th edition. Translated from the Pali of the Digha-Nikaya by T. W. Rhys Davids. Oxford: Pali Text Society, 2002.

Dietler, Michael. "Theorizing the Feast: Rituals of Consumption, Commensal Politics, and Power in African Contexts." In *Feasts: Archaeological and Ethnographic Perspectives on Food, Politics and Power*. Edited by Michael Dietler and Brian Hayden, 65–114. Washington, DC: Smithsonian Institution, 2001.

Dorit, Robert. "Biological Complexity." In *Scientists Confront Intelligent Design and Creationism*. Edited by Andrew J. Petto and Laurie R. Godfrey, 231–249. New York: Norton, 2007.

Douglas, Mary. *Purity and Danger: An Analysis of Concepts of Pollution and Taboo*. London: Routledge, 2007.

Elias, Norbert. *The Civilizing Process: The History of Manners*. Translated by Edmund Jephcott. New York: Urizen Books, 1978.

European Commission. "Food and Feed Safety." 2012. http://ec.europa.eu/food/food/sustainability/index_en.htm.

European Parliament. "Report on How to Avoid Food Wastage." 2011. http://www.europarl.europa.eu/sides/getDoc.do?type=REPORT&reference=A7-2011-0430&language=EN.

Flanagan, Thomas. "The Agricultural Argument and Original Appropriation: Indian Lands and Political Philosophy." *Canadian Journal of Political Science/Revue canadienne de science politique* 22, no. 3 (September 1989): 589–602.

Food and Agricultural Organization of the United Nation. "Food Loss and Food Waste." http://www.fao.org/food-loss-and-food-waste/en/.

Freud, Sigmund. *The Standard Edition of the Complete Psychological Works of Sigmund Freud*. Translated from the German under the general editorship of James Strachey, in collaboration with Anna Freud, assisted by Alix Strachey and Alan Tyson. Psychoanalytic Electronic Publishing. http://www.pep-web.org.libproxy.smith.edu:2048/static.php?page=standardedition.

Galanter, Marc. *Competing Inequalities: Law and the Backward Classes in India*. Berkeley: University of California Press, 1984.

Galanter, Marc. "Untouchability and the Law." *Economic and Political Weekly* 4, no. 1/2 (January 1969): 131–170.

Gale, Jason. "India Failing to Control Open Defecation Blunts Nation's Growth." *Bloomberg*, March 3, 2009. http://www.bloomberg.com/apps/news?sid=aErNiP_V4RLc&pid=newsarchive.

Gates, Anita. "Tammy Faye Bakker, 65, Emotive TV Evangelist, Dies." *New York Times*, July 23, 2007, A21.

Gee, Sophie. *Making Waste: Leftovers and the Eighteenth-Century Imagination*. Princeton, NJ: Princeton University Press, 2010.

George, Rose. *The Big Necessity: The Unmentionable World of Human Waste and Why It Matters*. New York: Metropolitan Books, 2008.

George, Rose. rosegeorge.com/site/about

George, Rose. "Why We Must Have Relief from the Toilet Barbarians." http://www.yorkshirepost.co.uk/news/debate/columnists/rose_george_why_we_must_have_relief_from_the_toilet_barbarians_1_4266255.

Gorringe, Hugo. "The Caste of the Nation: Untouchability and Citizenship in South India." *Contributions to Indian Sociology* (n.s.) 42, no. 1 (April 2008): 123–149.

Gould, Stephen Jay. *The Structure of Evolutionary Theory*. Cambridge, MA: Harvard University Press, 2002.

Greenblatt, Stephen. "Filthy Rites." *Daedalus* 111, no. 3 (Summer 1982): 1–16.

Gregson, Nicky, and Louise Crewe. *Second-Hand Cultures*. New York: Berg, 2003.

Hake, Sabine. "*Saxa Loquuntur*: Freud's Archaeology of the Text." *boundary 2*, 20, no. 1 (Spring 1993): 146–173.

Hawkins, Gay. *The Ethics of Waste: How We Relate to Rubbish*. Lanham, MD: Rowman and Littlefield, 2006.

Hiroki, Ryuichi. *Tokyo Trash Baby*. Arcimboldo, 2000. DVD.

Hirschman, Albert. *Shifting Involvements: Private Interest and Public Action*. Princeton, NJ: Princeton University Press, 1982.

Hume, David. *Dialogues Concerning Natural Religion*, 2nd edition. Edited by Richard H. Popkin. Indianapolis: Hackett, 1988.

Japan Management Association. "Just-In-Time-Toyota." In *The Industrial Design Reader*. Edited by Carma Gorman, 211–213. New York: Allworth Press, 2003.

JayBird. "Someone Went Through Mary Louise Parker's Trash and Told Page Six about It." *Celebitchy*, October 27, 2008. http://www.celebitchy.com/18327/someone_went_through_mary-louise_parkers_trash_and_told_page_six_about_it/.

Johnston, Mark, and Gary D. Stormo. "Heirlooms in the Attic." *Science, New Series* 302, no. 5647 (November 7, 2003): 997–999.

Kahn, Charles H. "Plato's Theory of Desire." *Review of Metaphysics* 41, no. 1, (September 1987): 77–103.

Kaza, Stephanie. "Penetrating the Tangle." In *Hooked! Buddhist Writings on Greed, Desire, and the Urge to Consume*. Edited by Stephanie Kaza, 139–151. Boston: Shambala, 2005.

Kitcher, Philip. *Living with Darwin. Evolution, Design, and the Future of Faith*. New York: Oxford University Press, 2007.

Knoedler, Janet, and Anne Mayhew. "Thorstein Veblen and the Engineers: A Reinterpretation." *History of Political Economy* 31, no. 2 (1999): 255–272.

Kolata, Gina. "Bits of Mystery DNA, Far from 'Junk,' Play Crucial Role." *New York Times*, September 5, 2012. http://www.nytimes.com/2012/09/06/science/far-from-junk-dna-dark-matter-proves-crucial-to-health.html?pagewanted=all&module=Search&mabReward=relbias%3Ar%2C%7B%221%22%3A%22RI%3A11%22%7D.

Kolata, Gina. "Reanimated 'Junk' DNA Is Found to Cause Disease." *New York Times*, August 19, 2010. http://www.nytimes.com/2010/08/20/science/20gene.html?module=Search&mabReward=relbias%3Ar%2C%7B%221%22%3A%22RI%3A11%22%7D.

Laporte, Dominique. *History of Shit*. Translated by Nadia Benabid and Rodolphe el-Khoury, with an introduction by Rodolphe el-Khoury. Cambridge, MA: MIT Press, 2002.

Larrabee, Eric. "The Great Love Affair." *Industrial Design* 2, no. 5, 1955: 95–98.

Lasch, Christopher. *The Culture of Narcissism: American Life in the Age of Diminishing Expectations*. New York: Norton, 1978.

LaViolette, Forrest E. *The Struggle for Survival: Indian Cultures and the Protestant Ethic in British Columbia*. Toronto: University of Toronto Press, 1961.

Leonard, Annie, with Ariane Conrad. *The Story of Stuff: How Our Obsession with Stuff Is Trashing the Planet, Our Communities, and Our Health—and a Vision for Change*. New York: Free Press, 2010.

Lerner, Max, editor. *The Portable Veblen*. New York: Viking Press, 1948.

Lindenlauf, Astrid. "Waste Management in Ancient Greece from the Homeric to the Classical Period: Concepts and Practices of Waste, Dirt, Recycling and Disposal." Ph.D. diss., University College London, 2001. http://discovery.ucl.ac.uk/1317693/.

Lippincott, J. Gordon. *Design for Business*. Chicago: P. Theobald, 1947.

Locke, John. *Second Treatise of Government*. Edited by C. B. Macpherson. Indianapolis: Hackett, 1980 [1690]).

MacDonald, Gordon. "Stray Katz: Is Shredded Trash Private?" 79 *Cornell Law Review*, 452.

Makalowski, Wojciech. "Not Junk After All." *Science, New Series* 300, no. 5623 (May 23, 2003): 1246–1247.

Malik, Bela. "Untouchability and Women's Oppression." *Economic and Political Weekly* 34, no. 6 (Feb. 6–12, 1999): 323–324.

Marche, Stephen. "The Case for Filth." *New York Times*, December 7, 2013. http://www.nytimes.com/2013/12/08/opinion/sunday/the-case-for-filth.html.

Martínez, Samuel. "The Struggle for Expenditure on a Caribbean Sugar Plantation." *Current Anthropology* 51 (2010): 609–628.

Masco, Joseph. "Competitive Displays: Negotiating Genealogical Rights to the Potlatch at the American Museum of Natural History." *American Anthropologist*, New Series 98, no. 4 (December 1996): 837–852.

Masson, Jeffrey Moussaieff, translator and editor. *The Complete Letters of Sigmund Freud to Wilhelm Fliess, 1887–1904*. Cambridge, MA: Belknap, 1985.

Mayer, Robert. "Dylan's Having a Heap of Trouble with His Garbage Can These Days." *Toledo Blade*, May 30, 1971, C6.

McKendrick, Neil. "Josiah Wedgwood and Factory Discipline." *Historical Journal* 4, no. 1 (1961): 30–55.

Mendelsohn, Oliver, and Marika Vicziany. *The Untouchables: Subordination, Poverty and the State in Modern India*. Cambridge: Cambridge University Press, 1998.

Milton, John. *Paradise Lost*. In *John Milton: The Major Works*. Edited by Stephen Orgel and Jonathan Goldberg, 355–618. New York: Oxford, 1991 [1674].

Müller, Gerd B. "Vestigial Organs and Structures." *Encyclopedia of Evolution*. Edited by Mark Pagel. Oxford: Oxford University Press, 2005. http:// www.oxfordreference.com.libproxy.smith.edu:2048/view/10.1093/acref/ 9780195122008.001.0001/acref-9780195122008-e-415?rskey=MjrzBT&result=1.

Murdoch, Iris. *A Fairly Honourable Defeat*. Greenwich, CT: Fawcett, 1970.

Myers, David B. "New Design Arguments: Old Millian Objections." *Religious Studies* 36, no. 2 (June 2000): 141–162.

Nagle, Robin. *Picking Up: On the Streets and Behind the Trucks with the Sanitation Workers of New York City*. New York: Farrar, Straus and Giroux, 2013.

O'Hagan, Andrew. "The Things We Throw Away." *London Review of Books* 29, no. 10 (May 24, 2007): 3–8.

Olivecrona, Karl. "Locke's Theory of Appropriation." *Philosophical Quarterly* 24, no. 96 (July 1974): 220–234.

PageSix.com Staff. "Prowlers Target Celebs' Trash." *New York Post*, October 27, 2008. http://pagesix.com/2008/10/27/prowlers-target-celebs-trash/.

Phillips, Adam. *Darwin's Worms*. New York: Basic Books, 2000.

Phillips, Adam. *Becoming Freud: The Making of a Psychoanalyst*. New Haven, CT: Yale University Press, 2014.

Plato, *Republic*. Translated by G. M. A. Grube and revised by C. D. C. Reeve. Indianapolis: Hackett, 1992.

Plato. *Symposium*. Translated, with Introduction and Notes, by Alexander Nehamas and Paul Woodruff. Indianapolis: Hackett, 1989.

Plato. *Two Comic Dialogues: Ion and Hippias Major*. Edited by Paul Woodruff. Indianapolis: Hackett, 1983.

Prashad, Vijay. *Untouchable Freedom: A Social History of a Dalit Community*. New Delhi: Oxford University Press, 2000.

Preus, Anthony. "Aristotle's 'Nature Uses . . .'" *Apeiron* 3, no. 2 (July 1969): 20–33.

Rathje, William, and Cullen Murphy. *Rubbish! The Archaeology of Garbage*. Tucson: University of Arizona Press, 1992.

Reid, Donald. *Paris Sewers and Sewermen: Realities and Representations*. Cambridge, MA: Harvard University Press, 1991.

Rieff, Philip. *Freud: The Mind of the Moralist*. New York: Anchor, 1961.

Rieff, Philip. *The Triumph of the Therapeutic: Uses of Faith after Freud*. New York: Harper, 1966.

Roelofs, Monique. *The Cultural Promise of the Aesthetic*. London: Bloomsbury, 2014.

Rogers, Heather. *Gone Tomorrow: The Hidden Life of Garbage*. New York: New Press, 2006.

Roget, P. M. *Animal and Vegetable Physiology with Reference to Natural Theology*, 2 volumes. London, 1834.

Rogovoy, Seth. "The Bob Dylan's Who's Who." http://expectingrain.com/dok/who/w/webermanaj.html.

Rolston, Holmes III. "Disvalues in Nature." *Monist* 75, no. 2 (April 1992): 250–278.

Sarkar, Tanika. "Gandhi and Social Relations." In *The Cambridge Companion to Gandhi*. Edited by Judith M. Brown and Anthony Parel, 173–198. Cambridge: Cambridge University Press, 2011.

Scanlan, John. *On Garbage*. London: Reaktion, 2005.

Schorske, Carl E. "Freud: The Psycho-Archaeology of Civilizations." *Proceedings of the Massachusetts Historical Society*, Third Series 92 (1980): 52–67.

Scitovsky, Tibor. *The Joyless Economy: The Psychology of Human Satisfaction*, revised edition. New York: Oxford University Press, 1992.

Sen, Amartya. "The Standard of Living: Lecture I, Concepts and Critiques." In *The Standard of Living*. Edited by Geoffrey Hawthorn, 1–19. Cambridge: Cambridge University Press, 1987.

Shaw, Bernard. *Man and Superman. A Comedy and a Philosophy*. Introduction by Stanley Weintraub. New York: Penguin, 2000 [1903].

Simmons, Dana. "Waste Not, Want Not: Excrement and Economy in Nineteenth-Century France." *Representations* 96, no. 1 (Fall 2006): 73–98.

Sloan, Phillip R. "'The Sense of Sublimity': Darwin on Nature and Divinity." *Osiris*, 2nd Series 16 (2001): 251–269.

Smith, Adam. *An Inquiry into the Nature and Causes of the Wealth of Nations*. Edited by Edwin Cannan. Chicago: University of Chicago Press, 1976.

Smith, Adam. *The Theory of Moral Sentiments*. Amherst, NY: Prometheus Books, 2000.

Special Correspondent. "Jairam Wants Social Barrier in Sanitation Broken." *The Hindu*, February 18, 2012. http://www.thehindu.com/news/national/jairam-wants-social-barrier-in-sanitation-broken/article2904583.ece.

Stoekl, Allan. "Excess and Depletion: Bataille's Surprisingly Ethical Model of Expenditure." In *Reading Bataille Now*. Edited by Shannon Winnubst, 252–284. Bloomington: Indiana University Press, 2007.

Storr, Anthony. *Freud: A Very Short Introduction*. New York: Oxford University Press, 1989.

Strong, Roy. *Feast: A History of Grand Eating*. London: Pimlico, 2003.

Stuart, Tristram. *Waste: Uncovering the Global Food Scandal*. New York: Norton, 2009.

Swann, Christopher. "GDP and the Economy: Second Estimates for the Second Quarter of 2012." *Survey of Current Business* 92, no. 9 (September 2012): 1–10.

Tagliabue, John. "A City That Turns Garbage into Energy Copes with a Shortage." *New York Times*, April 30, 2013, A9.

Tennyson, Lord Alfred. *In Memoriam*. Norton Critical Edition, edited by Erik Gray. New York: Norton, 2003.

Trigg, Andrew B. "Veblen, Bourdieu, and Conspicuous Consumption." *Journal of Economic Issues* 35, no. 1 (March 2001): 99–115.

United States v. Scott. 975 F.2d 927 (1st Cir. 1992).

Veblen, Thorstein. *Absentee Ownership and Business Enterprise in Recent Times: The Case of America.* New York: B. W. Huebsch, 1923.

Veblen, Thorstein. *The Engineers and the Price System.* New York: Viking Press, 1954 (1921).

Veblen, Thorstein. *Essays in Our Changing Order* Edited by Leon Ardzrooni. New York: Viking Press, 1945.

Veblen, Thorstein. *The Instinct of Workmanship and the State of the Industrial Arts.* Introduction by Dr. Joseph Dorfman. New York: Sentry Press, 1964 (1914).

Veblen, Thorstein. *The Place of Science in Modern Civilisation and Other Essays.* New York: B. W. Huebsch, 1919.

Veblen, Thorstein. *The Theory of Business Enterprise.* New Introduction by Douglas Dowd. New Brunswick, NJ: Transaction Books, 1978 (1904).

Veblen, Thorstein. *The Theory of the Leisure Class: An Economic Study of Institutions.* New York: Modern Library, 1931 (1899).

Whewell, William. *Of the Plurality of Worlds: An Essay. Also a Dialogue on the Same Subject,* 2nd edition. London, 1854.

Whiteley, Nigel. "Toward a Throw-Away Culture: Consumerism, 'Style Obsolescence' and Cultural Theory in the 1950s and 1960s." *Oxford Art Journal* 10, no. 2 (1987): 3–27.

Why Didn't I Think of That? Bright Ideas for Housekeeping, Garden, Kitchen and More. Memphis: Wimmer, 1993.

Wiessner, Polly, and Wulf Schiefenhoevel, editors. *Food and the Status Quest: An Interdisciplinary Perspective.* Providence, RI: Berghahn Books, 1996.

Wilde, Oscar. *The Importance of Being Earnest and Other Plays.* Edited by Peter Raby. New York: Oxford University Press, 1995 (1893).

World Health Organization. "Water Sanitation Health." http://www.who.int/water_sanitation_health/monitoring/jmp2012/fast_facts/en/.

Wray, Matt, and Annalee Newitz, editors. *White Trash: Race and Class in America.* New York: Routledge, 1997.

Yeo, Richard R. "The Principle of Plenitude and Natural Theology in Nineteenth-Century Britain." *British Journal for the History of Science* 19, no. 3 (November 1986): 263–282.

Zangwill, Willard I. "The Limits of Japanese Production Theory." *INTERFACES* 22:5 (September–October 1992): 14–25.

Zimring, Carl. "Dirty Work: How Hygiene and Xenophobia Marginalized the American Waste Trades, 1870–1930." *Environmental History* 9, no. 1 (January 2004): 80–101.

INDEX